Mortgage Risk:

A Blueprint for Smarter Origination

Mortgage Risk: A Blueprint for Smarter Origination / Anne Elliott – 2017

ISBN: 9781521871058
NON-FICTION: Mortgage Risk
NON-FICTION: Loan Origination
NON-FICTION: Loan Underwriting
1. Mortgage 2. Risk 3. Loan, 4. Underwriting, 5. Underwriter 6. Home Loan

Published by Digitology
Los Angeles, California

Introduction and Acknowledgements

Underwriting is the perfect fit for my analytical skills, curiosity and grasshopper attention span. Somehow I stumbled into a position where I was paid to think.

I started underwriting in my twenties and I never wanted to graduate from it. I remember details of loans with less effort than people's names. I've grabbed files out of underwriters' hands until technology changed the industry, after which I asked for the loan number or pulled up a chair and said "Let's look at this loan together."

There are so many people to thank. Norm MacLeod, John Dixon, Doug Jones, Jim Follette and Roy Downey helped me to understand the nuances of underwriting and management. Matt Willard and Sherry Light kindly voluntarily read this book in draft form and provided feedback. Sharon Price shared her expertise on the Transactional chapter and Greg Stephens shared his on the Appraisal and Valuation chapters.

Enriching my underwriting experience were Beth McDow, Ashley Oberst Dingler, Suzette Fernow, Jennifer Downing, Sheila Brachman, Jacob Keigan, Kelley Johnson, Kelly Darraugh Black, Joan Harrell Domanski, Adam Ferrary, Sharon Price, Gary Engel, Kim Foster, Sheila Spence, Shelley Varble, Carol Mnoian, Alice Vilanian, Mark Barry, Marc Condensa, Robert Sasser, Dave Farrell, Jack and Karen King, Marcie Melendy, Rosie Comet, Beryl Poole, Sue Kropp, Gary Ekgan and many others. Each of you has taught me more than you will ever know.

Thanks to Cousin Ken (the real estate attorney), Cousin Kip (the closing agent, maybe not forever) and Cousin Gail, whose love and anecdotes improved this book. Also to Daniel Gat and David Fein who shared their expertise about retail loan origination and real estate sales respectively. Thanks to Erik and Marc of Hara Nelson Physical Therapy, where I've spent considerable treadmill time thinking about risk. Thanks to friends and acquaintances who knowingly or unknowingly shared their loan experiences. Thanks for volunteer editor Sue Unterman who doesn't remember her loan experience but excels at close work, Karen Bergen whose professional editing skills trump mine, and David Westwood without whose help this book would still be a lengthy file in Pages.

Finally, much love and appreciation to Donald, who helped with formatting and anything complicated technically, and who far before this book was conceived listened to countless loan stories and only protested occasionally.

TABLE OF CONTENTS

How This Book is Organized

Chapter 1, *Underwriting Basics,* is fairly self-explanatory.

Chapters 2 through 8, *Loan Application* through *Transactional Issues,* correspond to traditional loan file order. Collateral is split up into Chapters 6 and 7 with the tangible aspects of property separated from appraisal aspects.

Chapter 8, *Transactional Issues,* discusses documentation including the purchase contract, title-work and subordinate financing.

Chapter 9, *Fraud,* merits it own chapter so fraud hounds can read it first.

Chapter 10, *Other Risk Considerations,* examines critical issues like marketability, equity, occupancy and reserves. Chapter 11 overlaps somewhat with the loan file chapters. The distinction is that Chapters 1 though 7 deal principally with documentation—what should be reviewed during underwriting and why. Chapter 10 integrates findings from documentation into risk evaluation.

Chapter 11, *Decisioning,* discusses the culmination of the credit review process.

Chapter 12, *The Meltdown and After,* examines underwriting before, leading up to and as a result of the meltdown.

Chapters 13 through 15 — *Borrowers, Underwriters* and *Loan Officers*— discuss the three principal players in the origination process. We sometimes forget that individual pieces of documentation collectively represent a person. Readers can gain insight into their own roles and the roles of those sometimes viewed as adversaries.

Chapter 16, *Life Lessons,* talks about insights gained through employment and home ownership.

Chapter 17, *Underwriting Management,* explores a variety of topics including training, workflow, conditioning, auditing and exceptions.

Chapter 18, *Forty Years, Three Loan Lessons,* presents three teachable loans. Other loan lessons are interspersed throughout the book. Most of them correlate to the adjacent text; a few do not.

Acronym Cheat Sheet, List of Loan Lessons and *Index* end the book.

Explanations and Caveats

1. I like and respect most loan officers even though it sometimes appears otherwise. Most LOs handle a complicated job well and are fun to talk to. The term loan officer is used generically for those who take the application and are the primary communicators with the borrower. For readers who perform that function and have another title, mentally substitute it. Thank you for reading this book.

2. In some companies underwriters do not get involved until a loan is ready to be decisioned. In those cases, processors should replace "processor" for "underwriter" as they read. Processors with expanded responsibilities should clearly delineate this on their resumes so those who assume processor is a clerical role give credit for all contributions.

3. Real estate agent is admittedly cumbersome, particularly in a long sentence. It is necessary to distinguish real estate agents from loan agents and real estate brokers since brokers have higher credentials. Realtor® was not used since not all real estate agents belong to the trademarked organization.

4. Those focused on procedural guidance may be disappointed. Procedures vary by lender and geography. The principles of risk are more universal.

5. This book contains a multitude of qualifiers—generally, typically, sometimes, potentially, possibly, and probably (yes, another) more not included on the list. Abundant qualifiers do not reflect indecision, but rather that there are few absolutes in underwriting.

6. Underwriting is an evolving profession. Portions of this book will lose pertinence or may be inapplicable to current practices. Dodd Frank springs to mind, since it occupies headlines currently and may be rescinded or truncated. This is part of the charm of the industry.

7. My lending point of view is unconventional. Breaking into underwriting in Beverly Hills made jumbo and super jumbo loans my initial frame of reference. Exposure to conforming product came later, but I grasped it well enough to serve several years on a Fannie Mae advisory panel. Over a decade of exception management led to a focus on risk, rules and flexibility. Although I went through FHA training and got my DE, I never underwrote a government loan and admit to limited expertise in government lending. I have even less expertise in compliance and closing.

8. Redundancies in this book are for the most part deliberate. Ideally readers will read it from cover to cover and refer to individual topics afterward. For reader convenience and also since information is better absorbed after multiple exposures, some concepts are repeated in different contexts.

9. Readers may tire of references to the meltdown. (The word could be used in a drinking game, but responsible underwriters indulge moderately and never during job-related tasks.) The meltdown is repeatedly addressed because of its impact and the pronounced differences between how matters were handled before (often referred to as traditionally) and after. I also apologize for the deliberate avoidance of synonyms. When reasonability is fully restored to the underwriting process, the topic can be bypassed or edited out.

10. Another word repeated so frequently that it may be annoying is credible. Stipulating that a letter of explanation or an appraisal be credible means that when there is uncertainty, a second opinion is advised. This should occur infrequently. Underwriter gut refers not to one's stomach but to the ability to identify high risk and deception.

11. The opinions and philosophies expressed herein are my own. They should not be construed as assurance that any loan is legally compliant, salable or will be repaid in a timely manner.

12. Loan Lessons are interspersed throughout the book. They were collected throughout my career, from friends and passing acquaintances. Some involve escalations which were decisioned while I had the authority to breach guidelines, and some are based on rationales that apply infrequently. Decisions such as disregarding major derogatory credit or supporting a limited credit history with financial management skills were not made in haste. They required both an open mind and considerable experience.

   Some of the resolutions may baffle readers. Be assured, each decision was made after thorough review of the loan file. The condensations are simplified for brevity's sake and also because time washes away some of the details. I believe life is a lesson, and you can be your own best teacher.

   If there is a loan lesson you want to share, email it to MRB@digitology. com. Please include your name and phone number. In the event that it is used in publication, you will be given full credit or, if desired, complete privacy.

CHAPTER 1
LENDING BASICS

The foundation blocks of underwriting were once the Four Cs: Capacity (or Capital), Credit, Collateral and Character. At some point Character was eliminated, and the number of Cs reduced to three. Since the industry has moved toward a regime of rules rather than foundation blocks, my suggestion is reconsideration of the basics, beginning with a substitution of the Four Rs for the Three Cs.

The four Rs of underwriting

Rules: Mortgage lending is rules driven, hopefully less so after more people understand that rules don't guarantee the best decision. Rules delineate program eligibility, comprise written guidelines and justify repurchase if the loan doesn't perform. Rules broken without justification, out of haste or because of inadequate training, are bad. Rules broken as a result of weighed analysis enable worthy loans to be closed.

Risk: Some people believe that if there are enough rules, the ability to evaluate risk is dispensable. This is incorrect. There are bad loans that fit into the box, and good loans that don't.

Reasonability: Occasionally an AUS-approved loan doesn't make sense or makes the underwriter uneasy. The problem can be questionable occupancy, instability or lack of credibility. An AUS engine cannot assess reasonability, but a talented underwriter can.

Respect: The vast majority of borrowers deserve our respect. Financially responsible borrowers buy what they can afford. Financially responsible self-employed borrowers are unlikely to destroy their businesses by extracting funds for down payment. Respect also includes not being intrusive unless there is justification. It is the underwriter's role to ensure that sufficient funds to close are verified and sourced but not to dissect discretionary spending.

The story of the loan

Every loan tells a story. The most familiar is John and Mary Buy a House, my label for an uncomplicated purchase transaction. Variations include John Buys a House, Maria and Sue Buy a House and so on. But on simple and complex transactions alike the story of the loan should be examined for plausibility.

The story of the loan is one of several elements that cannot be captured on a spreadsheet or integrated into an AUS decision. Luckily, the majority of loans are not complex and make sense.

A loan's context matters as much as its attributes. If a loan is illogical or an issue needs clarification, questions should be asked. If the response is not satisfactory, the loan may not merit approval.

See *What the AUS doesn't see*

Johnny Paystub

Johnny Paystub is the employment equivalent of John and Mary Buy a House. Johnny's earnings are easily definable. The borrower is salaried or is paid hourly on a regular schedule with few if any complicating factors. Income should be reviewed for a declining trend, instability or lack of sustainability. If no negative factors exist, the underwriter can move on.

Loans are like snowflakes

Every mortgage loan is different. Some differences can be discerned by a computer engine but not all. Others require a thoughtful person who is able to recognize the nuances, i.e., an underwriter. The time involved to review a loan varies since some loans need little attention and others need more. My standard response to how long it takes to underwrite a loan was "How big is a dog?"

Balancing risk

Part of the underwriting process is evaluating the strengths and weaknesses of the loan. The strengths have to be legitimate. Bad decisions have been justified citing long-term ownership when the borrower has recent mortgage lates, stable employment when the borrower is in a floundering industry and responsible credit when the borrower has excessive debt. An AUS approval is not a compensating factor.

Some loans have weaknesses or complications but are still approvable. Spotty credit is less significant when mortgage payments have consistently been paid on time. Unimpressive reserves can be offset when there is a large cash investment or property improvements. An over-improved property may be acceptable when the borrower has a strong equity position.

Some weaknesses cannot be offset. PropertIes with geologic instability or environmental contamination represent unacceptable risk. Equally toxic are borrowers with plummeting income or long-term irresponsible credit. A loan that is marginal in several respects probably doesn't deserve to be closed.

Risk principles

Creditworthiness: Creditworthiness is the demonstration of money management skills and likelihood of timely repayment. Assessment is based on credit history plus related factors such as support obligations and legal items. Strategic default has taught us that creditworthiness may be situational, and affordability does not assure repayment. See *Strategic Default*

Affordability: Timely repayment ceases when the borrower can't afford the payment. This occurs when there is reduced income or too much debt combined with inadequate savings. Lack of affordability is usually reflected in high debt ratios. It is less concerning when the borrower has proven ability to manage commensurate debt responsibly (assuming consistent income) or when qualifying income is conservatively derived.

Sustainability: Both employed and self-employed borrowers have the potential for erosion of earnings. Consider those in at-risk industries, or with limited earning careers like professional athletes and most people when they retire. There is lower potential for default when there is a solid equity position.

Marketability: In the event of foreclosure, focus moves from borrower and the property to the property and whether the lender will be repaid in full. This is why well-supported value is essential and why non-mainstream properties are problematic unless LTV is so low that the lender will likely be made whole.

Key loan-related quotations

- "If I don't understand a loan, I don't want to buy it." Tim Griffin

- "Don't torture the borrower." Carla Navas

- "Don't lend to a marginal borrower on a marginal property." John Dixon, paraphrased

- "Jumbo loans are not big conforming loans." Rosie Comet

- "Equity breeds character." Roy Downey

- "Most bad loans aren't bad in just one respect. They are ugly all over." Roy Downey

- "Every loan is a snowflake." Anne Elliott (long before this book was envisioned)

Welcoming change

Those who can't embrace change should consider another line of work. Volume is alternately overwhelming and alarmingly low, guidelines relax and then tighten up, and new technology replaces previous advances. At the beginning of my underwriting career, appraisals were handwritten, guidelines were in three-ring binders and loan files were in manilla folders.

The three game-changing events were credit scoring, AUS decisioning and the meltdown. All were facilitated by technology and all are mixed blessings. Credit scoring gave the impression creditworthiness was captured in a three-digit number, but it also demonstrated that other factors beside untimely payments predict performance. AUS decisioning caused some companies to believe underwriters were obsolete, but it also prevented arbitrary decisions. The meltdown taught us that universal homeownership was a flawed goal and, afterwards, that too much oversight can be just as harmful as not enough.

The basic elements of underwriting are constant. Credit, capacity and collateral are the three cornerstones but there are endless nuances. The best underwriters have a firm grasp of the basics and adjust to the changes.

CHAPTER 2

LOAN APPLICATION

Traditional application functions

A loan application serves several purposes:

- To initiate a mortgage transaction

- To provide key information to determine qualification.

- To provide a residential and employment history, and contact data for verifications.

- To provide declarations from the borrower regarding core issues including occupancy, citizenship, support obligations, history of major derogatory credit and the integrity of the contents of the application.

- To provide basic property data including the complete address and, on refinances, details on the borrower's history of ownership.

- To provide information on sources of income, current and future housing expenses and funds to close.

- To provide details on all monetary obligations.

- To enable a financial assessment of the borrower.

The more complete the application, the better the loan decision.

The expanded application

About two decades after the last revision, a redesigned Uniform Residential Loan Application has been rolled out. Mandatory use begins January, 2018. The changes are profound.

The obvious change is the application's length. The previous version had five pages, including one continuation sheet. The revision has seven pages for borrower information, four pages for each additional borrower, two pages for lender information, a one-page unmarried addendum plus an optional continuation sheet.

The expansion allows space for military service, gifts and grants, homeowner education and counseling, trust vesting, Indian County Land Tenure, and seller and other credits.

The presentation has changed. The old application packed the maximum fields in minimum pages. The revision has ample white space. The old application was businesslike. The revision is applicant-friendly. It speaks in clear language; assets are described as "things you own that are worth money." The revision is designed so the applicant can complete the application without assistance. There are suggestions about potential sources of income (21), potential sources of funds to close (13 account types and 10 additional sources), liabilities (5 debt-related, 3 support obligations, job-related expenses and other). If the borrower is allowed to complete the application, conditioning should be reduced, loan review simplified and some annoying worksheets potentially eliminated.

The application is so welcoming that the applicant may miss the emphasis on full disclosure. With a signed application, in addition to the previous declarations the applicant will have attested to disclosing alternative names, no primary housing expense, non-arm's-length employment, job-related expenses, ownership interest of 25% or more, family relationship or business affiliation with the property seller, mixed use property, borrowed funds, bridge loan proceeds, new credit, lender agreement to accept less than the outstanding mortgage balance due, changed or new application data including any other real estate contracts or any written or oral agreements. Per the application, information provided must be true, accurate and complete. Comprehensive disclosure protects the lender while making the borrower responsible for casual oversights and deliberate omissions.

The two fields I will miss are years of education and improvements made since purchase. Years of education can provide a comfort level for a loan with higher ratios and shorter job tenure if the borrower is a recent graduate with a marketable skill. Improvements made since purchase cannot be reconstructed elsewhere and could be critical on a refinance. Whether previous proceeds were invested in the property or, better yet, personal funds were spent is worth knowing. This can sometimes be gleaned from the appraisal, but very possibly without specification of whether renovations were done prior to or during current ownership, or non-existent.

I don't recall ever meeting a form revision with enthusiasm. This one deserves it.

Double-apping

Traditional triggers for double-apping are pricing and borrowers fearing they will not be approved. The more marginal the borrower, the greater the number of applications.

The newer driver is the easiest approval possible. With an industry that shifted emphasis from homeownership for all to treating every borrower with suspicion, even qualified borrowers rate their approvals for the difficulty involved in satisfying the conditions.

Double-apping is wasteful for all parties.

Other application-related topics

See *The loan application, How a complete application benefits the loan officer,* and *Full asset disclosure* in the *Loan Officers* chapter.

CHAPTER 3

CREDIT AND OBLIGATIONS

A brief history of credit scoring

Credit scoring began during World War II, when the diversion of able-bodied men to the war effort forced companies to hire women. Because of their inexperience and gender, females were considered incapable of evaluating credit without a tool. The earliest scoring systems were used by department stores and utility providers. Qualification for a credit card or the size of utility deposit was based on a point scale for criteria such as property owner or tenant, years at current residence, job classification and annual income.

The mortgage industry waited until the 1990's to embrace credit scoring. With the development of automated underwriting, an objective system for quantifying credit quality was necessary. As the industry increased its reliance on credit scores, FICO adjusted its scoring model to make it more predictive for mortgage-specific events. Mortgage defaults merited greater impact than auto repossessions, and multiple inquiries to mortgage lenders and auto dealerships over a limited period of time counted as one. Over the years, FICO has continued to refine its scoring models and continues to test correlation between credit usage and mortgage performance.

Lessons from credit scoring

Before credit reports included scores, credit analysis consisted of evaluating whether obligations were paid on time or how long after the due date. Late payments required explanation, and severely late payments or major derogatory credit could result in loan denial.

Understanding the component factors in a credit score increases the ability to predict loan performance. The five categories that contribute to each score are payment history (35%), amounts owed (30%), length of credit history (15%), new credit and types of credit (10% each.) Payment history includes legal items, and new credit includes inquiries.

Thirteen percent of Americans have scores of 800 or higher. On average, the high scorers have four to eight credit card accounts, no late payments in the past seven years, at least one major installment loan (mortgage or auto) with no lapses, an average of ten years credit history and a few accounts with twenty years of good history, less than three inquiries in the past six months, revolving utilization less than 35% of the account credit limit, and no bankruptcies, foreclosures, judgments, charge-offs or collection accounts.

Understanding contributory factors allows for better decisioning but also enables manipulation to enhance score levels.

Feeling the score

To gain a hands-on understanding of credit scoring, find a report with three disparate scores. Aim for one score each in the 800s, 700s and 600s. Highlight each bureau code in a different color. Reviewing each bureau's data individually enables a comparative analysis of what triggers each respective score. This exercise is not time-consuming since disparate scores usually apply to borrowers with shallow credit.

What's a low score?

Years ago, a 620 score represented the threshold between prime and subprime. Scores below 620 still qualified through a flexible array of subprime loan programs. Post-meltdown I've witnessed a 738 score described as "lower." The pendulum has swung far from pre-meltdown days. Our standards are comparable to a judgmental parent viewing an A- as an undesirable grade.

A 620 score is accurately viewed as marginal, but a 738 score is not low. More accurately, it is respectable but not exemplary.

Even an impressively high score can be suspect. It can be generated with deferred student loans, authorized user accounts or limited evidence of creditor confidence. Conversely, an unimpressive score can have relatively minor blemishes combined with minimal established credit or timely credit combined with heavy utilization. A thoughtful underwriter analyzes credit sufficiently to assess credit quality and is not dependent on score.

High score, questionable credit

Authorized user accounts: The intended use is for parents or a spouse to give a mature child or a less financially able spouse access to a credit card. One improvement in the scoring engine post-meltdown was to reduce or eliminate the impact of authorized user accounts. Those underwriters recalling the deviousness of authorized user accounts where a stranger's credit was rented to give the impression of robust credit or offset derogatory credit need not disregard current scores as non-representative.

Unlikely credit history: Most people don't wait until they're forty to open their first trade-line. Most people with above-average income have above-average high credit limits. When a credit history doesn't fit the borrower, questions are appropriate.

Doctored credit: Credit repair companies post signs on telephone poles and buy radio ads promising to increase credit scores. This is accomplished by disputing accounts with creditors, who are legally mandated to prove in a short time period that the derogatory credit is valid or retract it. The efficiency of credit cleansing companies combined with the inefficiency of creditors works to the non-deserving applicants' advantage. Another tactic is negotiating settlements with creditors in exchange for deleting derogatory ratings. For borrowers with isolated inaccuracies, errors can be cured personally with a phone call or email, or the impact may be so minimal that elimination is unnecessary. The cleansing companies work the system for deadbeats.

Shallow credit: Credit and debit cards are steadily replacing cash and checks. Although cash is steadily losing ground, younger credit users opt for fewer trade-lines. Some depend on a company credit card or one in their parent's or spouse's name, but when a borrower doesn't have a single open revolving account with a respectable high credit limit, the borrower's ability to function financially is in doubt.

Non-predictive credit scores

Not all credit scores are predictive. Seasoned and robust credit histories score more reliably than limited or newer credit histories. Scores based on insufficient data may not accurately forecast loan performance.

Personal circumstances may cause a credit score to be non-predictive. A recent graduate responsible only for personal expenses must adjust when housing and other personal expenses are no longer covered by parents. Retirees must change spending habits when paychecks cease. A high score before a life event does not assure a continuing high score, although good financial management skills suggest continuing responsible behavior.

Some believe that less than three trade-lines produce a non-predictive credit score. This varies case by case. A limited number of trade-lines with minimal use and/or short payment histories can yield a non-predictive score. The fewer the trade-lines, the more a single credit lapse will adversely affect the score. However, three or less trade-lines with seasoning and depth, especially if one is a mortgage or auto loan, can yield a valid credit score.

See *Manipulated credit*

Why read the credit report?

It is sometimes tempting to short-cut reading the credit report. Don't. The score level is not the only pertinent content. The report provides insight into a borrower's ability to handle the requested mortgage loan in many respects:

- Whether the credit history is newly-established or seasoned

- Creditor confidence as reflected in high credit limits

- Whether outstanding consumer debt (i.e., excluding mortgage and business loans) is minimal, moderate or excessive proportionate to income.

- Whether repayment has been timely, irresponsible or inconsistent

- Whether derogatory credit, if any, is widespread or restricted to certain accounts, and recent or dated. Late consumer debt payments but timely mortgage payments demonstrate prioritization working to the lender's advantage. Late mortgage payments and timely payments on consumer accounts may indicate questionable prioritization, hardship strategy or the potential for strategic default if equity is minimal. Be aware that some equity loans are classified as other than "M" (mortgage) accounts.

- Authorized user or disputed accounts that could invalidate the credit score

- Major derogatory credit like bankruptcy, foreclosure or foreclosure equivalent, vehicle repossession or a severely delinquent mortgage history

- Severely delinquent support obligations reflecting on ability to repay and character

- Fraud alerts to be investigated and cleared before loan closing

- Legal items such as outstanding tax liens to be paid or otherwise resolved before closing

- Whether credit usage is consistent with the borrower's age (except for those who have lived outside the country) and income level

- Whether address references correspond with the application's residential history and also reflect on stability

- Whether employment references correspond with the employment history on the application, and evidence multiple positions or growth in one field

- Whether a written explanation by the borrower should be requested

- Whether insufficient established credit requires non-traditional credit or addition of a co-borrower

- On manually underwritten loans or factors indiscernible to the AUS engine, whether loan approval should be granted.

After reviewing the credit report, the underwriter should have the ability to provide a concise description of credit usage.

Evaluating credit

Before credit scoring became an industry tool, credit was described as perfect if there were no derogatory ratings or legal items. Reviewing FICO's educational materials increased awareness of indicators other than timeliness and default. Major triggers include:

Quantity: The number of trade-lines and the types of accounts are relevant. Installment accounts and mortgages carry more weight than revolving accounts. Too many revolving accounts reduce the score level.

Quality: Untimely payments decrease the score. The more delinquent a payment, the greater its impact. Legal items such as bankruptcies and tax liens negatively impact score levels.

Seasoning: Mature accounts have a positive effect on the score level. As derogatory ratings become more dated, their impact on the score gradually decreases.

Utilization: This is the percentage relationship between the account balance and the high credit limit on revolving accounts. The higher the utilization individually and cumulatively, the more financially out of control the borrower appears. Higher credit limits indicate that creditors trust the borrower to repay. They elevate the score level unless an account has high utilization.

Inquiries: A high number of recent inquiries suggests the potential for increased debt and possibly applicant desperation. To be equitable, FICO reduces or "de-dupes" the number of inquiries from mortgage originators and auto dealerships within a short span of time; the borrower is likely shopping for one mortgage or vehicle.

Normal credit usage

The average number of trade-lines has decreased after the meltdown. Years ago having numerous credit cards was considered a positive especially with upper-end accounts. The meltdown and subsequent recession changed that perception along with loss exposure from identity theft and large-scale data breaches. Newer credit users don't see the need for many credit cards. Their parents and grandparents have closed accounts they aren't using.

The recession also changed spending habits. Consumers were motivated to pay down debt and reserve cash-out transactions for non-frivolous circumstances. Notwithstanding college graduates with student loan obligations, an increased percentage of people control outstanding debt and make higher than minimal monthly payments.

Handling credit responsibly may be family-learned behavior, like doing homework before playing. If your family believes in timely payments, chances are you will also. Or growing up in an environment that is excessively frugal or wantonly wasteful may lead to an abrupt change of direction.

Trended credit

Trended credit is Fannie Mae's inspired contribution to risk assessment. The bureaus provide a look-back of revolving account payment histories for up to thirty months. Excluded are accounts open less than six months, those without payment activity in the last twenty-four months, authorized user accounts and those in dispute or reported lost or stolen.

Trended credit provides insight into whether revolving accounts payments are the minimum, the full balance or in between. Applicants making partial payments perform better than applicants making minimum payments, and applicants paying off balances in full perform best of all.

As of this writing, trended credit is not reflected in the credit score directly. It is factored in indirectly through utilization (the proportion of account balance to high credit limit) but probably not relative to its importance as a predictor.

Trended credit histories also reveal whether account balances have been paid down, and if so, gradually or with a lump sum. Short-term good behavior aids in qualification but can be misleading as to ability to repay. Long-term good behavior indicates capacity and can justify higher debt ratios.

Although it is likely that the FICO scoring engine will be tweaked to reflect diligence of repayment, trended credit should be reviewed as a key demonstration of financial management.

Shallow credit, pre- and post-meltdown

Pre-meltdown, approving loans with shallow credit demonstrated bad judgment. But what constitutes shallow credit has changed.

Shallow credit was previously exemplified by unseasoned trade-lines with low credit limits. Typical starter accounts were health clubs, mall retailers and furniture stores. A trade-line with a financial institution was likely a secured credit card with a credit limit of $500 or less.

Today minimal credit usage does not necessarily reflect inexperience or lack of creditor confidence. Fiscal responsibility is demonstrated by restrained use of credit, sometimes so restrained that proof of non-traditional credit is required. Credit use should not be considered shallow if the accounts are seasoned and evidence creditor confidence. Five-figure credit limits on revolving accounts with mainstream financial institutions should not be confused with three-figure credit limits from retailers or health clubs. One has substance and depth; the other does not.

Credit usage is generational. Those recovering from the Great Depression were afraid of borrowing. Their children and grandchildren— Baby Boomers, GenX and GenY—take pride in credit approvals. The smarter ones use it carefully.

It has become normal for younger consumers to self-limit credit usage. They see little need for multiple department store and gas company credit cards. They correlate numerous trade-lines with excessive debt. Their restraint is not for lack of opportunity. They recycle credit solicitations in the mail and shake their heads at cashiers pitching revolving accounts. They shop more online and utilize the bankcard with the most attractive reward program.

Applicant profiles have evolved. Restrained credit is often accompanied by more than minimal savings. First-time borrowers are older. Those living with family likely could afford rent but are preparing for the responsibility of homeownership. Many have advanced degrees or other training that makes them employable even in tougher job markets. Their credit history may have started at the beginning of meaningful employment.

Quantifying credit requires more effort than counting trade-lines. In assessing sparse credit, what matters most is timeliness, duration and creditor confidence as evidenced in the high credit limit. A single three-year-old revolving bank line with a $10,000 high credit limit displays more substance than three minor revolving accounts.

Cautious credit is a more fitting description than shallow credit. Even seasoned credit-users have wisely opted to close accounts they aren't using. What the industry should be more wary of is applicants of any age with substantial outstanding consumer debt or periodic refinancing for debt consolidation.

See *Non-traditional credit,* a sub-topic of *Inclusionary lending*

The scary side of shallow credit

Borrowers with truly shallow credit may not deserve a warm welcome.

Negative profiles associated with shallow credit are young and unproven, previously incarcerated and credit cleansing graduates. Loans for applicants fitting into any of these categories should be underwritten cautiously, even with an AUS Accept. The outlier profile—when the borrower has no or minimal established credit—should be accompanied by a stable employment history. Even better is a history of savings and more than a minimal down payment.

Smart debt, stupid debt

Underwriters reviewing credit reports only long enough to locate the credit score and calculate debt ratios are shortcutting the underwriting process. A credit report is a key indicator of financial underwear, containing insights that even the borrower's relatives and closest friends may be unaware of.

Many underwriters conclude that $60,000 in outstanding revolving debt is excessive, but this depends on the borrower. Consumer debt should be viewed proportionate to annualized earnings, and individual circumstances should be taken into account. Family earnings of $50,000 with $60,000 in consumer debt is out of control, but it is less alarming with household earnings of $200,000. Consumer debt becomes more justifiable when it incorporates unreimbursed business expenses or costs of property renovation or a wedding, especially if the event occurred recently. Ideally there is a self-imposed plan to pay down the balance relatively quickly. More alarming is $60,000 of debt when there is an upcoming life event, going from a two-income to a one-income household or any major reduction in household income level.

Student loan debt has been traditionally considered a smart debt, but is not always. Unless there is a full scholarship or parental support, those choosing a college and field of study should consider their cost. Student loan debt of $200,000 is justifiable for a veterinarian but less so for a social worker. Before parents assume the burden of their children's student loan debt, they should consider long-term affordability. Whoever enrolls in a for-profit trade school should consider whether formal training is necessary for the position, whether the skill is in demand and whether compensation will repay debt over a period of years, not decades.

Auto loans are thought to be smarter debt than auto leases. Those enjoying the frequent vehicle turnover provided by a shorter lease period disagree. Car leases are more justifiable when auto expenses are deductible. The smartest car-owners use savings instead of auto financing, and smarter yet are those who keep cars until the cost of repairs justifies replacement.

The degree of dependence on consumer debt is quantified by the gap between the housing and the combined debt ratios. Outstanding mortgage debt exceeding original purchase price should be viewed as a red flag, especially on a cash-out refinance, unless the appraisal confirms proceeds have been used on property improvements. Insight can be gained through a written explanation for use of funds on prior refinances and equity loans.

Closed and open accounts

Although closed accounts represent unusable credit, they may give insight into credit management skills. Closed by creditor indicates deficient repayment if the account history shows late payments. With no evident performance issues, it is possible that an account was closed by the creditor for inactivity. Closed by consumer can reflect changed spending habits or an effort to enhance credit scores or deter identity theft. If a credit history shows responsible credit use and an upper range score, there should be no distinction between open and closed accounts in the consideration of credit quality. Closed accounts are factored into credit scoring engines until they become so dated they are irrelevant to current usage.

Some loan programs require a minimum number of open trade-lines. Such insistence is a throwback to the time when many accounts were considered normal and is outdated. Some people prefer separate revolving accounts for personal and business purchases, use certain cards beneficial for international travel, or participate in affinity programs offered by retailers, airlines, alumni groups, charities and the like. If no motivation exists, one seasoned open revolving account with a high credit limit is sufficient for normal and emergency needs. Its reflection of creditor confidence along with a mortgage or rental rating, if available, should be considered sufficient.

Ratings on timeshares

There is some confusion whether poor performance on a timeshare is equivalent to late mortgage payments. It is not. Since a timeshare loan is not secured against real property, it is an installment loan.

International credit reports

For those relatively new to this country, an international credit report may provide more insight into creditworthiness than non-traditional credit, which demonstrates payment performance on obligations no reasonable borrower would ignore, like rent and utilities. Credit scores on international credit reports may not correlate to our credit scores. Therefore, analysis is required. Most pertinent are payment timeliness, amount of outstanding debt and the presence of significant accounts like auto loans, mortgages and major bank lines. It may be necessary to convert foreign currency into American dollars.

Since many originators do not lend to foreign nationals and since most returning from interim employment use credit established in their home country, international credit reports are seldom necessary.

Business credit reports

Business credit reports were standard documentation at the beginning of my career. Since there was no credit database for businesses, borrowers disclosed their business credit relationships and the credit company called them. Not surprisingly, very little negative was reported.

There are now databases for business credit reporting and scoring, but business score levels are not synchronized by the providers like personal scores are. With their increased cost, reliance on a single bureau is more likely. Experian's score range from 0 to 100, FICO's from 0 to 300, and Equifax from 101 to 992. Business and personal score factors are somewhat similar but there are interesting differences: Experian's model divides late payments into 1 to 30 days and 31+, also delineating accounts paid before the due date. Other factors are the number of 30-day due lines of credit, lines of credit used in the past twelve months, collection accounts up to seven years old, the last twelve months of payment histories, and the age of the business. Experian also offers a business failure risk score ranging from 1000 to 1880.

The only current major investor requirement for business credit reports is manually underwritten FHA loans. This sounds counterintuitive but a troubled business could justify denial on an otherwise approvable FHA loan.

Commercial banks may have sufficient internal data to assess business strength. Personal and business credit management skills usually correlate.

At any rate, business credit reports in the twenty-first century presumably provide more meaningful content than previously.

Long-term obligations

A recurring debt is not the same as a long-term obligation. The first is discretionary, and the second is obligatory. Only long-term obligations should be factored into debt ratios.

The classic definition of a long-term obligation is any debt with a repayment period of ten months or longer. This includes any revolving account with a balance of at least $100 (a figure which has remained unchanged for decades), any installment account with ten or more remaining payments, auto leases (unless there is replacement transportation), real estate loans, time-share payments, support obligations, garnishments, and any other legal or contractual obligation.

What differ from long-term obligations are recurring debts such as dry cleaning, house cleaning, personal care (e.g., hair cutting and coloring, manicures), private school tuition (unless the borrower is contractually obligated to continue for greater than ten months, which is unlikely), tutoring, pet daycare and country club dues. These are discretionary expenses with no contractual requirement for continuation.

Long-term obligations, unreported

The credit report does not comprehensively itemize debt. Private-party financing and support payments are not reported. They and other miscellaneous obligations should come to light if the application is completed conscientiously.

Borrowings against savings and securities may surface on depository statements. They should not be included in debt service. Borrowing against personal assets even if repayment extends for longer than ten months can be excluded from long-term obligations; if there is inability to repay or the conscious decision to stop repayment, the account holder is reimbursed by the assets. Borrowings against savings must be taken into account in asset assessment. The asset balance should be decreased by the amount of the outstanding obligation.

Personal loans may be a concern. Loans from relatives or close friends are typically in lower amounts with a lump sum or no set schedule of payment. Repayment may be tied to an event like inheritance or sale of an asset. There may not be a written agreement or, even less likely, a secured interest.

Payday loans are another source of borrowing not reported to the credit bureaus. For homeowners, they are a remote possibility. Working in our industry's favor is that payday loans are unsecured, with lower loan amounts (averaging $375) and with demographics dissimilar from mortgage borrowers (younger, less educated and with annual earnings under $50,000). Payday loans are technically not long-term obligations. The potential for rollover is high and the average payday loan takes two hundred days to repay—far longer than the next payday.

Intense scrutiny of depository statements

The motivation for thoroughly reviewing bank statements sounds justifiable—ensuring the validity of debt ratios. But for various reasons, the practice is ill-conceived and unnecessary.

• The practice is intrusive. Borrowers resent being probed and cross-examined by lenders.

- There are minimal findings because long-term obligations typically appear on the credit report. Those obligations that don't appear on the credit report fall into predictable categories:

    1. Recently acquired or privately-financed real estate

    2. Support obligations

    3. Repayment of unsecured personal loans

All three should be disclosed if the application process is thorough. Since borrowers don't understand how qualification works, they usually tell the truth. Undisclosed real estate loans can be ferreted out through a property search database like MERS. Alimony payments are deductible on personal tax returns. Bank loans should surface on depository statements and VODs, and payday loan customers and loan applicants have minimal overlap.

Undisclosed long-term obligations may surface from time to time. A quick review of depository statements for recurring payments of significant size occasionally yields results. Dissecting depository statements and requiring borrowers to explain items deemed suspicious may be entertaining to underwriters. But if quantified in terms of risk and reward, these activities are a poor use of time.

Deferred obligations

Traditionally deferred obligations, usually student loans, could be excluded from debt ratios if the deferral period was at least one year. Consistent with Dodd-Frank, deferred payments or a minimum percentage of the debt is required to be included in qualification despite the period of deferral or forbearance. The GSEs, FHA and VA have some flexibility on debt ratios at least for a while.

This approach is equitable in some situations and inequitable in others. It is most unfair for borrowers whose education is costly and prolonged, with compensation increasing substantially after training is completed—like physicians. Their student loan burden may preclude qualification during internship and residency even if the starter house is relatively modest. See *Doctors*

Portfolio lenders insightful enough to deviate from a one-size-fits-all approach may benefit with long-term customer loyalty.

Short sales and forgiveness

Borrowers and even some mortgage professionals confuse forgiveness with exoneration. Mortgage debt forgiven in part or in full doesn't automatically mean the borrower is blameless, or that less than full repayment is exempt from credit assessment.

There are instances when lenders reach out to borrowers and offer to reduce their mortgage balance. This occurs less frequently than short sale default and is usually precipitated by investor desire for improved equity position, regulatory pressure or location in a municipality severely impacted by the meltdown. Under such circumstances, the lender should provide written confirmation that the reduction of monies due was not initiated by the borrower.

Strategic default

Strategic default is failure to repay when there is financial capability of repayment. Motivation is lack of equity combined with unwillingness to wait for property values to rebound. The phenomenon was a product of the meltdown, and the term was not in common usage until approximately 2010. The closest equivalent was walk-away, which could either be strategic or the result of life events.

The lesson of strategic default is that equity is at least equal to creditworthiness in determining performance.

The concentration of strategic default depended on location. The communities most affected had commonalities. Some had depressed economies. Others expanded from speculation. Bedroom communities distant from employment centers suffered when centrally-located homes became available at distress pricing. The phenomenon could be compared to a communicable disease, and where it was more prevalent default had less stigma. Affluent areas suffered less because of deeper equity positions, higher savings, more desirable locations and more stable ownership.

Strategic default was in part fueled by poor borrower choices to cash-out repetitively, qualify based on unverifiable income and aggressively acquire investment properties.

Post-meltdown, many people believed a pattern so widespread must not be the borrower's fault, a sentiment that was encouraged by the media and elected officials. Many in the industry resented those who should be held responsible but were perceived as victims.

The dilemma is how to treat borrowers who have strategically defaulted. Guidelines allow for serious credit lapses to be disregarded after a defined period of time. Excusing bad behavior encourages recurrence of bad behavior. Depending on the program, an applicant with a strategic default or buy and bail may not merit purchase money financing without a sizable cash investment. Allowing higher LTV cash-out refinances may also be questionable. The issue may be academic because of inability to distinguish between a standard default and a strategic default. With qualified and responsible borrowers, strategic default should fade into obscurity as quickly as it came into prominence.

How job stability and high reserves killed a loan

The borrower's letter of explanation was detailed and well written. He defaulted on a mortgage because of a chain of unfortunate events. His wife had multiple unsuccessful pregnancies that disrupted their lives. He started working at home in order to take care of their young children, but this became increasingly difficult because of the long commute for her medical appointments. Their dream home was remote from family as well, and making payments was difficult with one salary instead of two plus the burden of medical bills. They had no other choice but foreclosure.

The borrower had been employed by a major tech firm for eleven years, and interest and dividend income suggested there would be ample reserves even after a 20% down payment. These factors cast doubt on the letter of explanation. Large tech companies provide excellent health benefits, and the high amount of reserves suggested there may have been resources to cure the default. Foreclosure appeared to be the expedient decision, not a necessary one.

Lesson: A convincing letter of explanation can mask reality. The real reason for default could have been an inconvenient location, sad memories and lack of equity.

Identifying hard money financing

Hard money financing is the best available option for borrowers with troubled credit. Investors are recruited through print and radio advertising assuring high return on secured investments. Most investors prefer to diversify with smaller investments in several properties rather than a large investment in a single property. Thus the higher the loan amount, the more investors. If title-work shows multiple names as the mortgage holder, it is a hard money loan.

The name of one individual (as opposed to a lending institution) does not indicate hard money financing. It can represent seller-carried financing or private party financing arranged by a CPA, business manager or money manager.

Credit counseling

There may be investor prohibitions or underwriter discomfort with borrowers who are going through or have gone through credit counseling. Whether it is justified is debatable. Three situations are possible:

1. People with excessive debt, delinquent payments, or both seek credit counseling to mend their ways. Lending to these borrowers is chancy especially if debt ratios are predicated on reduced payments negotiated with the creditor. Credit counseling should therefore be verified as being no longer in force, with a sufficient time elapsed to demonstrate a pattern of responsible credit use.

2. Those whose credit abuse problem is more mental than actual. This situation can be compared to someone with only a few pounds to lose enrolling in a weight management program.

3. People whose remedy for credit mismanagement is credit cleansing. With this situation, the lender cannot assess the extent of derogatory credit because it may have been deleted from the borrower's credit history. See *Doctored credit* in *High score, questionable credit*

Not lending to applicants in credit counseling is justified. Payment plans may not be reported in the credit report and the payment histories used in the scoring model may be under-reported. A borrower given a reduced rate making timely payments may have no negative impact on the score level. If a creditor accepts less than the full balance as part of the agreement, "settled for less" may or may not be noted on the credit report.

Credit counseling evident on the credit report should be a red flag.

Credit counseling entered for remedial purposes should not be confused with homeownership and generic credit counseling designed to proactively promote responsible credit and homeownership practices.

Super prime and near prime

Since prime and subprime were apparently insufficient, two additional credit-ranking classifications have been added. Super prime breaks out the highest strata of prime borrowers, and near prime allows imperfect borrowers to be spared the stigma of subprime. Both terms are ego boosters.

The specific definitions vary by lender. The lowest super prime score likely is 720 or 740. Three lender definitions for near prime range from 581 to 659, from 600 to 680, and from 660 to 720. Interestingly, the first and third have no overlap and their combined range spans 139 points.

Ideally, near prime could provide improved financing options with equitable pricing, and super prime could offer more attractive pricing reflective of actual risk. Or, both may fade away as short-term phenomena.

Letters of explanation

Letters of explanation are like toilet paper. There's a world of difference between the best and the worst.

Prior to automated underwriting, explanations were required for every blemish on the credit report. Borrowers responded with heart-wrenching tales of woe, steadfast denials of fault, unconvincing excuses and sometimes the truth. Recurring themes were checks lost in the mail, extended vacations, department store returns credited to the wrong accounts, and—for upper-end borrowers—negligent bookkeepers since fired. At closing some borrowers refused to sign letters they had no part in writing.

The first generation of AUS conditioning required fewer letters of explanation. The rationale was that evaluation of credit quality should be based on factual data and that inaccuracies were best handled by disputing, not explaining. I disagree. An honest letter of explanation gives insight into credit management skills. The dishonest ones often are transparently untruthful, although I fell for an articulate sociopath's convincing letter. His loan was a first payment default.

Abuse of the system does not justify abandoning the system. No explanation can save abysmal credit. Conversely, no explanation is necessary for inconsequential lapses. But an explanation for somewhat negligent credit can help decide whether to be conservative on qualifying income or how to handle a property with marketability issues. Pertinent circumstances include dated and clustered lates, dated major derogatory credit, scattered lates after major derogatory credit, an imperfect mortgage history or credit-related issues found elsewhere than the credit report (like judgments on title-work or garnishments on pay-stubs).

A few letters remain lodged in my memory. An explanation of late payments caused by simultaneous high medical expenses and interrupted income ended with "It was ketchup soup for a while but we survived." A letter about seasoned funds stated the borrowers "saved all the money we could not possibly spend." Both letters were endearing and acceptable. An eye-opening letter described devastating property damage after an earthquake to justify mortgage default. The loan was denied since FEMA financing was readily available and the property was in an unaffected area. Not long after, the same loan request was received from a different originator with a letter blaming default on devastating family illness.

Supporting documentation may not support the borrower's case. I tangled with an underwriter defending a foreclosure caused by health issues. When I classified it as a buy and bail, she pointed to sixty pages of documentation on the borrower's medical and legal expenses. "Why legal bills?" I asked. For the surrogacy, she explained. Because the borrowers prioritized having a child and a larger house over repaying their mortgage, approval was not justified.

One gauge of authenticity is specificity. Generic answers are unconvincing. The more specific the detail and original the wording, the more believable it is. For more critical decisions, supporting documentation may be helpful. Bankruptcies are not the only events that merit sorting into the extenuating circumstances bucket or the financial mismanagement bucket.

A good rule of thumb is the more numerous the untimely payments and the more extended the time period, the more likely the borrower is irresponsible. A cluster of late payments within a limited time period is less concerning if sufficient time has elapsed. Least convincing are page-long letters summarized as "not my fault, not my fault, not my fault."

Factual details in the borrower's own words tell the best story. Loan officers or other assisters tend to simplify. For borrowers who are too busy or unable to write, the explanation can be dictated to the loan officer or processor and certified by the borrower as true before closing. Letters of explanation should be read for substance, credibility and whether flexibility is justified. This requires analysis, not a mechanical sign-off that the condition was received.

My lesson about inconsequential lapses was learned from a feisty and highly qualified borrower who refused to write a letter. When I learned of her refusal to address a single and dated thirty day revolving late, the condition was waived.

See *Inquiry letters*

The aged parents

The retired couple had credit blemished by three trade-lines each with recent multiple 30-, 60- and 90-day late payments and a score slightly below the program minimum. But the accounts were student loans and the borrowers were more likely to be co-signers than students themselves. A letter from the borrower's daughter, an attorney and judge pro tem, explained that she took full responsibility for the late payments that occurred while she was traveling. Untimely payments were isolated to student loans and student loan payments were verified to be paid by the daughter. This established a comfort level with the borrowers' creditworthiness.

Lessons: Several trade-lines with recent multiple late payments can wreak havoc on a credit score and mar a history of otherwise responsible credit. A logical explanation and proof of contingent liability absolved the borrowers of responsibility.

Inquiry letters

Pre-meltdown I was convinced that inquiry letters were a waste of effort for both the writer and the reader. Out of thousands read, only a few conveyed meaningful information. The most memorable stated that the self-employed borrower had just leased several autos for his sales staff.

Since the meltdown I've changed my opinion. Borrower-signed letters can be critical if future default occurs. Inquiries resulting in obligations are undisclosed debt. If the default can be tied to borrower misrepresentation, culpability is with the borrower rather than the lender.

Describing credit and obligations

Positive terms: seasoned, mature, timely, prudent, as agreed, exemplary, minimal, moderate, restrained, unblemished, prompt, spotless, responsible, cautious

Negative terms: unseasoned, shallow, limited, sparse, sloppy, blemished, irresponsible, excessive, erratic, major derogatory credit, severely delinquent, severe delinquency, substandard, negligent, subprime

Neutral terms: debt, consumer debt, non-mortgage debt, long-term obligations, timeliness, debt service

Synonyms for untimely payments: lates, derogatory ratings, delinquencies, not as agreed, lapses, blemishes

Terms quantifying frequency: consistently, periodically, recent, dated, sporadic, isolated, often, rarely, occasionally

CHAPTER 4

ASSETS AND FUNDS TO CLOSE

The benefit of full asset disclosure

A complete application requires full disclosure of assets. Tolerable exceptions are low balance accounts and what constitutes overkill for those with ample savings. Short-sighted originators fail to recognize that well-documented assets strengthen a file with some deficiencies and facilitate an accurate prediction of loan performance. The ability to save, or preserve inherited or other lump-sum assets, demonstrates sound financial management. Credit should be given—literally as well as figuratively—to borrowers prepared for homeownership.

Unless there is a significant equity position, affordable expenses and stable income, the amount of reserves is pertinent. Underwriters wondering about undisclosed savings can look for interest and dividend income on tax returns, bearing in mind they look less impressive when interest rates are lower.

Average borrowers enter into purchase transactions when personal savings have reached the threshold necessary to close. These borrowers may merit loan approval. However, minimum reserves combined with other risk factors may result in marginal qualification and future default.

Never assume the borrower has no more assets than verified. Casual origination or fear of resultant follow-up documentation may explain the omission.

See *Reserves* and *Reserves on investment properties*

Accessible liquidity

Some modes of savings have greater accessibility than others.

The most accessible funds are in checking and savings accounts. Stock holdings and mutual funds are also liquid, but sales commissions and capital gains liability decrease spendable funds. These accounts also have the potential for fluctuations in value, and selling early may sacrifice future profits if the stock is currently undervalued or on an upward trend.

Time deposits such as Certificates of Deposit (CDs) typically have penalties for early withdrawal or premature closing, or interest charges if the CD is used as loan collateral to avoid penalties for early closure.

Liquidating retirement accounts may result in both penalties and tax liability, and some employer-sponsored accounts may prohibit withdrawal even in the event of hardship.

When borrowers defer liquidation because of penalties or inopportune timing, the effect on risk may be minimal. Replacement funds will most likely be temporarily borrowed (usually from the holding institution or a relative) and repaid when the CD matures or the stock has appreciated. Payments are unlikely during the interim and interest is typically minimal or non-existent. Assuming the asset is verified to be owned by the borrower, personal short-term borrowing differs from borrowing from an unrelated party in a formalized business transaction. Understanding the potential of temporarily borrowed funds should not result in requiring proof of account liquidation or ignoring investor guidelines. Investor guidelines in most cases require verification of a specific dollar amount but not proof that funds were drawn from accounts verified.

It is more important to verify adequate funds to close than to know specifically from which account funds to close are drawn. Savvy borrowers will draw funds from accounts with lower profitability. This is good financial management, not fraud.

Gifted funds

Restrictions on eligible donors for gifted funds are in most instances justified. Parents and grandparents are most likely to gift and are least likely to take action if funds were gifted short-term. Siblings are less likely to have permanently discretionary savings for someone else's down payment. Godparents are less likely to gift large amounts to someone else's child unless they are childless. Cousins are problematic because the relationship is more distant, the age range issue can be similar to siblings, and there is a greater chance of misrepresented relationship with different surnames. Fiancés should be considered equivalent to non-borrowing spouses, and aunts, uncles and lifelong friends equivalent to cousins.

There are circumstances when a relative not on the official list or "like family" is bestowing a genuine gift. If there is opportunity for flexibility it should be considered on an exception basis or with investor approval. In such cases, the gift letter is essential for two reasons. The letter must discuss motivation specifically and convincingly, and a notarized signature is probably prudent. The letter can be used as evidence if the donor attempts to rescind or the lender discovers misrepresentation.

Gifted funds from multiple sources may be a burden to document but evidence a giving and generous family. Crowdfunding is a relatively recent phenomenon that sometimes meets gift guidelines and may become more prevalent. See *Crowdfunding*

A large gift, either in dollar amount or percentage, is as significant as personal savings in mitigating risk. Donors with the resources to bestow a sizable gift are apt to take a continuing interest in the property and offer additional financial support in event of distress.

Some underwriters disapprove of gifted funds when the borrower is not a first-time buyer. To my knowledge their discomfort has not been incorporated into written guidelines, at least on a widespread basis. Gift funds for non-FTHBs are easily justified if the borrower needs a different home because of changed circumstances, is relocating to an area with higher housing prices as well as with alternative scenarios. If the borrower is relying on gifted funds, lacks savings (which may be considered by the loan officer to be unnecessary) and debt ratios are high, the loan could have elevated risk. With equity in a departure residence, there may be a silent second to be repaid after the property is sold. Families seldom operate like mortgage lenders and are unlikely to formalize an advance with a recorded lien, interest charges, interim payments or—if a pending sale falls through—litigate.

Two experiences influenced my somewhat flexible attitude toward gift funds. I obtained 90% financing on my first home purchase. The 10% down payment came from my generous parents and was gifted to me several months before the closing date. My purchase was in a condominium being converted from apartment units. Since I moved in as a tenant, there was sufficient time to season the gift.

The second experience involves family friends. The husband recently earned his MBA and began work in a corporate position. Their first home was purchased with 90% financing and two 10% gifts, one from each set of in-laws, only one documented in the loan file. One gift provided the down payment and the other purchased appliances and furniture for the family of four.

Major investors are aware of early fund transfers—monies transferred in advance of seasoning requirements—and believe they are unlikely to require repayment. Despite not having 5% of my own funds, my loan performed without lapse. So did the loan made to our family friends, despite both sets of in-laws receiving reimbursement.

These anecdotes should not be construed as permission to misrepresent.

See *A Gift unlikely to be a gift* and *The gifted child*

The Chinese daughter

The concern on this loan was the six gift letters each accompanied by a wire transfer for $50,000. Two gifts were from the borrower's parents and the other four were from uncles and aunts, all living in China. The underwriter thought this looked suspicious and could be fraud.

The borrower earned her MBA from the University of Southern California and accepted a position with the major accounting firm where she previously interned. The established relationship helped support employment stability; seasoned and moderate credit with a high score supported financial responsibility.

$50,000 was the standard amount on wire transfers used to avoid scrutiny by the Chinese government, so the six gift letters were not alarming. The borrower had completed USC business school without student loan debt. Rent on a downtown Los Angeles loft exceeded debt service on the new condo. Previous rent and the absence of student loans confirmed her parents' wealth. These factors helped establish a comfort level with the loan.

A month or two later, I discovered a differing opinion. A loan request for a young Chinese couple with graduate degrees now employed in Silicon Valley tech positions had a loan amount exceeding $1,000,000 and sixteen gift letters. The package had been referred to Legal for review, and they recommended decline because of potential repercussions from the multiple gift letters.

I discussed both loans with a colleague, a senior executive in the fraud protection group. He agreed the loan was acceptable if wire transfers were accepted by a U.S. depository institution. He agreed with my approval.

Lesson: Written guidance don't always cover all bases. Although I don't regret my decision and believe that the lawyers were overly prudent, this issue merits additional research and collaborative discussion. I predict that if $50,000 wire transfers from China prove to be an obstacle, funds will be transferred earlier and will be fully seasoned at time of application.

Other sources of funds to close

Accumulated savings are thought to be the most preferable source of down payment. This is logical when monthly savings correlate with increased housing expense, but savings over a prolonged period for a minimal down payment may not assure a strong borrower.

Sales proceeds are inferior to personal savings, some believe. This minority opinion has greater validity when there is short-term ownership and rapid appreciation.

Refinance proceeds of a recently-acquired personal residence providing the down payment on another owner-occupied residence can be risky. If the departure residence is converted to an investment property and borrowers are allowed to perpetuate a recurring pattern, there can be a chain of investment property acquisitions, all with owner-occupied pricing and possibly shallow equity and negative cash flow. Motivation may also be buy-and-bail. A single instance may be acceptable if short-term occupancy is satisfactorily explained.

An **inheritance** can be considered a gift from a person who is no longer living. This should be documented with written confirmation from the executor, trustee or attorney handling the distribution and proof of transfer of funds.

Tax refunds are equivalent to personal savings in one respect. If the borrower took lower deductions, the funds would be seasoned in a depository account. They do not demonstrate ability to save, though.

Bonus income if a seasoned component of compensation is the equivalent of pain-free savings inasmuch as funds are anticipated but not spendable until they are distributed. However, a bonus also is not evidence of ability to save. Some underwriters believe that if a bonus is used for down payment, it should be excluded from income qualification. This conclusion should be applied selectively. If the bonus was recently distributed, debt ratios approach maximum and reserves are limited, the borrower may have questionable affordability until the next distribution. However, if ratios are below maximum and/or the borrower has sufficient reserves, repayment should not be jeopardized. If the bonus is a one-time award from the employer, which occasionally occurs in a small business for a long-term employee, the employer should confirm in writing it is not a loan.

Grants come from municipalities or larger corporations. Municipalities facilitate home ownership for those with limited means, and employers contribute to demonstrate appreciation for loyalty or to offset employment locations with high housing costs. Grants may be forgiven after a stated period of time, often five to ten years. If the property is sold prior or converted to tenant occupancy, forgiveness can be nullified or prorated.

Gambling and lottery winnings must be sourced. If the borrower is not the direct recipient of the winnings, the direct recipient should be treated as a gift donor.

Challenges in verifying funds to close

The purpose of sourcing funds to close is ensuring they are the borrower's own. The purpose behind the purpose is minimizing the potential for an unsecured loan requiring repayment or a silent second lien requiring repayment and decreasing the borrower's equity position.

The larger the down payment in dollar amount and equity percentage, the more likely it can be acceptably sourced. For borrowers with limited financial resources, the solution may be borrowed funds.

Sale of stock requires commissions due if a brokerage is involved and tax liability if value has appreciated and there are no offsetting losses. This applies to stock in a publicly-held company, as opposed to a closely-held corporation. If the stock holding is not verified through a brokerage or financial management account statement, web research or other form of authentication is necessary. If research is unsuccessful, a tactful way of determining whether a company's stock is publicly or privately held is asking where the stock is listed.

Sale of stock in a closely-held corporation (which occurs infrequently) requires a formalized agreement of sale and verification of sale proceeds. The business's value should be established with a credible balance sheet. With a partial buyout, future income may also be impacted. A historic average cannot be assumed to continue, and income predicated on a lower percentage of ownership could be considered projected, especially if borrower ownership decreased from majority to minority. Similarly, a **business buyout** could be acceptable with documentation of the transaction—ideally, a professionally-prepared contract—and proof of receipt of proceeds. With a full buyout, other sources of income should be considered, unless the contract includes provisions for a guaranteed paid consultancy for extended time period and preferably a history of receipt.

Business funds are a common source to close for the self-employed. There is industry concern that reallocating business funds for personal use will impair the business. A few lenders disallow use of business funds entirely. It is unlikely that a successful and seasoned business owner would jeopardize the entity generating income to finance homeownership. But many business owners leave profits in business accounts as a money management strategy or to accumulate a year-end bonus equivalent. With C corporations, there is tax benefit to retained earnings.

Lenders have developed worksheets for assessing effect on the business, some helpful and others overly complicated. Complicated worksheets should be optional for proficient underwriters able to justify use of business funds without completing a tedious spreadsheet of questionable value.

A CPA letter attesting that withdrawal of business funds will not adversely affect the business has been a standard requirement. Some non-conforming investors are adopting alternatives. Since most CPAs do not have hands-on involvement in their clients' businesses, the CPA statement is most likely based on review of prepared returns and/or profitability, longevity and confidence in the owner's ability to make sound financial decisions. This is precisely what an underwriter considers without the need for a cash flow worksheet or a CPA endorsement.

Cash on hand and **mattress money** are industry terms for personal savings that cannot be sourced. This is acceptable under FHA guidelines and may be acceptable under some affordable housing guidelines with a borrower profile of minimal credit and depository usage, and written substantiation of how funds were accumulated. Cash businesses, garage sale proceeds or large accumulations of spare change are relatively benign sources of savings. One borrower explained that converting savings to quarters saved in a five gallon water container was the only effective method of not spending money. The risk of tax liability from undeclared income is less likely when the borrower is a low to moderate income earner.

Mattress money is seldom if ever acceptable on jumbo loans. Unsourced funds, formerly referred to as stated assets, were a documentary option for a limited span of time. A Beverly Hills borrower offered to show me the thousands of dollars of cash in her safety deposit box. I declined the offer and the loan.

Offshore funds can be complicated. Borrowers who have emigrated from or have relatives living in another country transfer their savings or receive gifts via wire transfer. The situation becomes more complicated with sale proceeds of foreign property, or when a foreign government restricts large sums of money exiting the country. It is unrealistic to expect a closing statement from most foreign countries. A letter from the closing agent—possibly an attorney, municipal official or bank officer—and proof of transfer may be the only option available.

One country with stringent controls on transfer of funds is China. With China's increasing prosperity, nationals are purchasing American properties as second homes or primary residences for their children. Because of limitations on maximum transfers, some transactions include multiple gift letters from various relatives. With no student loan burden, high monthly rental expense and an unencumbered luxury car referenced on the application it is reasonable to conclude ample non-borrowed funds to close.

Checking accounts

In a normal interest rate market, considerable money in a checking account is a red flag. Most people place longer-term savings in an investment earning more than the bare minimum, which is generally anywhere other than a checking account. But when interest rates are rock-bottom low and/or when the stock market is not trending upward, a checking account becomes the default choice of where to keep savings until market conditions improve.

To test seasoning, divide year-to-date interest by the number of months that have elapsed year-to-date. The lower the average monthly interest paid, the shorter time the money is seasoned in that account. This approach is less useful when interest rates are low or when the down payment is minimal. When bank statements show funds are sufficiently seasoned, be less concerned.

Retirement accounts

Savvy underwriters and auditors should understand that updated retirement account statements are less critical than updated checking account statements. There is tax liability and possibly penalties when funds are withdrawn and not redeposited in another retirement account within a limited period of time. These impediments also explain why retirement accounts are a poor resource for down payment, except as discussed in the next paragraph.

Discounting a percentage of retirement assets is no longer required by the GSEs but no doubt some overly-conservative institutions will continue using the discounted approach in their ongoing quest to minimize risk. This not only distorts financial strength but is over-simplified in other respects:

1. When borrowers reach retirement age, penalties are not charged. There is tax liability but that is also a factor in gross income.

2. Some market environments are less stable than others. In any case, prudently-invested retirement savings commonly appreciate over time.

3. Tax liability on Roth IRAs occurs at time of deposit, not at time of withdrawal.

4. Disincentives are minimized per a government provision for emergency use of funds. This currently allows a one-time withdrawal of $10,000 (or $20,000 for married couples) for purchase of a house, either one's own or a gift, and also to avert foreclosures, which is more appropriately an emergency use.

In an ideal world, all liquid and retirement accounts would be assessed at face value and some discretion would be allowed on "outdated" retirement account statements unless funds were needed to close.

Co-vested accounts

Some investors require a full access letter from the co-vestee if the co-vestee is not party to the loan.

Jointly vested personal accounts allow full access to all vestees. Vesting as a conservator or power of attorney does not entitle full access. A business account may require dual signatures on a check. Personal accounts have no such provision.

It is statistically probable that funds in any co-vested account were not equally deposited by the accountholders. The principal contributor is most likely the person whose address is on the statements. Unless there is criminal coercion, the principal contributor had the choice of adding another person as a co-vestee or a beneficiary. Once the account is co-vested, the funds are jointly held and can be fully accessed by either party.

Repayment of debt

The thoughtful underwriter has a right to be skeptical when someone with insufficient seasoned funds to close is coincidentally expecting repayment of a debt in the necessary amount at the opportune time. Under the right circumstances, it can be acceptable. What is required is proof of original transfer of funds and proof of reimbursement. It is intrusive to require the reason for the loan. What is critical is some proof of funds going out and a reasonably similar amount being deposited. The amounts may not be identical since there may be incomplete repayment or interest paid.

A gift unlikely to be a gift

When borrowers have equity in a property pending sale or own securities or accounts that are not liquid, gifted funds may be a temporary loan that will be paid off when the property is sold or the investment liquidated. This could be viewed as misrepresentation but it more appropriately should be viewed as a gift that may or may not be needed some time in the future.

A gift from a sibling, a real estate agent

A relationship between close relatives is deeper and more long-standing than a transitory business relationship. Since the donor's role as real estate agent is temporary, funds given to the buyer should be considered a gift, not a concession. A gift from another interested party, e.g., a free property inspection from a sister-in-law would be similarly acceptable. Heavily discounted closing services from the cousin of a non-related real estate agent falls into the unacceptable category.

Equity sharing

Equity sharing is not a gift but is sometimes represented as one. It is a practice that over the decades has gained and lost traction. A want-to-be homeowner with minimal savings is paired up with an investor seeking returns higher than depository rates. This is a business transaction, far removed from an agreement between family members or a community-based affordable housing program, both designed to help the buyer. The private investor's motivation is profit, and the arrangement is formalized by signed contract with an established date (often five years from purchase) when the investor must be paid off through refinance or sale of the property.

The first lien holder may be totally unaware. Red flags are gift letters from non-immediate or unlikely relatives, non-credible source of funds explanations, recently-opened accounts and no history of interest or dividend income. There also may be missing pages or vague references in purchase contracts.

Equity sharing legitimized

Unison's business plan brings a new element to equity sharing—transparency. The first lien holder is aware there is secondary financing. The borrower has to pass a twenty-question test demonstrating understanding of the arrangement. The institutional investors are aware the return on investment may be delayed as long as thirty years.

For homebuyers with at least a ten percent downpayment, Unison provides matching funds without out-of-pocket expense until the equity-sharing relationship is terminated. Occupancy must be primary or, on a more restricted basis, a second home. The borrower benefits from lower lender pricing, no private mortgage insurance cost and reduced housing expense. Thus, loan qualification becomes easier and discretionary income increases. Unison will subordinate to a rate and term refinance or with cash-out equalling no more than the pay-down of the original first lien. The equity-sharing arrangement cannot be terminated during the first three years, which discourages those unsure about the near future and short-term investors.

Unison's process requires loan approval by their own staff, who have underwriting and appraisal expertise. They review loan documentation and also visit the property. In one case, they identified a foundation issue that eluded the lender, resulting in cancellation of the purchase. The grateful homebuyers ultimately purchased another house that passed the review. Unison makes it clear that they do not cherry-pick properties but will not commit on those that are over-improved or have other manifestations of impaired marketability.

Upon termination, Unison receives a portion ranging from 35% to 43.75% of appreciated value. If value depreciates, Unison absorbs the loss. There is a provision for appreciation attributable to property improvements, which are assessed at contributory value, not original cost.

This opportunity started with non-conforming borrowers as their target audience but may be extended to conforming loans with at least a twenty percent down payment. Unison is currently working with a limited number of lenders but plans on expanding both their client base and geographically.

Will Unison's vision on equity-sharing prove viable for all parties? Investors benefit most when there is minimal fallout. The greater the equity position, the less likely homeowners will default. The longer the term of ownership, the higher the accrued equity. Because they have delayed homeownership, the current generation of homebuyers is more likely to purchase a forever home. But some will move up, relocate or extract equity for personal needs or to terminate the equity-sharing arrangement, preferring to pay out less earlier than more later.

Time will tell.

Crowdfunding

Crowdfunding seems like an innovative means of accumulating funds to close. My first exposure came with an invitation to lunch. The instigator was a young attorney struggling to come up with his own down payment and envisioning others with similar circumstances. The intermediary was one of his clients, a provider of venture capital. Together they were exploring a start-up for crowdfunding down payments. I asked the attorney whether all of his personal crowdfunding would be gifted. Not all, he responded. This complicates matters, I said.

A valuation site blog mentions a flat five percent "out of the gate" fee for crowdfunding down payment contributions. The fee seems excessive, although fees on other crowdfunding sites can be up to ten percent. Deducting out fees points to crowdfunding being an investment from strangers. Gifted funds from established relationships would be likely transferred directly.

The same blog also mentions "gifts from family and friends are usually acceptable," adding that every donation must be documented. Non-industry crowdfunding sites at best have a blurred line between funds gifted and invested, with non-industry crowdfunding sites not distinguishing between what is and is not investor acceptable.

Those investing through crowdfunding must be warned that repayment is not guaranteed. I warned the young attorney about required disclosure of potential risk, as well as vetting of providers' financial strength with speculative investments. Investors, especially friends and family apt to view purchase transactions optimistically, need to be aware their investment could be lost. Borrowed funds, if handled appropriately in a recorded lien, would resemble hard money borrowings with the sources' names accompanied by their percentage of contribution.

The workaround to gifted funds from ineligible donors is seasoning. Crowdfunding as an alternative to tangible wedding gifts is acceptable if the couple waits long enough to convert the funds into a down payment. Although this circumvents lender requirements, from the homebuyers' point of view it represents a more mature long-term use than a lavish honeymoon or tangibles less likely to appreciate.

Crowdfunding converted into seasoned borrowed funds formalized with donor-to-borrower unrecorded loan agreements or recorded after the fact remains misrepresentation.

If crowdfunded mortgage financing gains momentum, it could become an alternative to institutional mortgage financing.

Windfall assets

Windfalls are funds obtained from sources like lottery winnings, gambling or inheritance. They can be used for down payment if acceptably sourced.

Windfall assets as a source of qualifying income are more problematic. If they are seasoned, they may be an eligible source of asset dissipation. If they are not seasoned, they should not be usable since there is no assurance the asset base will be preserved. The exception is gamblers with a verified history of recurring winnings.

The lottery winner

Superficially this loan was an easy approval. LTV was just under 20%. Credit score was in the mid 700s. The loan amount was likely predicated on affordability, since DTI was 44%. And the loan purpose was to extract as much cash-out as possible.

The borrower had lottery winnings with a single-payment net distribution of $500,000. The majority of winnings—$400,000—went to the cash purchase of a newly-constructed home, but of the remaining $100,000 only $10,000 was left.

This loan was justifiably denied. There was little evidence of responsible financial management and questionable affordability. Sufficient equity to refinance again has not been a convincing justification post-meltdown. The best decision for the borrower could be to sell the dream house and downsize.

Loans to lottery winners can be be difficult to justify. I've seen a handful, and this wasn't the first cash-out request. Except under extenuating circumstances, creditworthy lottery winners shouldn't need cash-out refinances.

Lesson: A loan with low-risk attributes can be a poor risk.

Sale of personal property

Some borrowers without sufficient funds to close resort to selling personal property.

The most frequently sold items of personal property seem to be vehicles and, in second place, guns. Other personal property may be sold, from artwork to jet skis. Essential documentation for any personal property is proof of sale including proceeds and, depending on who the buyer is, proof of fair market value. The latter is less critical if the purchaser is not an individual but a bona fide business related to the item being sold. Presumably a used car lot will purchase a used car for an equitable wholesale price.

A bill of sale is typically used to document transfer of personal property. Although forms are readily available online, an improvised agreement should be acceptable as long as it contains details including the date, a brief description of what is being sold (preferably 2014 Honda Civic, not just "auto") the sales price and the names and preferably signatures of buyer and seller. Businesses selling used cars should have forms including the business name, address, etc.. Sale proceeds should also be verified.

Proof of fair market value has been simplified by online resources. Don't expect that the sale price coincides exactly with the tool used to support fair market value, since the value of personal possessions varies according to model, added features and condition, and also whether the buyer is eager to buy or the seller is desperate to sell. A used motorcycle sold for resale would be not purchased at top dollar, although an artwork sold to a private party might.

When an applicant is selling his or her sole vehicle, consider whether the borrower has an alternative method of transportation if it is a locational necessity.

Some personal items sold may be non-arm's-length accommodations, but if an item has supported value and the rest of the loan has merit, the sale can be accepted at face value.

Rental credit applied to closing

When a tenant is purchasing a property, credits from rental payments may be applied for the down payment. Only the portion of monthly rent paid above fair market rent should be credited toward down payment. Attempts to credit a higher portion of rents paid probably reflect inadequate savings for the applicant and a property seller willing to close with reduced proceeds. The amount of excessive credits should be deducted to arrive at an adjusted sales price.

When a non-tenant is purchasing an investment property, tenant credits such as security deposits and prepaid last month rental payments should be transferred from the current owner to the new owner. These funds are not a seller concession. They should be preserved by the buyer for future reimbursement to departing tenants, replacement rent or necessary repairs.

When reserves matter more

1. Fluctuating income

2. Less than stable employment

3. Limited remaining years of employment See *Age Discrimination*

4. Untested income source, e.g., rental income on a two-to-four unit purchase

5. High DTI/marginal affordability

When reserves matter less

1. Stable income with high probability of continuation

2. Probable unverified assets (check interest and dividends income on 1040s, if available)

3. Appreciating income or conservative approach to qualifying income

4. Generous relatives (as demonstrated by a gifted down payment)

5. Convertible assets, such as equity in real estate

Sufficient savings to repay the loan

Some believe that elevated risk like a high DTI can be offset if the borrower has enough verified savings to repay the loan. This assumes in event of hardship the borrower will be willing to deplete personal savings in order to avert default and/or reduce monthly debt service. The assumption is contingent on motivation. The concept of strategic default was inspired by borrowers with sufficient savings failing to repay. Motivation may be driven by character but is more likely driven by equity.

Describing savings

Positive: Ample, comfortable, strong, impressive, diversified, well-invested, accumulated wealth, prosperous, trust fund baby, steadily or diligently saved, financially secure

Neutral: Sufficient, satisfactory, adequate, seasoned, matching contributions, employer-augmented, possibly understated, publicly-traded stocks, investment portfolio

Negative: Insufficient, inadequate, unimpressive, barely enough, barely adequate considering (borrower's) level of income, illiquid, inadequately sourced, penny stocks

Types of accounts: Liquid, retirement, IRA, Keogh, certificate of deposit, CD, brokerage, securities, bonds, tax-exempt bonds, mutual fund(s), investment portfolio

CHAPTER 5

EMPLOYMENT AND INCOME

Compensation variations

The most common sources of income are employment, self-employment and investment. There are additional sources and the potential for overlap.

Salaried or hourly: This is the most prevalent and most basic source of employment income—Johnny Paystub at his most elementary. Minor complications are overtime and part-time work. Standard guidance is that qualifying income is derived from current base, with overtime trended and averaged. Base income should be tested for stability. Lack of consistency can be negative (as with recurring absences or short-term layoffs), neutral (family leave) or positive (because of an increase in base pay.) Part-time pay can be steady or irregular because of varying hours worked per pay period or number of days worked, such as for substitute teachers on short-term assignments. The degree of regularity can be determined through analysis of pay-stubs (including year-to-date earnings) and W-2s. Don't assume that all adjustments increase income. Infrequently, an employee's compensation is reduced, typically when business profitability wanes or when the employee is reclassified in a less responsible position.

See *Testing qualifying income, Newly increased compensation* and *Johnny Paystub*

Shift work: When compensation varies according to the time of day or day of week worked, pay-stubs appear complex. Hospital nurses are the classic example. Earnings increase for nighttime, weekend and holiday shifts and for specially skilled assignments. Increases for cost-of-living or merit should be taken into account. When the monthly average for the last two calendar years and year-to-date supports appreciating income with teetering qualification, a shorter-term average may be justified.

Fixed income: Fixed income calculations are usually easy. Social security and most pension benefits are reassessed annually with increases tied to cost-of-living. Survivor social security benefits cease when the minor turns eighteen. Pension distributions from defunct companies may not increase. Annuity payments can extend through the recipient's lifetime or cease at the end of a defined period. The duration of annuity income and social security dependent benefits should be determined for underwriting purposes. Since qualifying income is at the current pension amount, whether the payment is fixed or increasing is usually irrelevant. The probability of a fixed pension payment is remote but should be researched if there is marginal qualification, adjustable rate financing and/or minimal equity.

Salary with incentive pay: Principal sources of incentive pay are commissions, bonuses and overrides. Commissions can be smaller (a segment of department store employees), larger (auto sales) or sporadic (a token amount for a cashier when a customer opens a branded revolving account.) Bonuses are paid at intervals—most often annually, quarterly or monthly. Frequency should be taken into account in qualification; a thirteen-month average should not be used immediately after annual bonuses are disbursed. Overrides are a percentage of a subordinate's commissions distributed to a sales manager or branch production to a district manager. Commissions, bonuses and override income should be trended and averaged. Be aware that some companies tweak incentive pay arrangements periodically. Also be aware that when incentive pay increases or decreases, base income can be adjusted as well, usually in the opposite direction.

Seasonal work: Examples of seasonal work are Christmas tree sales, firework sales, snow removal, swimming pool maintenance and lifeguarding. Farm workers may harvest multiple crops during different times of the year. There should be a documented pattern of seasonal employment over at least two or three years. With demonstration that hours worked annually are reasonably consistent and periodic pay increases, the most current year average is justifiable.

Temporary work: Temporary employment can be a short-term solution until something better comes along, or a long-term solution for someone not wanting to work full-time. Temporary work can be obtained through an agency or companies hiring temporarily for fill-in work. Earnings should be consistent or appreciating over at least two or three years.

Commissioned: A relatively few employee positions are solely commissioned. Because of minimum wage laws, more likely is an arrangement where workers receive minimal hourly compensation structured as a draw against commissions or are independent contractors. See *Draws as compensation*

Independent contractor: Independent contractors work on an irregular or freelance basis, often a balance between the level of business activity and when the contractor wants to work. Examples are real estate agents and consultants. Income is typically reported on a 1099 with personal expenses (if any) written off through a Schedule C or a personal corporation.

Income is typically averaged over two full years because work activity may be seasonal.

Self-employed: Considerations for self-employed individuals are their company's ownership type, percentage of ownership, size and industry. Income is typically trended and averaged over two years. See *Evaluating sole proprietors, Evaluating corporations* and *Evaluating partnerships plus other applicable topics in this chapter.*

Investment: Investors generate income (or losses) through investment of liquid and retirement assets, ownership of residential or commercial property, partnerships, joint ventures and the like. Income takes the form of interest, dividends, capital gains (or losses) and Schedule E income. Income is typically averaged over two years, with the exception of rental income which the GSEs (and some other investors) now allow to be averaged over one year.

Multiple sources: Most common is income from employment, self-employment or retirement benefits combined with investments in depository, security accounts and/or investment properties. Investments may be diversified to assure a a balanced investment strategy, asset conservation and a steady income stream. For qualifying purposes, each source should be considered individually. Take into account that with a comfortable asset base, income can be maximized or preserved depending on current and anticipated future needs.

Other: Child support terminates when the child reaches the age stipulated in the settlement agreement, most commonly at eighteen or after four years of college. **Spousal support** is dependent on the length of the marriage and recipient's ability to self-support. It can extend for a specified number of years or lifetime, or until remarriage of the recipient. If there is evidence of a court-mandated payment because of changed circumstances, use the amended figure. **Gambling or lottery winnings, inheritances,** some **capital gains** (e.g., sale of business or personal residence that will not be replaced) are typically non-recurring and ineligible for qualification. However, professional gamblers may have a history of consistent declared earnings. Similarly, real estate investors may have recurring capital gains if they adjust their holdings on an annual basis. When such patterns are evident, income can be used in qualification. If windfall assets are preserved and generate income, investment income can be used in qualification.

Industry-related subtleties of employment

Autopilot does not work for qualifying income. Before doing the calculation, consider the line of work and consistency of earnings. In some cases, written justification is necessary.

Educators: Some public school systems issue paychecks only during the school year. Others give the option of compensation over ten or twelve months. If a teacher receives only ten paychecks, either the annual salary should be divided by 12 or gross pay per pay period should be multiplied by 10 and divided by 12. Year-to-date averaging is inequitable if there are no paychecks during summer or if salary increases in the fall.

Second jobs: For educators and others, summer positions are available at day and sleepover camps, and water and theme parks. Some venues may need help during winter breaks as well. If employment or similar employment is seasoned over two to three years, it can be used in qualification.

Athletes: The contract with terms of employment and compensation should be closely reviewed. The likelihood of three years continuance is a pertinent issue. Professional athletes do not have lifelong careers; age and injuries take their toll. Approval for a 35-year-old player with three years remaining on a no-cut contract is easily justified. Approval for a 33-year old free agent is not. At 70% LTV with millions in verified reserves, asset dissipation should be considered.

Union employees: As an alternative to working for one single employer, unionized tradespeople have the option of receiving job assignments through the union. Income can be consistent or inconsistent, and year-to-date income may come from multiple sources. The solution could be a union-prepared manifest of earnings.

Construction and entertainment workers: Many in these industries are employed on a project basis. When the office building or television series is complete, they look for another assignment. Income for these borrowers should be averaged. If W-2s and year-to-date income show inconsistent earnings, averaging over an extended period may be the best approach. Some individuals work more steadily than others in the same line of business. Examples of those less susceptible to intermittent employment are employees of larger builders with a succession of local tracts and daily television shows with minimal re-runs. As long as income is proven to be stable, such borrowers can be handled like salaried employees.

Tip-supplemented Income: Many people in the food service, hospitality, personal care and other industries rely on tip income. The situation complicates loan qualification because some tip income may not be declared. There are several ways of dealing with this situation.

With tolerable debt ratios and payment shock, approval is justified. With insufficient declared income, the options are a co-borrower, a program allowing qualification with bank statements, or delaying purchase until declared earnings reflect actual earnings.

Real estate agents: A minority of real estate agents are employed rather than independent contractors. They most likely are commissioned, and their income and number of hours worked is seasonal.

See *Part-time employment; Doctors; Entertainers and athletes; The special case for other borrowers* and *Cash businesses*

Borrowers with more than one employer

In some lines of work, it is normal to have multiple employers either simultaneously or consecutively. The construction trades or the entertainment industry often hire on a project basis. This applies even to long-running television shows whose seasons may consist of eighteen or twenty-six shows annually. Dental hygienists may work at various practices one or two days per week and nurses at more than one hospital, care facility or private duty assignment.

The most prudent approach for qualifying income is a 2- or (when employment is less steady) 3-year average of earnings. This balances inconsistent assignment lengths and compensation levels.

The most inappropriate approaches for deriving qualifying income are from the most current or from the lowest base compensation, since neither takes into account periods of idleness between assignments or concentrated periods of employment. Unemployment benefits can be averaged into qualifying income if tax returns confirm a recurring history of benefits.

Time management may be a concern with a borrower holding two full-time jobs simultaneously. It is not unusual for nurses to hold two full-time positions each with three twelve-hour shifts per week. But for offices and other businesses with standard weekday business hours (including nurses working for medical practices rather than hospitals) two full-time jobs may be misrepresentation. Depending on compensation, earnings from weekday and weekend positions (or day and evening positions) can give the impression of double full-time employment. A letter clarifying time management and tax return transcripts can resolve the situation. Since aspiring homeowners take on second jobs to save for a down payment, ensure that tenure in both positions is sufficiently stable and there is intent to continue if both incomes are needed to qualify.

Employed by a family business

Employment in a family business has long been considered a red flag as evidenced by the GSE requirement for tax returns to validate income. Compassionate relatives may willingly enhance earnings to facilitate qualification. Transcripts are a more reliable means of authentication, provided that the tax returns from which the transcripts were generated were not late-filed or amended.

Underwriters who believe that employment income verified by tax returns requires averaging over two years are in error. This depends on the nature of the compensation (i.e., salaried, hourly or incentive-based), not the borrower's employer.

When a borrower is newly employed by a relative, ensure that the skill set and compensation are reasonably consistent with previous employment. It should be expected that title and income will be elevated somewhat. Validation can be obtained through depository statements showing net deposits consistent with pay-stubs if transcripts are not yet available.

Concerns should not obscure the positive aspects of a family business (as evidenced by the number of businesses striving for a family atmosphere.) Working for loved ones can be a wise choice. Opportunities for advancement may result more quickly than in an impersonal company. Job security should be less at risk unless the business is in distress or the employee assumes that hard work is optional.

In a family business, compensation may be linked to need as well as contributory effort. An employee advancing from renter to homeownership may receive a generous bump in compensation. This situation may seem alarming but may be justifiable if the company demonstrates profitability which could have been disbursed earlier. Written support can be obtained from the company owner or accountant if there is a reluctance to share business tax returns. If the increase appears excessive, an alternative is advising restructure with a reduced increase plus a lump sum bonus as a family gift. (What is excessive should not be gauged by standard increases for non-family businesses.) A reduced loan amount will allow a more conservative approach to qualifying income while a larger down payment provides a higher probability of performance. In either case, a family business is unlikely to put a close relation in a position of questionable affordability.

See *Newly increased compensation*

Part-time employment

Part-time employment is usually viewed in terms of personal experience—working after classes or weekends in an entry-level position for minimal pay. However, some part-time positions are skilled and secure.

Consider a retiree who transitions to a 20-hour workweek after decades of 50-hour workweeks, or a healthcare worker who prefers two (or more) part-time positions to one full-time position. Technology has facilitated part-time opportunities, eliminating the need for commuting while connecting via phone and texting.

Part-time employment should be evaluated case by case. The borrower's level of expertise, consistency of earnings and tenure are relevant considerations. Stability ensures that there is a good fit from both the borrower's and the employer's point of view.

Re-employed or returned to the workforce

"Return to the workforce" is the industry term for a borrower who left employment voluntarily, did not work for an extended period of time and relatively recently became re-employed. Common rationales for leaving the workforce are home-schooling, caring for aging parents or a career break, but valid non-standard motivations exist as well. The industry norm is six months since rehire, ensuring that re-employment is stable, a good fit and not orchestrated for qualification purposes.

If compensation includes commissions, overtime or a temporary draw, six months may not be adequate to use non-salaried income in qualification. A change in field may require additional tenure as well. If the borrower returned to previous employment, a full six months may not be necessary to ensure stability.

Factors affecting re-employment are economic conditions, the lapse since previous employment, and supply and demand in the borrower's field. After ten years of home-schooling three children, my sister-in-law returned to work. This occurred while Florida's economy was devastated as a result of the meltdown. She went on six job interviews and received five offers as a licensed physician's assistant. Neither stale job skills nor Florida's financial crisis impacted her ability to be re-hired. Although she has since changed positions several times, she remains in the workforce despite having two younger children, both attending public school.

Returning to the workforce differs from re-employment after unemployment following a termination, a layoff or business shut-down. Since cessation of employment was involuntary, the six month threshold does not apply, but proven stability of re-employment is a valid consideration.

VOEs, pay-stubs and electronic verification

Originators have a choice of how to verify income. Variants are the amount of data received, reliability, time involved and cost.

The Verification of Employment form has been considered less reliable than pay-stubs and W-2s. It takes little effort to write in inflated earnings, embellish a job title or fabricate income that doesn't exist. Factor in a cell phone number answered in business mode and all appears above-board. Human error is more likely on VOEs than through compensation documents.

Pay-stubs and W-2s are not guaranteed reliable either. Technology enables the creation of convincing income documentation. Decades-old practices of whiting-out actual earnings and inserting higher figures have been rendered largely obsolete.

The positive aspect of VOEs is breakdown of incentive compensation, the opportunity for comments by the employer and contact data for whoever filled out the form. VOEs are helpful for the newly hired or promoted. Probability of continued employment is less instructive than in previous years; responses are more apt to minimize legal exposure than be frank.

W-2s and VOE figures can be tested for reliability against tax transcripts. Awareness of VOE red flags such as round numbers and improbable job titles, and validation through withholding tables remain valid. Pay-stub net income can be tested against depository statements.

Electronic verification has the highest reliability but is not available for all employers. The originator is provided with a breakdown of a borrower's base, bonus, commission and other earnings. This data allows trending of the previous years' incentive income, which is not broken down in W-2s. It also provides job title, start date and termination date for previous employment.

Newly increased compensation

Increased compensation just prior to or during the origination process is either normal or questionable. Assuming two months of loan origination and an annual raise, about one-sixth of employed borrowers will have adjusted compensation during the process. Probability increases for borrowers who initiate home purchase after receipt of an expected salary increase or bonus distribution.

If the borrower works for a larger company, and the increase is reflected on pay-stubs with net income reflected on depository statements, there should be little cause for concern. If the percentage of increase appears improbably high, a written explanation from the employer is warranted and proof of successive deposits may be prudent.

For small or family-owned businesses, a raise may be contrived in order to facilitate qualification. Huge salary increases occur rarely with seasoned employees of established businesses. If the amount appears improbable, obtain an employer explanation. Proof of receipt may not be sufficient since the pay increase can be short-term. A statement from the business owner confirming the increase in compensation can provide documentation to authorities if the loan fails to perform.

For family-owned corporations, there may be a reasonable explanation for even a sizable increase in earnings. Since corporate earnings are taxed at a lower rate than individual earnings, increased earnings may be deferred until there is an immediate need for funds such as when a renter becomes a homeowner. The test for the legitimacy of a salary increase would be whether business returns evidence retained earnings or increased corporate profitability. Business returns may not be available if the borrower is not an owner; however, a CPA letter should suffice.

See *Employed by a family business*

Unreimbursed expenses

The GSEs no longer require employee expense deductions to be deducted from qualifying income, unless the borrower is a commissioned employee. Other investors may retain the traditional posture of deducting expenses for all borrowers. Their stance is unduly conservative when the expenses are discretionary. Teachers voluntarily purchase school supplies for their classrooms, and department managers may spring for birthday cakes. If in either case affordability becomes a problem, it is far more likely the treats will discontinue than the mortgage will become delinquent.

The stigma of self-employment

The following examples demonstrate how the industry is unduly conservative with self-employed borrowers:

- Intense scrutiny of business funds used to close.

- Insisting on a two year average of tax-return income, even when profit and loss statements show steadily increasing income. In such cases, a one-year average of the most recent year should be acceptable.

- Even worse, insisting on a one-year worst-case average.

- With a year-to-date P&L, not distinguishing seasonality from declining income.

- Excluding discretionary pension contributions in qualification.

- Requiring a history of distributed income despite steadily accumulating retained income and the liquidity behind it.

- Treating business debt (i.e., notes due in less than one year) unrealistically. Business loan due dates are short-term so pricing can be negotiated; repayment is not demanded from sound businesses.

- Not distinguishing seasoned and profitable businesses as lower risk.

Discomfort may be attributable to self-employed borrowers being a minority of the borrower population. Many fear the unfamiliar. Caution with unseasoned self-employed borrowers is prudent. Excessive caution with all self-employed borrowers is why many end up with low-risk portfolio loans from their business bank.

Self-employment risk

The industry considers self-employment to be a red flag. This doesn't mean that all self-employed borrowers are higher risk than all employed borrowers. For businesses less than five years old, stability is assessed by reviewing two or more years of tax returns, concentrating on stable growth and profitability. Mature businesses demonstrate business viability by longevity, the long-term proven ability of the borrower to meet financial obligations, and accumulated savings, including retained earnings for an incorporated borrower.

The function of the business matters. Some types of businesses will have continued demand for the foreseeable future—attorneys, plumbers and morticians come to mind. But technology changes some of the roles we have taken for granted. Decades ago, booksellers would have easily fit into the "consistent demand" category. In industries like apparel and food, demand is consistent but products and delivery evolve. Luckily, underwriters are not held responsible for predicting how various occupations will evolve over the coming decades.

Transaction type also matters. When a business is relatively new (less than five years old) or when the line of work is on downtrend, high LTV cash-out refinances for self-employed borrowers or employees with non-transferrable skills have elevated risk.

25% ownership interest

The industry standard is that 25% or greater ownership interest is considered self-employment. This guidance is appropriate most but not all of the time.

If a business is owned by five brothers each with a 20% share, should none of them be considered self-employed? If a son-in-law is given a 25% interest in a seasoned business by his father-in-law who owns the remaining 75%, how self-employed is the son-in-law? The answers can be found in the two following topics.

The important considerations are documentation and qualifying income. Two years' corporate returns should be obtained under both of the above circumstances to demonstrate the health of the businesses. With either borrower, justification for qualifying income would be based on atypical circumstances. When a guideline applies questionably to an atypical situation, how it is handled should be defendable and justified in writing.

See *Employed by a relative* and *Employed by a family business*

Five brothers

The borrower was one of five brothers with a chain of retail stores. The business was held in a partnership with each brother having an equal 20% interest. The pivotal issue on the borrower's loan was whether to consider him self-employed or not.

The classic delineator of self-employment is a 25% or greater ownership interest. However, in this situation all brothers were equally self-employed.

Concluding self-employment resulted in additional required documentation and averaging income over a two-year period. For this loan, more documentation and a conservative approach to income was the judicious decision.

Lesson: The strongest underwriters understand when underwriting conventions should be disregarded. Since all five brothers have equal ownership interests, each of them should be considered self-employed.

The son-in-law

This situation is the hypothetical counterpart to the Five Brothers loan. The pivotal character is the co-borrower in a purchase transaction on a primary residence. The co-borrower owns 25% of a family business founded by his spouse's parent, who owns the remaining 75%. Assuming the son-in-law's position is adequately seasoned, the central issue is whether he should be treated as self-employed.

Especially during the first few years, the son-in-law's compensation will be more dependent on the opinion of the majority owner than the profitability of the business. As time progresses, he should gain in compensation and authority. Salary increases will likely be more generous than for an unrelated employee, and job security greater. Whether flexibility in deriving qualifying income is justified depends on other aspects of the loan including trends of his earnings and corporate profitability, and whether an unconventional approach to income is necessary.

Regardless of how qualifying income was derived, standard documentation for a self-employed borrower should be obtained.

Lesson: The most insightful underwriters understand when industry conventions justifiably merit flexibility, even on a fictional loan. The son-in-law's 25% ownership represents a minority interest compared to his father-in-law's 75% interest, so if the borrowers did not qualify using a two year average, assess overall risk. If he had been employed long enough to ensure stability with increasing base salary, the case could be made that current compensation reflected the end of apprenticeship more than company profitability. Stable and consistent earnings should be documented with several pay-stubs. The write-up should comment that if the borrower's ownership was 1% less at 24%, treating him or her as not self-employed would be a non-issue.

Newly self-employed

Unseasoned self-employment is believed to be a major risk factor. Standard guidelines require at least two years self-employment, if not two years documented by tax returns.

Some borrowers appear to be newly self-employed but are not because the date of incorporation is not the start date of the business. Some businesses begin as sole proprietorships and incorporate later. Law and accounting firms may re-incorporate when partners change or depart. Developers may incorporate each project separately. A person transitioning from one practice to another may have an established clientele.

Pertinent considerations are whether only the name is new, whether there is a stable and loyal client base, and proven capability or high likelihood of managing and growing a business. If what appears to be unseasoned self-employment is viable, the circumstances should be addressed in writing by the borrower's tax preparer or financial advisor.

Conversely, a seasoned business with new ownership is not necessarily a stable situation. Equilibrium changes. The new owner may be a poor people manager, alienate the customer base or be otherwise incapable of running a profitable business.

Entrepreneurial types

Entrepreneurial borrowers (encompassing many self-employed and largely commissioned individuals) think differently from underwriters. We value prudence. They take chances. Their mindset prompts actions underwriters perceive as financially risky, such as purchasing based on current income rather than a historical average. For an entrepreneur, actions such as liquidating equity or retirement savings for seed money or business expansion, maintaining minimal liquidity, valuing a lower payment over a shorter amortization are reasonable behavior. However, entrepreneurs should be sufficiently savvy not to endanger their credit score or risk losing their home.

If refinance proceeds are disclosed as being used for business purposes, a counter-offer to rate and term may be tempting. Before you do, if your institution has a business banking relationship, consider speaking with the account managers. Do not underestimate their insight into the company's financial strength. Rationale for loan approval may be feasible.

If there is no relationship but your company offers business banking services, consider suggesting someone in that group contact the borrower. A business loan may be a more appropriate than a residential mortgage.

Trendy businesses

New businesses spring up, multiply through copycatting and franchising, and then fade out—much like fads in fashion. Once there were many instant printers and cupcake bakeries, and now there are fewer. Regrettably, bookstores are being replaced by online megastores and electronic readers. Once-popular businesses will be replaced by ventures not yet imagined.

A key issue in underwriting any source of income is sustainability. Since it's difficult to deny (or counter-offer) a loan to a business owner who demonstrates solid earnings over the last two years, trend gross income as well as profitability and consider requiring a larger equity position if you have significant concerns. Ample reserves may not be a valid compensating factor without a significant equity position. If the business is in jeopardy, the borrower may prioritize cash infusion to the business over mortgage payments.

If a business owner requests a cash-out refinance, specific use of proceeds should be required and reviewed. Will proceeds be spent on a move-up to the borrower's dream home, seed money to explore franchising or to augment already lagging sales? A letter from the borrower's accountant or business banker may provide clarification.

Cash businesses

Some owners of corner stores, flea market vendors and childcare workers declare what they earn but possibly not all.

If the undeclared portion of earnings is low, the borrower may still qualify.

There is little sympathy for those not paying their share of taxes. Repercussions are potential tax audits and less favorable financing. Income qualification from bank statements—common in pre-meltdown subprime financing—remains available but on a less widespread basis. Smaller business banks may qualify on account activity and waive tax returns. What they probably won't offer is a thirty-year fixed-rate loan.

The man selling hubcaps from his front yard

The sole proprietorship for used hubcaps sales generated losses in both tax return years. The issue was whether the recurring loss had to be incorporated into qualifying income.

The borrower was retired. I envisioned his wife telling him to find something to occupy his time. So he took his collection of used hubcaps, bought more as needed and opened a business in his front yard. It had little chance of profitability. There was potential for undeclared cash income, though.

The Schedule C cash flow losses were $5,000 and $8,000, with the larger loss in the more recent year. There was no long-term storefront lease and no one was forcing the old man to continue in an unprofitable business—aside from his wife, who preferred him out of the house.

Lessons:

1. *Depending on the investor, losses may be ignorable.*

2. *When evaluating an unprofitable business, consider whether continuation is discretionary and the ramifications of closing including contractual overhead.*

3. *Termination of an unprofitable business may be prompted by the IRS, which eventually loses patience with tax-sheltering losses.*

Evaluating Schedule Cs

A sole proprietorship and single owner LLC are the least complicated forms of self-employment. A sole proprietorship by definition has only one owner, although some could be called mom and pop businesses. A borrower can own multiple sole proprietorships and single owner LLCs and file a Schedule C for each.

Qualifying income is relatively simple to calculate: net income or loss adding back non-cash expenses which include depreciation, depletion and amortization. Qualifying income is traditionally averaged over two years. If a business has less than a two year history of earnings, it is usually deemed unseasoned and excluded from qualification. Some originators will not allow qualification without two years reported on tax returns.

Nuances include:

Trending: Whether a business is growing, shrinking or stable is an essential risk consideration. Earnings should be compared year-by-year over a minimum two-year period plus the year-to-date P&L. If earnings are declining, it is traditional to average over the most recent year only. However, this approach may be ill-advised if the declining trend is significant and is continuing.

See *When income needn't be averaged*

Reliability: Net/gross ratios test the reliability of the profit and loss statement and late-filed tax returns. Profitability can be inflated by underestimating expenses. Income can also be inflated, but this ruse fails if verification of gross receipts is requested. (Gross income can easily be substantiated for commissioned individuals.) Reliability testing involves dividing net profits by gross income during each reporting period and comparing the ratios. A stable business typically has expenses roughly proportionate to income from year to year. A start-up's initial financial statements typically show lower profitability due to start-up expenses and a new customer base.

Most investors do not allow qualifying income from a profit and loss statement, but a three year old business with consistent or growing profitability in the second and third years should not be hampered by a less profitable first year. A twelve month average of the company's second year is a reasonable compromise. Review of current year data for reliability and trending is more essential than with a seasoned business.

Affordability: When a sole proprietor yields high debt ratios, it may be helpful to analyze expense write-offs to see whether any appear discretionary. Distinguish hard expenses like rent and cost of goods from soft expenses such as travel and entertainment. Soft expenses can be increased in profitable years and reduced in less profitable years. Although discretionary write-offs cannot be factored into qualifying income, a borrower with soft write-offs may be able to handle higher debt ratios more easily than a borrower with no or fewer discretionary write-offs.

Unprofitable businesses: The critical issue with unprofitable businesses is whether losses will be recurring and the business is still viable.

Some ventures can be closed with minimal repercussions. Examples would be direct sales (such as cosmetics, candles or cookware) and in-home businesses. When a business has no contractual liabilities such as facility or equipment leases, minimal overhead or inventory, it is unrealistic to believe that the business will continue generating losses over the coming years.

Double-counting: Expenses that are written off through the business should not be double-counted in qualifying ratios. The two most likely are auto expenses and business use of home. Since vehicles often have both business and personal use, only the portion of the payment attributed to personal use should be included in debt ratios. For business use of home, the write-off can be added back to net income.

Evaluating corporations

Corporations are more complex forms of ownership. They require separate returns, but also allow more than one owner (except for LLCs), limited personal liability and in some cases deferral of income. There are three types of corporations, each with its own tax reporting format:

1. **C Corporation, Form 1120:** Within the 1120s Form 1125-E, Compensation of Officers provides a breakdown of salaried earnings and the percentage of ownership during the corporate year. If ownership is 25% or higher, returns for two years should be obtained. The corporate year usually coincides with the calendar year but not always. When it does not, do not average two overlapping periods, for example W-2 earnings with 1120 officer compensation. Income is declared on a W-2, and there is potential for Schedule A corporate interest income. Since corporations are taxed at a lower rate than individuals, profits can be retained in the corporation rather than distributed to ownership at corporate year-end. Compare beginning and year-end retained earnings (currently page 5, line 25) for trending purposes. Potential sources of qualifying income are W-2 earnings; apportioned share of depreciation, depletion and amortization; the borrower's share of discretionary pension and profit-sharing contributions (which may not correspond with percentage of ownership); and the borrower's share of taxable income assuming retained earnings show an increase. Whether potential sources of qualifying income are usable depends on the investor and the percentage of ownership interest. When a borrower owns 100% of the corporation, the borrower's potentially higher salaried earnings and the resultant lower tax liability on corporate income or retained earnings for that year should be taken into account in qualification. This also applies to discretionary pension contributions. The lower the borrower's ownership interest, the more difficult it is to justify use of non-salaried corporate income.

2. **S Corporation, Form 1120S and K-1:** The percentage of ownership position is shown on the K-1. The corporate year may or may not coincide with the calendar year. Qualifying income should be taken from the W-2, K-1 and Schedule E. Additional potential sources of qualifying income (depending on investor requirements) are apportioned share of depreciation, depletion and amortization and the borrower's share of discretionary pension and profit-sharing contributions (which may not correspond with percentage of ownership). Interest, dividends and capital gains generated by the business also can be included in qualifying income.

3. **Limited Liability Corporation (LLC) as a Schedule C:** This reporting format is used when the borrower owns 100% of the company. The

corporate year always coincides with the calendar year, and there is no potential for retained income or pension contributions. Qualifying income is derived as with a sole proprietorship.

Personal corporations, also known as loan-outs or pass-throughs, allow a borrower to have income channeled through the PC instead of paid to the borrower personally. This enables an additional layer of write-offs for expenses and pension contributions, and also shelters the borrower from personal liability. Personal corporations are most likely to be S or limited liability corporations.

Evaluating partnerships

Partnerships fall into three general categories:

1. **Small professional partnerships** have a relatively small number of partners in the same line of work like dentistry, architecture or accountancy. Each owns a percentage of the business. Compensation may be proportionate to percentage of ownership or the amount of income generated by the partner. Qualifying income is typically taken from a two year average of distributions, assuming there is a stable or upward trend.

2. **Large professional partnerships** such as doctors in an HMO or attorneys with a major law firm have dozens or hundreds of partners.. Shares of ownership can be less than one percent. Managing partners run the company, and locations range from one to many. Qualifying income is taken from a two-year average unless the borrower has recently been promoted from associate to partner, when income usually increases substantially. Using a shorter average may be supportable if all or an established portion of compensation for partners (or subcategories like obstetricians or litigators) is driven by function, not individual or business profitability.

3. **Investment partnerships** have general partners who manage the investment. The role of limited partners is to provide capital. Investments vary widely—from residential or commercial investment property to windmill farms to any kind of business start-up. These partnerships are typically structured so limited partners buy in with a non-recurring capital contribution. The major share of profit may not be distributed until the investment is sold or exhausted.

Partnerships report on Form 1065 with a K-1 for each individual partner. The full Form 1065 is not required loan documentation unless the borrower has a 25% or greater interest. Cash flow for the most part is reflected in three figures on the K-1. Positive cash flow is indicated by withdrawals/distributions and guaranteed payments. Guaranteed payments are seen infrequently. Negative cash flow is indicated by capital contributions. The figure declared on the borrower's Schedule E reflects the borrower's proportionate share of investment gain or loss but not cash flow. Unreimbursed partnership expenses should be deducted from qualifying income unless verified to be non-cash losses.

Almost all partnerships have a one-time buy-in fee but far fewer have recurring capital contributions. For professional partnerships, distributions are the partners' compensation. Mid-term distributions are less common in investment partnerships. When a capital contribution is non-recurring, it can be excluded from qualification.

The final distribution of investment partnership profit can be included in qualifying income if there is a pattern of recurring income from similar investments plus current ownership of enough remaining partnerships to assure probability of continuing income. In such cases it is equitable to deduct capital contributions from qualification. Even though they are non-recurring on an individual basis, they are recurring when there is a pattern of reinvestment.

The motivation in owning investment partnerships has traditionally been long-term profits and short-term taxable losses. Whether a partnership functions as a tax shelter should be evident in whether there is a taxable loss but no negative cash flow. An example would be an investment property whose rent covers PITI, repairs and upkeep but which generates a taxable loss because of depreciation. Tax codes have been amended to disallow passive losses except when offsetting passive income.

When there are many investment partnerships, qualifying income can be calculated by creating a spreadsheet. This simplifies calculating annual cash flow and also helps identify partnerships with non-recurring capital contributions (evidenced by negative cash flow in the earlier year only) or likely final distributions (evidenced by positive cash flow in the later year only).

Profit and loss statements

Documenting year-to-date profitability before closing is better in concept than in reality. There is potential for inflated gross income, underestimated expenses, blatant fabrication or rough estimates, which explains why incorporating P&Ls into qualifying income is considered overly aggressive. To test reliability, compare the net/gross income ratio and test individual P&L expense items against those on tax returns.

The absence of depreciation and owner earnings should not be taken as irregularities. They are encompassed in profit, and business owners may take draws until salary is determined at year-end.

Seasonality is an essential consideration when the P&L covers less than a full year. Halloween costumes seldom sell before fall and even in temperate climates people wait to buy grills until the weather warms up. A costume manufacturer's P&L ending in August would give the impression of a declining business, and nine month P&L for the barbecue store would exclude the three least profitable months of the year. The extent of seasonality can be less obvious. Per the manufacturer and online distributor of model trains, 70% of sales occur during the Christmas shopping season and sales fall to 20% of the monthly average during the summer months.

When a P&L is unrepresentative because of seasonality, business income should be trended over full years. If income is stable or appreciating, a profit and loss statement serves little real purpose. If declining profitability is a concern, options for borrowers with easily verifiable gross earnings are copies of checks or depository statements, or for a commissioned salesperson, a company-prepared manifest of commissions. Another option is written confirmation from the tax preparer (preferably a CPA or enrolled agent) that earnings have stabilized.

With a meaningful decline in profitability, the reason for the decline should be clarified. Consider pending the loan until updated tax returns become available and can be supported with transcripts. When there is substantial equity and ample savings, declining income may not be a deal-killer. See Declining income

With Dodd Frank legislation in force, waiving a profit and loss statement may mean the originator is at higher risk, even when it is irrelevant to the risk decision.

When P&Ls matter more or less

More necessary

- Declining income

- Newer businesses

- Businesses with fluctuating income

- At-risk businesses, where internal or external forces suggest vulnerability

Less necessary

- Established and stable businesses

- Personal corporations where W-2 income is the key component of gross income. (See the last paragraph of *Evaluating Corporations*)

- Seasonal businesses where a partial year P&L is unusable for trending and therefore non-representative

- Small business or tradespeople like gardeners unlikely to maintain detailed financial records until year-end. These borrowers often fit into the established and stable business category.

Audited P&Ls

An audited profit and loss statement is considerably more expensive than having tax returns prepared. With tax returns, preparers usually accept income and expenses as represented by the taxpayer unless errors or omissions are detected. Inflated income correlates to higher tax liability, and fear of audit also motivates honesty. The preparation of an audited profit and loss statement requires individual items of income and expense to be confirmed, entailing hours of tedious work for the preparer and a resultant hefty bill.

Balance sheets

The pro-P&L lobby tends to be pro-balance sheet, but the critical issue is how the presence of a balance sheet strengthens a loan file.

Balance sheets for sole proprietors or uncomplicated corporations usually do not include much pertinent information. Assets are business funds, accounts receivable, professional property and equipment, and for some businesses such as retailers and manufacturers, inventory. Liabilities are short- and long-term obligations. The difference between assets and liabilities is owner equity, which ideally should be entered on the financial statement in the loan application as an asset.

The rationale of a balance sheet is to identify debt extended to the business. If there is personal liability the debt usually appears on the credit report. If not, failure to disclose it is misrepresentation. Borrowings for larger businesses are obtained through business banking relationships. They can be secured by business assets or unsecured.

This is another instance where Dodd Frank legislation has resulted in requests for needless documentation.

The viable loan the investor rejected

The underwriting manager was angry. His site had closed and delivered a non-conforming loan that fit easily into the box, but the investor had required repurchase. Why? There was no formal balance sheet.

The borrower was employed full-time in the tech industry and had a tech-related sole proprietorship whose minor loss was factored into ratios. The borrower had submitted a year-to-date profit and loss statement but, like many sole proprietors, had no idea what a balance sheet was. Since he was savvy enough to explain that his home-based side business had only a checking account and no liabilities, the reasonable solution was a signed statement to that effect. Unfortunately, the investor thought otherwise and required repurchase of the loan.

The inability to sell this loan was incorporated into new-hire training, and after one such session a new loan officer approached the underwriting manager and correctly identified the investor requiring repurchase.

Lesson: Over-zealous adherence to rules can be as mindless as casual disregard.

Non-cash losses

Even novice underwriters know that depreciation can be added back. Most understand it represents a non-cash expense write-off. That is, the cost of the property or equipment is written off over several years rather than entirely in the year of purchase.

There are two additional non-cash expense write-offs: depletion (natural resources such as oil, minerals or timber) and amortization (capital costs and other intangible assets). They occur less frequently than depreciation but can be added back too.

A loss carry-over (previously called a loss carry-forward) represents a historical loss. Since it was incurred before the corporate or calendar year being considered, it can be excluded in qualification.

PAL is the acronym for passive activity loss. These are paper or actual losses on investments which the borrower does not actively manage. If documentation verifies a paper loss, it can be excluded from qualifying income.

Early- and late-filed returns

Salaried borrowers and those with uncomplicated returns usually file by April 15. Not coincidentally, early filers typically receive refund checks.

Self-employed borrowers and those with complex returns are more apt to apply for an extension.

People with minimal income are exempt from filing.

Flakes may be non-filers.

When tax returns aren't filed until after the extension period expires (mid-October, currently) and especially when two years' returns are filed simultaneously, income may be inflated to facilitate qualification, with intent to refile later. Since there is the potential to file amended returns, the presence of transcripts should not be reassuring. The red flag is the late date of filing.

Late-filed returns can be paired with identity theft from a person whose earnings are below the filing requirement. Another option is a consensual arrangement with a low-earner who is paid a few hundred dollars. Bogus tax returns are late-filed to provide income documentation with transcripts validating the returns. The person whose identity was stolen or rented out becomes the straw buyer on a property with inflated value. Early payment default is a certainty.

Tax transcripts

Transcripts are a relatively effective and inexpensive method of pre-closing quality control. Although misrepresentation is more probable with self-employed borrowers and there is greater cause to validate integrity with higher loan-to-values, some originators and investors obtain transcripts on every loan. A sampling targeted to higher-risk originations with some random selection could be adequate.

For borrowers who are not self-employed, the decision is whether to order tax transcripts or W-2 transcripts. Admittedly tax transcripts complicate the process by disclosing side businesses and investments, both profitable and unprofitable. Look under the couch cushion and you might find nothing, loose change or dirt. The deciding factor could be the presence of red flags in the file. It's best to identify misrepresentation in advance to a request for repurchase or loan default.

CPAs, accountants and other tax preparers

The credibility of written supporting documentation rests on the contents and the writer's professional credentials. Not every borrower employs a certified public accountant whose statements provide the highest level of credibility. After passing rigorous examinations, CPAs have continued scrutiny from monitored audits during the initial years of practice and must adhere to high ethical standards. Underwriters should be aware that CPAs have limited accessibility at certain times of the year not restricted to the first half of April.

Some accountants have college-level degrees in accounting. Others benefitted when the job title of bookkeeper was elevated into accountant years ago. They and tax preparers may have no formalized education other than training provided through employment. Those with certification usually reference their credentials in written communications.

Enrolled agents are certified by the IRS. They must pass a three-part exam (unless with past IRS employment in certain positions), participate in continuing education and be re-certified every three years.

Business management firms with wealthy clientele typically are owned and staffed by CPAs or CFAs (Chartered Financial Analysts). Responsibilities include preservation of capital and, for some clients, mundane tasks like bill-paying. If the borrower is a client of a business management company, the management-level contact typically has the credentials and professional designation to provide a credible letter of explanation.

Trending self-employed income

With some exceptions, sound underwriting requires trend assessment. Trending requires two years tax returns (if available) and a current P&L (if pertinent.) More than two years' data is prudent when income is inconsistent, fluctuating or questionably sustainable. Intangibles worthy of consideration are stability and long-term viability. A lending decision without trending should occur with well-established businesses when the intangibles can be assessed visually or when qualifying income is a minor factor.

Qualifying with a single year's returns is likely available only when granted in an AUS decision (which protects the originator) or through an established relationship with a portfolio lender. In either case, there is likely solid equity and high probability of repayment.

It depends

Businesses in their third or fourth year may not yet show yet stability. The most desirable alternative is not a P&L but a third year of tax returns. Reviewing three years' returns should not be construed as requiring a three year average of income. This would be unfair since start-up years typically have greater expense and lower income.

Mortgages or notes due in less than one year

A major difference between mortgage loans and business loans originated by commercial banks is the length of the loan term. Business loans are usually made for less than five years. This enables the bank to re-assess business strength and adjust pricing. Payoff is not required unless the business is floundering or the business owner is not loyal to the bank. Banks have no incentive to call notes due from well-regarded customers.

One approach to business obligations due in less than a year is verifying assets for payoff. This may not be viable but it does not mean that the business is in distress. An alternative is obtaining written confirmation from the lender confirming that the loan will or will likely be extended. This and a comfort level with business tax returns should be sufficient.

The entertainer with declining income

The borrower was an entertainer with a reputation for partying. His credit report was clean and verified income was impressive. Since this was a super-jumbo loan, I submitted his package to the investor and was surprised to learn they weren't leaning toward approval. Their concern was declining income.

The file included three years' personal and corporate tax returns. Salaried income was stable for the two earlier years but reduced in the most recent year when the borrower had sold a major investment with resultant capital gains. I asked the investor whether the eight-figure capital gains the previous year was taken into account. No, it wasn't because of the absence of a three-year recurring history. I asked whether eight figures in capital gains might reduce the need for personal appearances. After a short silence, I was told the loan would be approved.

Lessons:

1. *When income is generated from multiple sources, minimized or deferred income can be deliberate. Even when sources of income aren't used in qualification, awareness of the full picture can help in evaluation.*

2. *A reasonable rebuttal can result in approval.*

Declining income

Declining income doesn't have to be a deal-breaker. The following are several rationales for loan approval:

- Debt ratios so low that even additional decline does not jeopardize affordability. A letter of explanation addressing the potential of stabilization is advised.

- Additional sources of income making the declining income less relevant.

- Significant equity combined with abundant reserves supporting the borrower's motivation and ability to repay.

- A rebounding economy. At the end of an economic downtrend, businesses (unless affected by other factors) are apt to trend upward.

- A well-qualified co-borrower, occupying or otherwise.

- Decline so minimal it is irrelevant.

The transaction type is relevant when there is declining income. A rate and term refinance with a slightly lower payment and/or a longer term, particularly when the new loan term is considerably longer than the current loan's remaining term, evidences desperation and may be too risky for prime financing. A rate and term refinance with a shorter term may offset concern with hardship. A cash-out refinance is suspect. Loan proceeds could be targeted for propping up a business, starting up a replacement business or providing the down payment on a less costly home. The purchase of a second home or investment property could be a move-down or a buy and bail, depending on equity in the primary residence.

If the borrower's CPA is willing to address the reason for declining income and potential for turn-around, this may be helpful in decisioning. Not all CPAs are involved in the operations of the business; their expertise may be restricted to income tax filing. However, a hands-on CPA can provide an impartial opinion or increase concern if that statement appears to be hedged.

Sympathy for the borrower is poor rationale for loan approval.

Fluctuating income

Fluctuating income should be distinguished from declining income. It occurs in various lines of work. Examples are attorneys who handle major cases, developers with longer-term projects and those in the entertainment industry. Options for supporting documentation are a chronological project list, a written explanation from the CPA and/or additional tax returns. Signed contracts for upcoming projects can also support the pattern.

The most justifiable method of handling fluctuating income is documenting a recurring pattern, e.g., alternating higher- and lower-earning years or two lower years followed by a higher year, and then averaging appropriately.

Projected income

Traditional examples of projected income were a beginning stockbroker with no history of commissioned earnings or an employee with less than a two year history of performance-based bonus income. Projected income has since expanded to a newly-hired academic before the school year begins or a recent retiree beginning to receive pension and social security benefits.

The traditional examples remain unacceptable. The expanded examples demonstrate the limitations of the one-size-fits-all philosophy. Projected income now encompasses a spectrum ranging from speculative to assured. To qualify a newly hired academic, a signed employment contract should be adequate even if pay-stub is not available prior to closing. Educators legitimately prefer to relocate before the academic year begins. To qualify the new retiree, an award letter or the equivalent is needed. For both examples, the dollar amount of qualifying income is not in question.

The greater risk for academics is not in the initial months of teaching but several years after if tenure is not granted. The greater risk for newly retired borrowers is inability to adjust to reduced income, more so if savings do not bridge the gap. If the industry is willing to accept the greater risks, it should reconsider the expanded definition of projected income.

Residual income

Residual income, also called disposable or discretionary income, is calculated by subtracting housing, other long-term obligations and an adjustment for each household member from net income. The remainder must meet the requirement for minimum residual income.

Residual income has traditionally been utilized in government and subprime lending. The test has most validity for borrowers with high DTI, marginal credit, minimal equity and large families.

Residual income is less pertinent for conforming loans and, to an even greater extent, jumbo product. It is not a GSE requirement even on affordable housing programs. Nevertheless some originators or underwriters calculate residual income on every loan.

On conventional loans other considerations give greater insight to affordability: DTI, the gap between the housing and combined debt ratios, ability to manage credit, proven ability to repay, reserves, savings pattern, equity position and transaction type.

Calculating residual income is worthwhile under limited circumstances. It can be a compensating factor for higher debt ratios on a manual underwrite.

Doctors

Medical doctors historically have been granted latitude in underwriting since as a profession they are stable and are compensated well. There are potential complications, as described below:

After completing medical school, an intern or resident may have limited financial resources but the desire to transition from renter to homeowner. Risk increases in a non-appreciating market if, with a low down payment, the doctor wants to move up after earnings increase.

Many doctors amass considerable student-loan debt. Unless the doctor opts for a full-time position helping mankind or has poor money management skills, ability to repay is likely. The problematic periods are internship and residency when debt is high and income is low. Qualification may be impossible if deferred payments are required to be factored into qualifying ratios. This explains why interns and residents whose income typically multiplies after residency often seek financing from portfolio lenders. They also may benefit from more favorable credit standards from private mortgage insurers.

Doctors in group practice may have some portion of compensation tied to personal and/or group productivity. Qualification may be impossible if the borrower can't qualify on base salary and doesn't want to wait two years to purchase a house. The solution for doctors in group practice or those who are self-employed for less than two years is financing with a portfolio lender or the commercial bank carrying the practice's business accounts.

Entertainers and athletes

Even with impressive earnings and the resultant ease of qualification, entertainers and athletes should meet the tests of sustainable income and/or a solid equity position. Entertainers may be one-hit wonders; athletes at some point are replaced by younger talent. Relatively few enjoy consistently high earnings throughout an extended career. Residuals and syndication fees rarely replicate original income, and those few broadcasting jobs require a different skill set and continuing audience appeal. Smart entertainers and athletes anticipate the limited longevity of their earning power—or listen to business managers who do—and save as well as spend. Equity and reserves matter more than debt ratios for these borrowers.

Investment in real estate is a sound tactic for entertainers and athletes and often part of their long-term business plan. Real estate appreciates over time and even partial deductibility shelters income. For primary and second homes, substantial down payment (based on percentage, not dollar amount) is advised unless the entertainer has proven staying power. For investment properties, at least a near break-even cash flow is optimal. Athletes depend on physical ability and lack of injury; the three years continuance standard may be inadequate in their case. Most high-profile borrowers end up downsizing, with accumulated equity converted into income after their incomes trend downward.

See *Industry-related subtleties of employment*

The special case for other borrowers

Some originators have special guidelines for doctor loans. Attorneys and CPAs may be included as well. Some degree of flexibility is also justified for the following:

- Borrowers in high-demand professions like nurses and other credentialed medical workers. Not only are they well compensated, but depending on position may be able to increase income by working outside of standard work hours.

- Borrowers with transferable skills. Even when employed by an at-risk company or in a declining industry, they may have the advantage over those with specialized expertise. Examples include those with technical and analytical proficiency, and exceptional salespeople.

- Borrowers with extraordinary job security and/or standardized negotiated compensation. This includes tenured educators, unionized workers and some government employees. Sustainability is a valid consideration. Much is dependent on the entity's continuing ability to deliver high levels of compensation and benefits.

- Promotability. Borrowers with education or special training at the beginning of their careers can advance steadily. Some demonstration of increasing responsibility and accompanying financial benefit should be evident.

These strengths can provide a comfort level and serve as compensating factors.

Rental income

The traditional two-year average of rental income has been reduced to one year, at least for some investors. The change is for the better, but what is best may depend on the situation.

The most recent year's Schedule E reflects the most current level of income and expenses. If, for example, cash flow for the most recent year was impacted by extraordinary expenses and interrupted tenancy, a dated average would be more indicative—assuming tenancy has stabilized and higher expenses are non-recurring.

When income differs from the investor-sanctioned method, written justification at minimum and supporting documentation as available should be provided. For restored tenancy, include a copy of the rental agreement and proof of monthly payments. For extraordinary expenses, provide the renovation contract or a cost breakdown supported by cancelled checks.

Rental income from non-residential properties

Lease agreements on non-residential properties have longer terms, five to ten years depending on usage. The shorter terms are for office space; the longer for retail, commercial and industrial space which is reasonable considering the likelihood of tenant-specific modifications. Consequently rents fixed for the term of the lease are rare. Non-residential rental agreement may include a "triple net" provision, which means that the tenant pays for taxes, insurance and other maintenance costs. If this is the case, the expenses should not be charged to the borrower.

Rental income from relatives

Some believe rental income is unusable when the tenant is a family member. The rationale is that the landlord/tenant relationship is non-arm's-length. Family members may think rental payments are optional and the landlord may not evict family. This theory fails to take into account that strangers can be deadbeats and landlords protect their investments.

Rental income from relatives therefore is usable. On purchase transactions, ensure that rental payments on the lease or rental agreement do not exceed market rent. Excessive rent is a legitimate red flag. The absence of a good faith deposit or rental agreement is not suspect because of the family relationship. If the relative proves unreliable, a replacement tenant can be found. On refinances, cash flow should be validated with tax returns or depository statements for less seasoned rentals.

Seasonal rentals

Well-located investment properties can command high rents during limited periods of the year. Typically the property is close to a winter sport, lake or coastal area. With a prime location, short-term tenants willingly splurge for close proximity to recreational or special event locations.

By definition, income from an in-season rental cannot be replicated year-round. On a refinance the most valid approach is to average Schedule E net income for at least two years. A shorter-term average is chancy even on a rate and term transaction, and a partial-year average would be misleadingly over-stated or under-stated. On a purchase, figures from a local rental agency or the seller's financial records (but not full returns) should be obtained. Reserves should be higher than with a standard income property since rental income may not start immediately.

Short-term rentals

Procuring short-term tenants through online services such as Airbnb may fall into the trendy business category. The concerns should be sustainability and tenant responsibility. Tenants are attracted by well-located premises, especially when they are larger and less costly than hotels. Those less responsible have been known to take advantage of off-site management by trashing the premises or refusing to depart without formal eviction. Tenants may become disenchanted—missing beds freshly made, bathrooms cleaned and onsite dining facilities. Resistance has come from condominium projects enforcing CC&R prohibitions on short-term tenancy and municipalities preserving affordable housing for local residents.

For underwriting purposes, there should be a two year history of consistent use as a short-term rental, and for condominium units, no restriction against short-term use.

Vacant houses

This topic isn't in the Property chapter because it deals with qualification on listed houses that are not yet sold. Some enlightened originators ignore debt service if property is under contract with imminent closing, but the traditional approach is to include its debt service in qualifying. The traditional approach under most circumstances is unduly conservative. If a listed house doesn't sell, there are two likely resolutions. Either the property will be made more desirable by reducing the asking price or increasing visual market appeal, i.e., staging or renovation, or it will be turned into a rental. In a normal market, properties don't remain unsold and vacant long enough to become long-term obligations. If there is inadequate equity, there is a chance default may occur, but equity can be determined through online research.

Even if the property remains unsold and vacant during the critical first several months after move-out, reserves are a more appropriate consideration in qualification than debt ratios. If the borrowers have limited reserves and negligible equity, punitive qualification is justified.

Asset dissipation

Many homeowners tap into savings as they age. Only those with ample resources or those who already have extracted equity through downsizing have no need to tap into savings.

Asset dissipation—also called asset depletion, asset amortization, asset utilization or other permutations—allows principal as well as interest and dividends to be incorporated into qualifying income. Allowable principal includes liquid assets (encompassing securities, mutual funds and bonds), retirement savings and (per select guidelines) sale proceeds of a home or business.

Fannie Mae and Freddie Mac share similar asset dissipation policies— both conservative, basically consistent but differing in minor aspects. Qualifying income is calculated using a hypothetical distribution amount amortized over thirty years. Both GSEs require a minimum 30% equity position, a minimum 620 score and the subject property to be a primary residence or second home.

Other investors have individualized approaches to structuring asset dissipation. Requirements differ as to eligible and ineligible funds, the portion of includable non-liquid funds, minimum qualifying assets, calculation of assets, calculation of rate of return or amortization period, and more.

This discussion is intended to introduce the general concept of asset dissipation. Qualification should be based on specific program guidelines.

Parsonage

Parsonage is housing allowance paid to clergy. Income can be included in qualification. Parsonage income is sometimes reported as Schedule C gross with flock-related expenses written off. If tax returns are part of submitted documentation, it is difficult to justify ignoring expense deductions.

Draws as compensation

A draw is not a salary. How a draw should be treated depends on whether the borrower is a new employee, an employee with vacillating income or self-employed.

For employees, a draw is an advance or loan against future commissions. For new employees, the draw arrangement can last for a limited time period until commissions are generated. New hires not meeting their employer's expectations for productivity will not only lose their draws but possibly their jobs as well. For employees with production variances, seasonal or otherwise, a draw helps with financial obligations during lower earning periods.

For self-employed individuals, income is determined by year-end profitability. Throughout the year draws are disbursed. For established businesses, the draw can be on target based on cash inflow, historic earnings, or deliberately understated to cover an owner's needs with a "bonus" distributed at year-end. If the draw exceeds a company's earnings, the owner may have to reimburse the company, reduce draw amounts or tap into retained earnings.

Whatever the situation, draw income should not be used in qualification. Actual income should be averaged.

Disability benefits

Before using disability income to qualify, determine whether benefits are permanent or temporary. This requires verification from the entity issuing the payments. Only permanent disability is eligible as a source of qualifying income.

The continuance of temporary disability is intrinsically undeterminable. Insurers paying temporary disability are unlikely to confirm long-term continuance, and a written statement from the borrower's doctor is speculative. "Temporary" refers to the duration of the benefit, not the medical condition. This situation is not parallel to maternity leave.

Stated income revisited

A one-word description of stated income pre-meltdown is travesty. The program exemplified industry abuse. Income was inflated to the amount necessary to qualify the borrower. When stated income exceeded the upper limit of reasonability, an inflated job title or additional sources of income were contrived. Some borrowers claim they were unaware of their stated income. They either failed to read the application before signing it, signed a blank application, or upon discovery of falsification decided not to derail the transaction. Or loan originators committed fraud and forgery.

Stated income guidelines were originally designed to help self-employed borrowers wanting to qualify on current earnings and those with cash businesses. Salaried borrowers and those living on fixed incomes were ineligible, and transaction types were limited. Borrowers were required to have significant down payments or equity in the property. This generation of stated income loans performed well.

Stated income abuse flourished as the industry took aggressive measures to make home ownership available to a larger segment of the population. Thresholds for equity and score levels gradually decreased. Salaried employees and those on fixed incomes became eligible. Stated income was allowed on expanded transaction types. The reasonability test required in underwriting grew increasingly difficult as the population of loans with documented income grew smaller. The rationale was that property appreciation mitigated risk, and that property values would continue on an upward trend indefinitely.

Some lenders are offering stated income loans with sizable down payments and responsible credit. This is not aggressive lending, except possibly in pricing. Risk is reduced on stated programs for lenders affiliated with brokerages or business banks. With an established relationship and an asset-based borrower or a profitable business, there should be sufficient financial data to offset the absence of tax returns. For other lenders, stated loans will perform well when all concerned act responsibly.

NINAs revisited

Initially, No Income No Asset (NINA) loans required a sizable equity position and a high credit score. They performed acceptably. As volume-hungry investors offered increasingly aggressive programs, NINA loans were originated up to 95% CLTV with credit scores in the mid-600s. With shallow equity, unknown income, unknown and unsourced assets and an undistinguished credit score, performance unsurprisingly suffered.

A mentor expressed his preference for NINA loans over loans with stated income and SISA (stated income, stated asset) documentation. His rationale was that NINA loans included no misrepresentation. His logic was validated post-meltdown, at least from the lenders' point of view, by limited repurchase requests.

Describing income and employment

Positive: Appreciating, steadily appreciating, stable, diversified, seasoned, long-term, established, well established, high potential (for promotion, appreciating income), in-demand, tenured, skilled

Negative: Declining, unstable, short-term, at-risk industry, fluctuating, intermittent, inconsistent, entry level (for a seasoned employee or applicant long-term in the workforce)

Neutral: professional, fixed (income), self-employed, full-time, part-time, seasonal, straight salaried, incentive compensation, unionized, entry level (for skilled positions or those requiring specialized coursework)

Ratio-Related: high, low, above maximum, below maximum, moderate, mid-range, increasing, decreasing, stabilized, affordable, easily affordable, questionably affordable, proven ability (to handle commensurate obligations)

CHAPTER 6
PROPERTY

Urban versus suburban versus rural

Urban areas once comprised upper-end and middle class areas plus what was politely called "inner-city." As expanding populations caused lengthy commutes and transportation costs increased, developers and eco-types repurposed central city properties. Gentrification resulted, and even car-centric cities like Los Angeles touted mass transport, added bike lanes and relaxed zoning on live/work projects close to light rail stations. Underwriting guidelines on mixed use properties have become less restrictive. As public acceptance of new urban housing options grows, availability of similar comparables will increase.

Suburbs have been depicted as cookie-cutter communities where conformity squashes individualism. However, as developers caught on that buyers value personalization and homes in maturing suburbs were renovated to their owners' tastes and needs, the stereotype began eroding. In some locations, belief in the cookie-cutter generalization holds true only for people who haven't visited the suburbs lately. Relative to urban and rural areas, suburban residential properties have higher conformity, and appraisers enjoy the relative ease of comparable selection and fewer adjustments.

Rural properties have traditionally been problematic for underwriters. Complicating issues include primary appeal, high land value, agricultural use and outbuildings. Underwriters unfamiliar with rural lending may not differentiate poor from limited comparable selection. Marketability may improve when telecommuting allows more employees to work off-site.

Each of the three locational classifications has its own distinct challenges. Since neighborhoods differ, evolve and are affected by economic conditions, challenges can change.

About fifty years ago, there was an exodus of homeowners from West Los Angeles to larger homes on larger lots in the San Fernando Valley. About twenty-five years later, another exodus occurred with homeowners from the San Fernando Valley moving even further out into Ventura County. Simultaneously, employment once concentrated in metropolitan Los Angeles has dispersed to the suburbs. The longer I worked, the farther I commuted. Cities grow, suburbs become citified, and rural areas turn into new suburbs.

See *Rural properties, Agricultural zoning, High land value—deal-killer or not* and *Commercial influence*

The nudist colony loan

The purchase transaction appeared ready to close when someone noticed comments in the appraisal mentioning location in a clothing-optional community. The appraiser disclosed that the property was in one of two adjacent tracts of clothing-optional homes in one of the Carolinas but the comparable sales were not in either tract. Unfortunately, the marketability issue was not noticed until a month after the appraisal date. See *Impaired marketability*

My resolution was conditioning for the most recent two or three comparable sales in the two adjacent tracts and the days on market for each. How recent the sales were and how long it took for the properties to sell were critical. I wondered whether marketing efforts extended to nudist websites or magazines, but this question remained unasked.

The appraiser's response indicated extended marketing times—hundreds of days. Since the borrowers were not providing a large down payment, impaired marketability resulted in denial of the loan. A motivation letter explaining that the borrowers were not nudists but liked the large lot size and resulting privacy was not sufficient to alleviate our concerns.

Lesson: Appraisals are worth reading, preferably sooner than later.

The grow-house loan

The basement of the property was being used as a grow-house (i.e., indoor marijuana farm) according to the appraiser. The appraisal referenced amped-up electricity to provide intense lighting simulating sunlight and a jerry-rigged irrigation system.

Qualifying income came from disability benefits for one borrower and earnings from his spouse's job. Credit was spotty with assorted minor lapses and a collection account or two. The depository statements showed numerous charges from fast food restaurants, pharmacies and pot shops. (Curiosity caused a departure from my usual reluctance to dissect depository statements.)

Although medical marijuana use was legal in the state, the loan was denied because zoning did not permit commercial use and basement modifications could result in health and safety issues.

Lesson: You can never anticipate what you'll learn from a thorough review of the loan file

Mainstream properties

A mainstream property is the opposite of a unique property. It is conventional and vanilla in all respects. It has broad market appeal. A minority of buyers think mainstream housing lacks character and individuality, but for the appraiser it represents a less complicated assignment.

Mainstream housing doesn't have to be bland. It can be personalized to the buyer's taste with furniture, accessories and wall decor. Savvy owners eliminate more permanent changes prior to listing for sale. A vivid purple bedroom can be repainted in a neutral color. An eliminated wall converting two bedrooms into one larger bedroom can be rebuilt, thus increasing marketability.

Non-mainstream properties

In urban or suburban areas, non-mainstream housing falls into several categories:

Custom homes are usually the most costly houses in an area. They are built to the owner's specifications. If concentrated in an upper-end neighborhood, architectural styles may be similar or varied—a two story colonial next to a two-story brick next to a one story contemporary. But if all the houses are well-constructed with curb appeal and well-maintained landscaping, the neighborhood will appear cohesive in an "all different but very nice" way. Excessively customized houses fall into the unique category.

Custom tract homes are relatively new in availability. They are higher-cost tract homes configured and upgraded to the buyer's tastes. Although they are thought to be customized by their owners, they likely should be classified at the pricier end of mainstream housing.

Quirky, eclectic and very individualized houses may be located in the "arts district" or scattered through otherwise normal neighborhoods. Especially in urban areas, you can find a modern minimalist structure surrounded by older ranch homes, a house painted in a glaringly bright color or one having a facade painstakingly embellished with a broken china mosaic. Unless the unique house can be easily converted to mainstream or the neighborhood includes a number of eclectic houses, appropriate comparables may be scarce or unavailable, and the property may have impaired marketability.

In rural areas, mainstream matters less because houses are further apart and assessed individually. Curb appeal is less important when a property is being purchased for lot size and agricultural use. An area transitioning from rural to suburban is likely to be populated with tract housing or, on a smaller scale, non-tract houses built by a developer who subdivided a larger parcel.

Unique properties

I have known underwriters who believe any properties described as unique should be ineligible for financing. I disagree.

Unique can be a positive or negative quality. The only house in the neighborhood on a double lot may be desirable because it has a larger yard and more privacy. The only house in the neighborhood backing to an active landfill is far less desirable.

The key is to assess whether the unique element is negative, positive or a combination of both. An example of combined elements is a house adjacent to a school. There may be increased traffic at times, footprints on the lawn and increased noise during school hours, but there is a short commute for the homeowner's children and reduced noise during off-school hours.

If the unique element is negative, determine whether the solution is loan denial or a more conservative loan offer, typically reduced LTV. If the element is positive, take into account the adjustment in the market approach to determine the extent of impaired marketability. This should be factored in determining the appropriate loan-to-value and loan amount.

Allowing maximum financing on the house sited on a double lot may be a poor decision if lot size turns the property into an over-improvement. The house backing to the active landfill has impaired marketability at best and possibly health and safety concerns.

Those fascinated by distinctive houses should consider looking at *My Passion for Design: A Private Tour* by Barbra Streisand. This 2010 coffee-table book has close to 300 pages, mostly pictures. It tells the story of how Streisand almost single-handedly (except for the construction crews) transformed three adjacent Malibu homes into a replicated 1790 mill home (exterior only), complete with color-coordinated koi pond and brook, barn, guest house and main house. Teaser: The master suite is not in the main house.

See *Over-improvements*

The retired legislator's house

The Midwestern legislator retired and hired a contractor to build his dream house. The exterior was impressive, two stories topped with a cupola. The interior, in the kindest terms, was basic. The lower floor had a garage big enough for two cars and a small tractor, a guest bedroom and bathroom. The second floor had a bedroom and bathroom, and an open-concept, all-purpose room including kitchen at one end. The cupola held an office.

The house didn't have air conditioning since the owner tolerated heat well. It also was built without washer-drier hook-ups since the owner's mother did his laundry. But the house was exactly what the owner wanted. It served all of his needs.

Lesson: Custom for one person can be undesirable to nearly everyone else.

Two-to-four units

Motivations vary for owning two-to-four unit properties, also called small income properties. Some buyers are attracted by the offset to housing expense. Others want close proximity to but privacy from extended family. Retired borrowers purchase real estate as a prudent investment with rental income replacing income from employment.

Loans on small income properties as a group perform less reliably than loans on one-unit properties, with increasingly poor performance as the number of units increases. Well-located properties tend to attract more stable and responsible tenants.

When underwriting a loan on a two-to-four unit property, consider the following:

Key appraisal points: The two-to-four unit appraisal form includes separate grids for rental comparables and sales comparables. The rental income section details pertinent information on each unit and compares current rents with market rents. Since most areas have a limited number of small income properties, comparable sales may require more adjustments than SFRs. The sales comparable grid is more complex than the single family grid because of detail on each unit.

Qualification: The default formula for conforming purchase loans allows 75% of gross rental income as qualifying income per actual rents on the appraisal. The 75% figure is used to allow for vacancy and expenses other than PITI. On refinances, the Schedule E provides actual income and expenses. Actual cash flow should be used whenever available; real numbers are preferable to hypothetical numbers. FHA requires three- and four-unit properties to be self-sufficient, which is reasonable especially when the borrower has limited reserves.

Affordability: High debt ratios, an inexperienced landlord and an older property with mediocre upkeep add up to questionable risk, which is amplified when the borrower lacks reserves. Borrowers who do not qualify on conforming programs may qualify under government programs.

Occupancy: Borrowers purchasing investment properties may be motivated to misrepresent occupancy to obtain more favorable pricing and a lower down payment. First-time borrowers may see small investment properties as the first step in a real estate empire. Others move out for more room or distance from tenants. A recurring pattern of flight should be taken into account on cash-out refinances. If a property is discovered to be non-owner occupied within a year of origination, the loan may require repurchase or repricing. When borrowers insist they will continue to occupy, make them aware of the repercussions for misrepresentation. Consider conditioning for a handwritten letter confirming intent for continued occupancy and specific use of proceeds. If necessary, the letter can be used to demonstrate intent to defraud.

Updated leases: Underwriters have been known to condition for updated leases, thinking they are similar to updated depository statements. They are not. When a lease expires, the owner can renew the lease. If not, the tenant transitions into month-to-month status. A change in rent does not require a new lease but written notification. Tenancy without a lease can continue for months or decades. Rents on the appraisal should be vetted by the appraiser. If the appraiser's authentication is inadequate, copies of rental increase notifications and tax returns should suffice.

Five-unit properties: Properties with five or more units are categorized separately from small income properties. If you encounter a four unit property with an accessory unit, possibly below grade, review the title-work and the appraisal to ensure the property legally has four units.

Five or eight units?

The borrower was a performer and was considered to be a free spirit. Her residence was legally an eight-unit apartment building, each with a kitchen, bathroom and combined living room/sleeping area. Her business manager said that the lower floor units were rented out to four single men and the upper floor had been modified into the owner's personal living space. A carpenter had added extra doors. One unit was used as guest quarters and the others for various purposes such as a dedicated make-up room and closet rooms for wardrobe, shoes and accessories.

The business manager asked whether the property had eight units or five units. I responded that it was an eight-unit property unless the upper floor had been permanently remodeled into one cohesive living unit. That would require a building permit and formalized conversion into a five-unit residence, which would also decrease value. I recommended when she moved out the extra doors upstairs should be removed and the openings drywalled, thus restoring the second floor to four living units. The current configuration would turn into a memory.

Lessons:

1. ***Temporary use isn't a zoning violation as long as it is in accord with permitted use. Modifications such as sinks installed to convert a living room into a dog grooming salon are not temporary and likely not in accord with zoning.***

2. ***Although five units are ineligible for one-to-four unit residential financing, the same lesson applying to the eight-unit property applies to one to four units as well.***

Factory-built housing

Manufactured houses are built in a factory. Double-wides and triple-wides are too wide to be hauled on a trailer down the highway so are assembled on-site.

Single-wides, double-wides and triple-wides (typically 16', 32' and 48' in width respectively) are typically rectangular. Houses with more complicated exterior footprints are most costly to build. Inexpensive stick-built houses may also be rectangular, but usually differ from factory-built because they have non-standard width.

Loans on manufactured housing are considered higher risk than stick-built housing for multiple reasons:

1. Loan performance is poorer.

2. The average borrower has a lower credit score and more problematic credit.

3. Most manufactured housing is less durable and shows wear earlier than stick-built housing. Consequently, value depreciates similar to automobiles rather than appreciating like stick-built housing.

4. In most areas, manufactured homes are less marketable. Much of the public does not distinguish between trailers and manufactured homes, despite the latter being permanently attached to a lot.

5. Permanent attachment may be impermanent. Appraisers and servicing agents tell stories of arriving at an address and discovering an empty lot where a manufactured house once stood. Stick-built houses are capable of being moved from one lot to another, but manufactured housing can be moved more easily.

6. Documentary requirements on manufactured housing (principally title- and appraisal-related) are complex.

7. Manufactured housing may be an affordable option in an appreciating market, but value suffers in a depreciating market when borrowers can afford more structurally sound and centrally located stick-built housing.

In some areas such as the Pacific Northwest, manufactured housing has better market acceptance and less of a stigma. Manufactured homes in California coastal communities may sell for prices consistent with or higher than luxury home prices in non-coastal states.

Several years ago when I announced that our correspondent division was discontinuing purchasing loans on manufactured housing, spontaneous cheering broke out. I cheered as well. For me, it meant fewer audit errors to research, less internal training and re-training, and no further repetition of my standard warning to originators: Assign manufactured housing loans to your most detail-minded and risk-savvy underwriters.

Be aware of distinctions between manufactured, modular and prefabricated housing. Manufactured housing is assembled in the factory and transported to the site. Modular is built in sections, transported and assembled on-site. Prefabricated housing is factory-built with panels or walls attached to framing on-site. Some view the minor distinctions between modular and prefabricated as inconsequential. Unless the appraiser distinguishes and the investor does also, it may not make a difference. In most cases, modular and prefabricated housing are typically considered the equivalent of stick-built by investors.

Factory-built housing revisited

Given recent improvements in manufactured housing, I'm considering eating my words. The original treatment above, written some time ago, had little positive to say. The following two updates do:

1. The *Hot Property* supplement of the *Los Angeles Times* recently featured an article headlined "Prefab homes for the sophisticated." Opening with comments about traditional prefab housing ("mega-builders who cranked out staid, cookie-cutter design lines") the article moves

on to describe "a new breed of home builders...branded architects... modernist styles with clean and often daring lines, light-infused spaces and lofty ceilings." Most of the article is devoted to four eco-friendly builders of upmarket prefab homes. Photos accompanying the article and the four company websites are impressive. Two builders are relatively affordable (for California) with pricing from $250,000 to $500,000 and $300,000 to $665,000. The other two range from under $500,000 to slightly over $1,000,000 and from $235,000 to $1,855,000. (All prices exclude site prep and land costs.) Pricing is said to be 20% below similar-sized stick-built housing. It is encouraging that economies of scale applied to mass-produced nondescript housing can turn out non-rectangular, moderately-priced, innovative and individualized housing.

2. A conversation with a fellow traveler revealed that she was on her way to Germany where she planned to build a shipping container house. Container homes are affordable, durable and making inroads in Europe, South America and Asia. The basic shipping container sizes are 20' x 8' x 8' (160 square feet) and 40' x 8' x 8' (320 square feet.) Structures range from one container to several. After returning from the cruise, I saw HGTV episodes of Container Houses, one a small lakeside vacation home and the other a two-thousand-square-foot house built out of seven containers. (The HGTV website shows an underwhelming total of five episodes.) When multiple containers are adjoined, container houses cease to be rectangular and take on a contemporary and industrial vibe.

What is off-putting about traditional manufactured housing, aside from the higher default rate, is uniformity combined with questionable quality. Stereotyping the manufactured housing industry was a faulty conclusion on my part. It is capable of change. Using the best selling point of their product—affordability—and expanding product lines for a wider audience indicates smart business sense.

Live/work units and mixed use developments

Live/work units are not newly invented. Grocers, tailors, doctors and other small business owners have lived behind or above their storefronts long before the contemporary resurgence justified by environmental protection. Some still do. The contemporary storefront equivalent is an artist's studio adjacent to other creative spaces in a converted factory.

Loans on live/work units appear to defy prohibitions against commercial use of residential property but are acceptable to the GSEs and some other investors. They must be permitted for dual use. Properties informally converted—like a residence next to a bus stop functioning as a convenience store—are not investor eligible. Also unacceptable are properties where commercial square footage substantially exceeds residential space or with considerable noise, noxious odors or potential health hazards—situations where commercial use negatively impacts residential use.

Live/work properties should be primary residences. The buyer of a mixed use property claiming second home occupancy was probably a straw buyer or seeking a source of rental income.

Mixed use housing has also been long-accepted. In urban areas, condo developments have been built above commercial usage on the ground level and, less frequently, luxury condominiums have been built above hotels. Mortgage financing is available as long as the percentage of commercial square footage is acceptable relative to total square footage. See *Evaluating Condominiums* and *Neighborhood Update*

Live/work and mixed use may be used interchangeably.

Row houses, zero lot lines and townhouses

Row houses are typically found in well-established urban neighborhoods, principally in northeast United States but also in other areas such as Baltimore, New Orleans and San Francisco. Row houses typically have brick or brownstone exteriors, and except for end units share an interior wall with the unit on either side.

Row houses may have been the inspiration for both zero lot line houses and attached townhouse-style condos. Zero lot-line houses offer a pricing advantage to the buyer and are profitable for the developer, with higher density if they are attached or improved lot utility with no setback if they are detached. Townhouse-style condos are similar to zero lot line houses in terms of pricing and developer profitability, but differ since they have association fees, CC&Rs and bylaws.

Brick construction between units common in row houses provides the benefit of sound insulation. Row houses and zero lot-line houses lack the separation that single family detached residences offer, so preferably should be compared to similar structures. They are legally single family residences—although not detached.

Student housing

Some underwriters are wary of lending on income properties near colleges and universities because of relatively short-term occupancy and excessive partying. There is consistent demand for conveniently-located housing in two-to-four unit properties and single family residences. Newer residences have been designed specifically for student usage, such as a four-bedroom residence configured so paired bedrooms share a bathroom or, better yet, with each bedroom having an adjoining bath.

These properties can be highly profitable to the owner. Lease agreements cover a full year or the academic year with rent compensating for potential vacancy during the summer. The leases are signed by students and their parents, or by the parents solely. Target tenants are graduate students or female undergraduates.

Kiddie condos

Kiddie condo is the industry designation for a unit purchased for occupancy by the borrower's offspring while attending college. Second home occupancy was previously tolerated by the GSEs with the tenuous justification that the property was an annex of the primary residence or that parents would co-occupy during visits. This rationale became unacceptable after numerous defaults during the meltdown.

GSE policy may differ when the "kiddie condo" is a detached SFR. Flexibility on condo units may be restored with sustained market stability. Or, it may not be restored because of the relatively short term of ownership or conversion to rental property combined with the higher incidence of default on condo units.

Rural properties

Rural properties are challenging to appraise and to underwrite for several reasons:

Non-residential use: Properties with significant acreage and/or out-buildings like barns, silos and loafing sheds are apt to be used for agricultural purposes. This will be declared on the Schedule F of 1040s, or possibly the Schedule E if acreage or facilities are leased out. Unless the property can be classified as a hobby farm, it is ineligible for residential financing. Fannie Mae's and Freddie Mac's charters specify non-residential properties as ineligible; even a stellar borrower and low LTV cannot reverse ineligibility.

Non-residential appeal: It is irrelevant that the borrower does not use the property for non-residential purposes. Primary appeal is the deciding factor. Key considerations are lot size and the value of the residential improvements relative to overall value. If the lot size is extensive, even a stunningly large and high-end residence may not qualify for conventional financing because of the acreage.

Value: The less dense the area, the more likely comparables will be distant, dated and dissimilar—translating to high adjustments. Value therefore will be difficult to define.

Marketability: With lower population density, rural areas have a smaller pool of potential buyers. Factoring in that homeowners prefer to spend more on their residences than their backyards, and also value proximity to employment, schools, services and stores, rural properties have decreased appeal and consequently increased marketing times. With technology enabling more people to work and shop at home, employment proximity and retail convenience may decrease as considerations.

Percentage of land value: Some companies have stringent rules about maximum percentage of land value. Underwriters should be aware that large lot size represents only one of three major causes of high land value, the other two being poor condition of the improvements and high-demand location. *See High Land Value—Deal-Killer or Not*

Foreclosure: Because of reduced locational marketability, a foreclosure sale on a rural property is more likely to result in monetary loss to the lender. The solution is below-maximum financing and, to a lesser degree, a well-qualified borrower.

See *Hobby farms versus working farms*

Agricultural zoning

Agricultural zoning should not cause property ineligibility. The specifics of the property matter more. In areas transitioning from agricultural to residential use, agricultural zoning may still be in effect despite the presence of residential subdivisions.

Some areas preserve agricultural zoning to prevent urbanization. In Hawaii, farm use is mandated in defined areas with consequences to the owner if the land lies fallow. In the Pacific Northwest, designated areas have mandatory tree farming. The Hawaiian properties are ineligible for residential lending, but depending on the amount of acreage dedicated to trees in the Pacific Northwest, the property may qualify as residential.

High land value–deal-killer or not

1. Loan requests should be declined on working farms where tax returns reflect significant non-residential activity or when primary appeal is not residential.

2. Be skeptical of lending on older houses where usage has shifted from single family to apartments, condo projects or commercial. If long-term residents with deep equity want a rate and term refinance or can provide documentation for a planned remodel, loan approval may be defendable. Owner-occupied purchases should be viewed with skepticism. If a property is being purchased as an investment property by someone in the real estate or construction industries, or as a primary residence with a non-occupant co-borrower in either field, it may be demolished as soon as building permits are approved.

3. Small houses on large lots may be purchased for future subdivision. However, a small house with a large lot may be attractive for a borrower who values privacy. The test is whether the borrower appears to be a long-term occupant.

4. When properties are dated or in disrepair, some can be restored and others are better torn down. If renovation is required because of health and safety concerns, or when the property cannot be occupied in time to comply with the trust deed, interim financing is more appropriate than permanent financing. For a tear-down, financing should be short-term since the secured property will soon be a vacant lot. Replacement financing will likely be obtained after the improvements are complete.

5. An in-demand location is acceptable as long as the neighborhood is residential. After I revealed to co-workers the percentage of land value on our West Los Angeles house, my short-term nickname was 85%. Having an in-demand location is a positive factor despite the size of the residence and/or the lot. Ask someone who owns in midtown Manhattan or Honolulu, who would probably consider our house affordable.

In every case, current and anticipated future primary appeal must be residential.

The tandem tandem bedrooms

The floor plan was unconventional at best. The house was long and narrow, and the bedroom-bathroom arrangement on the second floor consisted of a single row of five bedrooms, each separated from the next by a bathroom. With no hall, the only way of getting from the bedroom closest to the street to the most distant bedroom was by walking through the three middle bedrooms and all four bathrooms.

The loan had strong compensating factors. The borrowers were impressively qualified. The property was oceanfront in Malibu on a guard-gated street. Lot size was normal for the street, with sales prices relative to the length of ocean frontage.

This loan has one more interesting facet. Occupancy was as a second home and the borrowers' primary residence was in Beverly Hills, about twenty-six miles away.

The loan was approved.

Lessons:

1. *The floor plan in other locations would cause impaired marketability. In Malibu it was a trade-off for higher room count and beach-front access in a protected and prestigious environment.*

2. *Second home occupancy that would be suspect elsewhere was reasonable because of the metropolitan vibe of the primary location and the beach vibe in Malibu, also the one-hour commute on a good day between the two.*

3. *Each loan should be judged by its individual merits.*

Hobby farms versus working farms

An underwriter advocated that a property was a hobby farm because the borrower could easily afford the Schedule F loss. The borrower's earnings from a tech position easily offset losses from the vineyard covering most of the residence's acreage. Relative to high-paying employment, the vineyard was the borrower's hobby. However, relative to Schedule F activity, it could not be considered minor agricultural use.

A key indicator of a hobby farm is minimal gross earnings. The vineyard had significant gross earnings but was far from profitable, even though the wine was sold commercially. There was no resemblance to a home garden or a 4H project. That the borrower could easily afford the loss was irrelevant to how the property was utilized.

Another consideration is primary appeal. A large house on moderate acreage could be attractive to a buyer looking for what could be called a kitchen garden—enough produce to supply the household—and privacy from neighbors. A small house on the same moderate acreage would only attract a buyer wanting to farm the acreage.

Marilyn's farm

Eric and Marilyn owned a spacious house in a low-density suburban neighborhood with an acre of avocado trees in the backyard. An irrigation system watered the grove, but the gardener came no more often than for a normal residence. Twice yearly a crew harvested the crop. Despite Eric referring to their backyard as Marilyn's farm and the Schedule F in their tax returns, this clearly constituted a hobby farm. The value of the property rested largely in the residential structure, not the small but profitable income from the avocados. Location was in an upper-end suburban residential neighborhood. Although an adjacent neighbor's backyard housed a few llamas, that property was not considered a zoo.

Lesson: It's not a working farm unless a primary appeal is agricultural use, despite what you call it.

The improved condo

I phoned a helpful real estate agent and asked if he had a few minutes. Brief silence. He said he was reading through some CC&Rs. I offered to call back. Brief silence. No, now is good, he responded. Thank you but first, David, why are you reading CC&Rs?

It turned out David's client was under contract to buy a condo with interior updates. The work had been costly, cosmetic for the most part but removing some walls to make the unit more "open concept." No permits were obtained. The City of Los Angeles technically requires permits for additions or upgrades requiring electrical or plumbing modifications. This is sometimes ignored for minor (and sometimes major) renovations with few ramifications. David had already advised a structural engineer's report but his buyer was concerned about future ramifications.

It is unlikely that a seller occupying the property would stipulate "as-is condition" in the purchase agreement. It would have been a red flag to the lender, the buyer and the conscientious real estate agent. It turned out the renovation was noted in a seller disclosure, one the lender did not require.

From a lender's point of view, much depended on the appraisal. It could merely state that the interior was recently upgraded, or it could describe the improvements in detail. If the absence of permits were mentioned and accompanied by the verbiage "workmanlike manner," the lender would likely take no further action.

As for the homeowners' association, it is improbable that there would be repercussions. Individual units in well-maintained projects likely keep pace with interior upgrades. Upgrading increases market value of the unit and in turn enhances value of other units within the project. HOA controls typically focus on exterior uniformity, structural integrity and disruptive behavior.

The final consideration is insurance. Removal of a bearing wall could intensify structural instability, especially if there is a natural disaster. The engineer's report should identify any shoddy workmanship on the remodel, providing a comfort level for both the HOA and the insurer.

Lesson: The best real estate agents do much more than sell. They guide their clients, share expertise and often serve as intermediary between buyer and lender.

See *the As-is condition* subsection of *The purchase contract*

Evaluating condominiums

Condominium unit ownership includes a living unit and a percentage share of the common area, which may include hallways, walkways, elevators, green space and amenities such as swimming pools and exercise rooms. A condominium also is a legal entity as defined within the CC&Rs and bylaws. Condominiums, commonly referred to as condos (with both terms in the singular referring to the project and an individual unit), take on varied appearances. A project can be a multistory building, adjacent buildings, a former two-to-four unit property converted to condominium ownership or detached homes looking just like single family residences.

Underwriting a condo loan is complex, since both the individual unit and the project must be evaluated. Aspects worthy of consideration include:

Owner-occupancy: The percentage of owner-occupied units is critical. With high tenant occupancy, the project feels like an apartment project. Tenants may disrespect the property, and landlords may skimp on repairs with a negative effect on livability and appeal. The percentage of owner-occupied, second home and tenant-occupied units per the appraisal or HOA questionnaire is critical to risk evaluation and investor eligibility. High tenant occupancy can cause a project to be non-warrantable. Showing the breakdown of occupancy status as "unknown" is evasive. The appraiser should be required to provide the data.

Covenants, conditions & restrictions (CC&Rs) and bylaws: These are formalized organizational and operating rules for the project, usually drafted by a real estate attorney from a template and consequently similar in most respects to other projects. Organizational controls establish the composition of the board of directors, the frequency of elections and the board's authority over unit owners. There may be restrictions on the age of residents, noise levels and hours of pool use, what kinds of vehicles can be parked and for how long, and architecturally-related rules such as exterior paint color. Occupancy controls typically include a minimum lease term to discourage short-term tenancy. Standard verbiage enables the association to convert delinquent HOA fees into a recorded lien. Underwriters should consider reviewing CC&Rs and bylaws until they can identify standard verbiage, after which the review process can be expedited or unnecessary in well-run established projects. The review process is simplified by investors who maintain lists of unacceptable or acceptable projects.

Budget: The project budget is pertinent reading for prospective owners and lenders. Key points are whether the project is operating at a loss and the amount of delinquencies, both of which impact a project's ability to operate smoothly. Also pertinent are reserves, which are funds set aside for future repairs and maintenance. With a troubled budget, warrantability may be jeopardized. Adequacy of reserves is especially critical in older projects; diligent accumulation of reserves in a newer project can avert special assessments later on.

Warrantability: If a project is warrantable, it meets investor guidelines—typically Fannie Mae or FHA. Traditionally, Freddie Mac follows Fannie Mae warrantability standards, and some non-conforming investors require Fannie Mae warrantability or have internal lists of non-acceptable projects. Although originators are not required to review CC&Rs, bylaws and budget, if the project is revealed to be non-warrantable, the loan may be considered ineligible and repurchase may be required.

Seasoning: Fannie Mae's traditional posture has been that an established project with high owner-occupancy, good maintenance and an in-balance budget evidences good health. This does not mean that all non-seasoned projects have higher risk. A newer project in a non-declining market with sound construction, a developer mindful about owner-occupancy and a realistic budget can be a rewarding investment. These factors also minimize future delinquencies and distress sales.

Ineligible projects: Investor-ineligible project lists should be checked before loan approval. Ineligibility typically results from too many units used as rentals, heavy foreclosure activity, condotel attributes or litigation issues. If possible, such lists should be embedded into an originator's loan origination system. Projects that offer personal service amenities such as medical care and meal service traditionally have been designated as ineligible. See *Condotels*

HOA fees: Monthly HOA fees cover operating expenses including property and liability insurance, taxes and upkeep on common areas, and reserves. In some projects they may also cover utility costs, cable television and staffing. Luxury projects may have doormen, valet parking, gym attendants and office personnel.

Too low HOA fees are shortsighted and too high HOA fees may be a deterrent to some potential buyers. If comparables have considerably higher HOA fees, the subject property may be compared to more desirable projects.

HOA questionnaires: A questionnaire signed by an HOA officer or management company representative is one component ensuring warrantability. In mid-2016 Fannie Mae finally issued a standardized industry form, stipulating that for some projects lenders may need to obtain additional information to fully assess risk. This places responsibility on the originator for ensuring that the questionnaire is basically consistent with the appraisal and does not reveal any areas of concern. Consider this a risk review, not automatic sign-off after the form has been received.

Amenities: Basic amenities include parking and laundry facilities unless they are incorporated into the individual units. Less common are workout rooms, swimming pools, playground and pet exercise areas. Luxury amenities are staff-related (doormen and receptionists) or facility-related (party rooms and community gardens). Amenities in non-urban areas may include tennis, volleyball or basketball courts and walking paths. In-demand amenities change with the times.

Commercial usage: Urban condominium projects may have storefronts on street level, office space above and shared parking below. The percentage of commercial usage must be acceptable to the investor. In the best interest of unit owners, there should be controls on businesses allowed, e.g., no odiferous restaurants or any venture with a raucous clientele. Fannie Mae historically allowed flexibility case by case when the maximum percentage of commercial use is exceeded.

Inside and outside comparables: The appraiser should attempt to provide comparable sales from the same project and similar projects in the vicinity. Depending on the size of the project, its stability and local market activity, model match comparables may not be available. Inside comparables are more critical but may not be available in smaller developments.

Condo versus townhouse: Some owners believe that if their residence is a townhouse, it is not a condominium. People who believe a condominium by definition has more stories than a townhouse are misinformed. The actual distinction is that a condominium is a mode of property ownership and a townhouse is an architectural style. The advantage of townhouse-style architecture is typically that there is lower density and there are no neighbors above or below. The downsides are that some buyers are deterred by units with interior stairs, and townhouse projects may have fewer amenities than high-rises.

Projects with detached residences: Some condo projects have the appearance of SFRs but are legally condominiums, possibly because of a desirable amenity (like a golf course) or because lot sizes are below the local zoning minimum. Amenities may be minimal and HOA dues so low they are collected through one annual payment. When a project comprises individual lots (as evident from the appraisal and legal description), owners are likely responsible for their own hazard insurance. Coverage for common areas is incorporated into the HOA assessment.

Vacation condos: Condominiums are marketable in second-home areas because pricing is more affordable and exterior upkeep is maintained by the HOA. Short-term rental can offset debt service but can be contrary to association rules. Short-term rental may also jeopardize second-home occupancy on a refinance depending on the amount of income generated.

In some locations premium rent can be generated during peak periods, so it is worthwhile to determine whether Schedule E gross income covers a relatively short time period. This requires documentation such as copies of short-term leases, a spreadsheet or ledger detailing dates and rents received and/or a written statement from a local rental agent delineating standard and premium rental pricing.

If the HOA contracts with a vacation rental agency or allows an online listing for units, second-home occupancy may be difficult to defend. If the rental agency is on-site at the project, the investor may deem it a condotel. On the other hand, if CC&Rs prohibit short-term rental use, advertising online or otherwise, this could cause repercussions for a borrower seeking rental income. See *Condotels*

Conversions: Condominiums converted from other uses have been stigmatized, sometimes unfairly. Projects built originally as mid-range apartments may require special assessments as they age, and conversions from motels may have inadequate size and cooking facilities, but well-built and -maintained apartments transition easily to individual unit ownership. Industrial buildings gutted and converted for residential use to contemporary expectations often blend open floor plans with original high ceilings and preserved architectural detail.

Separate metering: This occurs in some older projects converted from apartments and may still be prohibited by some investors. For borrowers, the trade-off may be a vintage building in a prime location and higher utility costs (incorporated proportionately to square footage into the monthly HOA fee) if other unit owners are less eco-conscious and/or frugal.

Two-to-four unit condominium projects: This classification covers two distinct property types. The common classification is small projects with individual units sold to individual buyers. Investor guidelines typically stipulate the minimum percentage of owner-occupied units and may require that the HOA be incorporated.

The far less common use is a project of two-to-four unit investment properties with HOA membership comprising owner-landlords. These are typically conversions of urban apartment projects. Not surprisingly, loans on these projects are commonly ineligible with residential investors.

The unwarrantable New York condo

The borrower was a youngish attorney purchasing a Manhattan condo. With two restaurants on the street level and only 30% owner occupied, the project was unwarrantable.

The project's low owner occupancy was the result of defaults after the meltdown and during the subsequent recession. Low owner occupancy perpetuated when units were purchased by corporations for visiting executives and clients; the units were affordable alternatives to hotels. The midtown location and restaurant amenities were also attractive to the single attorney borrower and the growing percentage of owner-occupants. The project's budget was balanced with no HOA delinquencies, and the appraisal indicated good interior and exterior upkeep.

Lesson: If a lender has the capacity for portfolio loans, unwarrantable should not necessarily mean it's a bad choice to purchase or lend on.

The unwarrantable Los Angeles condo

The borrowers were qualified in all respects, but the condo unit they wanted to buy was unwarrantable because five of fifteen units were developer-owned. The usual conclusion with a five-year-old condo with one-third unsold units is impaired marketability—but I knew otherwise since the project was a mile from our home. The situation forced me to seek out another rationale.

The key to the puzzle was the age of the project. It was completed when the real estate market was still in distress. The developer had the choice of selling the units for bargain prices or retaining them until the market recovered. He chose not to sell. As the market improved, he had the choice of listing all the units at once or gradually.

The appraisal offered some insight. Of the ten sold units, all were owner-occupied. The best comparable was in the same project, identical in room count and within 20 square feet in size. It sold six months earlier for $25,000 less. The appraisal also included two listings in the adjacent building, also five years old and with HOA fees identical to the subject. They were listed for $25,000 higher than the subject's value. Both buildings had common ownership.

The developer delayed and then staggered sales to maximize profits and minimize tax liability. In a distress situation, he would have sold the units earlier.

Lesson: The conventional conclusion is not always the correct conclusion.

Condominiums mainstream and specialized

Initially condominiums were a less costly alternative to detached residences. Most were apartment conversions with a growing number of new structures modeled on apartments, and a scattering of motel conversions.

Condominiums gained acceptance as developers incorporated features that appealed to a wider range of buyers. Finishings in kitchens and bathrooms resembled those in single family residences. Square footages increased, and floor plans included features like laundry rooms and walk-in closets. As projects spread out from urban to suburban locations, lower-density townhouse-style developments accommodated buyers willing to share interior walls with neighbors but not wanting footsteps above.

Condominiums appealed to an increasingly broad segment of homebuyers but also including specialized market segments:

Urban lofts: Conversions of commercial and industrial buildings into residential units featured high ceilings, open multipurpose floorspace and preserved architectural details. These units attract younger and hipper buyers than traditional condos and suburban SFRs. The repurposing of older buildings appeals to the eco-conscious while retro details attract those resistant to tract housing.

Luxury developments: Developers realized that high-end units appealed to buyers ranging from young professionals to empty nesters, anyone seeking reduced square footage with no compromise in quality. Features include doormen, valet parking and reception offices manned round-the-clock—deliberately evocative of higher-end hotels. In locations with high housing costs, buyers are not resistant to four figure HOA fees.

Active Adult communities: Dedicated retirement communities cater to assorted income levels. Housing is tailored to senior needs and a restful atmosphere through age restrictions. The community center offers a variety of recreational and social activities. Active adult developments flourish in sunbelt states like Florida and Arizona but have found market demand in many locations.

Urban infill: Developers saw potential in buyers preferring metropolitan to suburban living. Higher-density multi-story structures have replaced dated and run-down housing. Economy of scale adds to profitability. Chicago exemplifies cities where newer condos are more desirable than dated single-family housing.

Cooperatives

Also referred to as co-ops, cooperatives are living units where the shareholder—equivalent to a condo unit owner—owns a percentage of the project and exclusive use of the specified unit. A share loan is equivalent to a mortgage. Maintenance and upkeep are covered by a monthly fee.

Cooperatives are concentrated in relatively few locations, notably in New York and New Jersey. Not all investors lend on co-ops, and many who do restrict financing availability to areas where units have proven marketability and with sufficient comparable sales. Some long-established cooperatives are so solvent that insurance coverage is deliberately below industry expectations; strong reserves compensate for higher coverage.

In the 1980s a cooperative project was located a few blocks away from my condo in West Los Angeles. Because co-op financing was (and remains) difficult to obtain in California, the only options were non-institutional financing or an all-cash purchase. Limitations on financing caused sales prices to be lower than comparable condo units. The co-op project eventually converted to a condominium.

Co-op loans require specific expertise for appraisal review and document preparation.

Restricted projects

Restrictions are incorporated into CC&Rs either by the developer or by the municipality.

A typical developer-prompted restriction for condos and PUDs is age, e.g., requiring occupants to be at least fifty years old. Residences have design features appealing to mature adults, and communities offer amenities and activities targeted for grown-ups. Grandchildren can visit but can't move in.

A typical municipally-prompted restriction is a limitation on household earnings. This is not traditional subsidized housing (although some developers may think otherwise) but is conditional to the developer obtaining permission to build or convert. Especially in areas with high housing costs, municipalities seek affordable housing for wage-earners such as teachers and police officers. In some locations, even a wider segment of the general population may be eligible. In Honolulu, a young attorney and his college instructor wife qualified. In Manhattan, there is at least one development with income restricted to $200,000 or lower. Controls on earnings may apply to an entire project or a percentage of affordable units in a project. Another example of municipally-prompted restrictions are Native American reservations where property owners are required to be tribe members.

The risk consideration is whether, in the event of borrower hardship or resultant foreclosure, there is an acceptable pool of potential buyers who qualify within the restriction. Developers usually conduct extensive market research before breaking ground, and moderate income earners covet housing close to their employment. If there is any doubt, days on market for the subject and similar properties should provide adequate direction.

Condotels

Condotels blend elements of condominiums and hotels. Some projects are affiliated with major hotel groups. Some cater to luxury buyers and others are affordable.

True condotels and some condominium projects with condotel attributes are GSE-ineligible. The investor's ineligible project list should be checked if there is any doubt before loan approval is communicated. Rationale for ineligibility should be evident in the appraisal, rental income tax returns (for a refinance), project website and condominium documents. A project on an ineligible list with no evident reason should be questioned; some are included for arbitrary or inconsequential reasons.

Red flag amenities are a front desk for registration, daily housekeeping and on-site food service. Other features endangering eligibility are disclosed in the purchase contract, CC&Rs and bylaws. These include limitations on owner occupancy during high-demand periods (summer or winter months, depending on the location, also holiday weekends), mandatory rental pooling and furnishings provided by the developer. Some units are designed with a lockable closet for the owner's personal possessions or with interior locks allowing subdivision of the unit into self-contained mini-suites. Such features effectively transform the property into de facto hotel rooms.

Both the developer and the purchasers of condotel units have the same motivation—profit. The developer generates profit without the need for commercial financing, and the unit owners willingly accept cash flow and potential profit in lieu of their rights of enjoyment.

Investors other than the GSEs find condotels or condominiums with condotel attributes objectionable, concurring that units have greater commercial appeal than residential.

Luxury homes

- Size isn't enough. A big house is not necessarily a luxury house.

- In most cases, location is amongst other luxury houses or with a coveted locational feature. In smaller towns, the doctor's house may be the only luxury house.

- Privacy is enabled by larger lots assuring distance from neighbors and sometimes an entry gate to discourage the unwelcome. (A luxury development in Southern California has a second gate protecting the most exclusive properties in the development.) In high-end condominiums or co-ops, privacy is facilitated by doormen or a front desk controlling access.

- Custom in design and detail. There have been attempts at luxury house tract developments, some more successful than others. The best offer an array of floor plans, exterior designs and upgrade options so the finished residences are distinguishable from tract housing and each other.

- Features assuring comfort and convenience such as ample bathrooms (preferably one per bedroom, extra for visitors and possibly with separated bathrooms and closets in the master suite), professional-quality appliances in the kitchen, perhaps an upstairs butler's pantry or an in-house elevator.

- Less commonly, ample square footage with a limited number of bedrooms.

- Amenities include features representative at the time of construction or foreshadowing future and more widespread trends. Years ago, tennis courts were desirable. Screening or media rooms came along later. Double sinks and walk-in closets started in upper-end houses and then expanded into mainstream housing.

- Amenities often include living quarters for live-in help and/or guests.

- Some people confuse luxury houses with ostentatious furnishings. Some interiors appear opulent but others are deliberately understated. They also can appear comfortable, messy or sorely in need of updating. In any case, the underwriter's role is not to evaluate furniture but rather to assess functionality and marketability.

- Actual age is irrelevant. There are gracious older homes and striking contemporary ones. High-end older homes maintain value through periodic upgrading and remodeling, structural and/or cosmetic. The number of bathrooms undoubtedly increased from the original structure. There may be no master suite but instead adjacent rooms compose the equivalent of a master suite, e.g., rooms repurposed for a sitting room, an office and a wardrobe room with built-in racks and shelves. Although upgrading sometimes includes amenities to current expectations, owners may prefer vintage detail.

Multiple kitchens

Multiple kitchens do not necessarily indicate multi-unit properties. Some ethnic or religious groups (Indians and observant Jews, for example) want two separate kitchens. Summer kitchens, i.e., an outbuilding used for cooking prior to indoor air conditioning, may still be found in vintage homes. Upper-end homes with guest houses or quarters for live-in help may include fully functional second kitchens. None of these usages constitute conversion of the residence into a duplex. A home I walked through when shadowing an appraiser had three kitchens: one fully equipped one on the first floor, a compact version in the below-grade housekeeper suite, and a butler's pantry on the second floor adjacent to the master suite. It was a luxury house, not a triplex.

What's a bedroom?

For appraisers, the defining point between a bedroom and a non-bedroom is that the bedroom has a closet. Some add that it also must have a door. Depending on the municipality, a bedroom may require a window.

Multiple bedrooms

Some residences other than those occupied by large families have numerous bedrooms. Boardinghouses may be out of fashion, but investment properties near universities may have boardinghouse-like configurations, with multiple bedrooms, shared bathrooms and a common area including kitchen. If close enough to the college, these properties can be very profitable. Similarly, beach properties attractive for family reunions or groups of friends can have profitable recurring annual rentals. (If occupancy on such properties is shown to be a primary residence or a second home, and the application does not indicate children, the underwriter may want to see tax returns.) Interior photos of multi-bedroom properties not near learning institutions or water amenities can reveal elder care or rehabilitation facilities, which are a blend between business and residential use. Primary appeal must be residential and use in accord with zoning.

See *Student housing* and *The nurse with too many bedrooms*

Below-grade square footage

In many parts of the country, living space below street level is common. A full basement doubles a one-story home's square footage and can provide safe harbor during extreme weather. Finished basements also provide extra living space. Unfinished space can be used for exercise and laundry equipment, for quiet space and for storage.

Particularly in the Pacific Northwest, suburban neighborhoods have been built on rolling hills. If any part of the below-grade area has windows and/or a door providing exterior access, it is considered a walk-out or daylight basement. Under certain conditions, living space below street level need not be treated as below-grade. Walk-out basements qualify.

If the full floor is not built into the dirt, as with pier and post foundations on hillside properties, square footage is counted as above-grade. Those believing living space below a residence's main floor constitutes below-grade are incorrect.

Although real estate listings may describe a house by its full room count and square footage, appraisers assess below-grade square footage separately and apply a lower square foot adjustment.

If below-grade square footage comprises a separate living unit, the residence is not considered to be a multi-unit residence even when there is no interior access between the units. It is treated as an accessory unit.

Traffic streets

Location on a traffic street has a negative effect on livability. Factors include congestion, reduced privacy, delays during departure and entry, possibly reduced street parking availabilty, and higher potential for traffic accidents. Single family properties on traffic streets tend to have shorter term ownership than properties on quiet streets.

Appraisal adjustments should be proportionate to the value of the property and the degree of noise and congestion on the street. Considerations include:

- Is location on a major traffic street with an elevated noise level, commercial usage and pedestrians, or on a neighborhood arterial street with local traffic mostly confined to morning and evening commute times?

- Are adjustments arbitrary or extracted from other properties with similar adverse influences?

- Is street noise mitigated by a sizable lot, ample setback or double- or triple-paned windows, or is quality of living compromised by external obsolescence?

- Is the street name or neighborhood prestigious, with residents willing to put up with some inconvenience rather than live elsewhere?

- Is the area transitioning from residential to mixed-use or commercial? If so, is the house being purchased as an investment rather than a residence?

Condominium developments, particularly high-rises, have less or no impaired marketability because of a traffic-street location. The projects usually have double- or triple-paned windows to mitigate street noise and may have parking accessed through a side street. Urban condo dwellers value locational amenities that offset a traffic street location. See *My first house*

For apartment buildings including two-to-four unit properties, location on a traffic street can be viewed as a positive at least for the owner, since replacement tenants can be recruited with signage facing the street.

Cul-de-sacs

The detriments of a traffic street don't exist on a cul-de-sac. The American equivalent is a dead-end street. The more appealing French term was adopted when suburban developers realized houses on cul-de-sacs could command premium prices because of reduced traffic. Newer suburban neighborhoods don't have efficient grid streets but rather meandering avenues and lanes, some short and leading nowhere. Cul-de-sacs allow children to play safely and at least the illusion of a congenial neighborhood.

Commercial influence

Residential properties in close proximity to commercial properties have been traditionally considered less desirable. With persuasive advocacy for the energy-saving benefits of live/work units and mixed use properties, the stigma of "adjacent to commercial" may fade somewhat. Living in close proximity to commercial properties may provide convenience or livability issues.

Consider the potential for elevated noise, traffic congestion, restaurant or industrial odors, adult entertainment with rowdy patrons—all of which present an unrestful environment for young children or quiet-loving adults. Extra-thick windows can mask noise but homeowners want a pleasant exterior environment as well as a comfortable interior.

When a neighborhood transitions from residential to commercial, some opt to relocate while opportunists see the potential for quick profit. Short-term residential rental may be the interim game plan; investment property is at least a truthful declaration. Be skeptical of borrowers moving down asserting owner-occupancy, or of non-occupying co-borrower situations where a developer or investor type is providing the down payment.

Transitioning from low-density residential with minor commercial usage to higher-density residential with increased commercial usage can impact property values negatively or positively. Households may view proximity to public transportation and other resources as positives.

Personal preference affects locational choice. Golfers view proximity to the fifth tee as a positive while non-golfers fear broken windows and disrupted sleep. Urban locations with integrated residential and commercial use seem to be trending toward mainstream.

See *Live/work units and mixed-use developments* and *Neighborhood update*

Swimming pools

How the industry deals with swimming pools defies logic, at least mine.

Appraisers have been requested to provide an additional comparable with a pool to support their adjustment and prove that pools are typical in the area. The adjustment is based on the pool's quality and condition; it is rarely a creative decision. If the underwriter can't figure out whether pools are more the norm in Arizona or Wisconsin, the appraiser's statement or an aerial view of the neighborhood can resolve the issue.

Several underwriters I have known were trained that unfenced, uncovered or empty swimming pools are a safety hazard. Their solution was to condition for proof that the pool had been filled with water or concrete and/or was protected by a pool cover or fence. The condition could invalidate the value conclusion if the property description changed and incur needless expense. Limbs can be broken by a fall into an empty pool, and there is the potential for drowning in a gated and filled pool. Borrowers should be trusted to protect themselves and their families, and homeowner insurance includes liability coverage in the rare instance tragedy occurs.

I spent several hours researching whether lenders actually experience losses resulting from loans on properties with swimming pools. I spoke with loan servicing management and legal departments. There were no findings, and no servicing complications, lawsuits or insurance claims. GSEs leave it up to the lender to ensure that health and safety issues are addressed. At last check swimming pools were not specifically addressed in their written guidance. For a comfort level, check with your own or your investors' servicing departments.

My conclusion is that swimming pool risk is our industry's urban myth. It could have started with an isolated loss or a fearful underwriter. This situation exemplifies how good intentions can translate into hassle and expense for the borrower or a lost loan for the originator.

The tiny house phenomenon

I confess an obsession with tiny houses. The topic may have little relevance years from now. But prior to the end of a phenomenon, it is difficult to predict longevity. The best we can do is analyze eligibility, market appeal and other factors with a direct effect on sustainability.

Those devoted to the HGTV and DIY cable networks could easily conclude that tiny houses are a hot trend in housing. Their virtues are extolled on shows like Tiny Home Nation and Tiny House Hunters, and the selling points are convincing. Small residences are budget-kind and ecologically friendly. Advocates extoll the joys of simplified living, increased discretionary spending and reduced dependence on material acquisitions. But after decades of increasingly bigger residences, how many of us are capable of downsizing?

The tiny house definition per HGTV and its sister station DIY is a freestanding residence of 500 square feet or less. Wikipedia's equivalent under "small house movement" is defined as 1000 square feet or less, and may be a precursor of the newer and more diminutive movement. The GSEs, FHA and VA have no minimum square footage requirements but require that value be supported by the appraiser, which translates to comparables being similar. Historically some investors stipulated minimum square footage, which was concluded to be "discrimination by effect."

There are two major manifestations of tiny houses:

• The first type is newly constructed, often portable structures engineered for maximum utility. Like tract housing, new tiny homes can be customized to a buyer's specific wants. Cost is predicated on base price plus selected upgrades. Features include loft bedrooms accessible by ladders or paddle steps, solar panels, multi-use tables built on hydraulic lifts, and miniaturized appliances like two-burner cooktops and combo microwave-convection ovens.

• The second type is existing structures rebranded as tiny houses. They vary widely in original quality, e.g. modernization and maintenance. Some second homes adapt more easily than primary residences, since they are traditionally smaller and may be designed with tuck-away sleeping accommodations and reduced storage space.

Tiny home financing has little (if any) consideration on cable television. Perhaps buyers have accumulated savings, accrued equity after downsizing or recent cash windfalls. But there must be buyers unable to pay cash. Even though tiny house prices are relatively low, not all homebuyers have the ability to write a check for their purchase. Insight is provided in rockymountaintinyhouses.com, which suggests financing by friends or family, loans arranged through builders certified as RV manufacturers for tiny houses with Vehicle Identification Numbers (VINs), and third-party peer to peer loans. Institutional options include unsecured or secured bank loans, possibly against the owner's own retirement account.

And what about opportunities for mortgage lenders?

Most of the tiny houses highlighted on televised shows or through Tiny House Listings are unsuitable or ineligible for mortgage financing. Some are closer to sheds than residences or cannot be permanently affixed to land, like converted campers and buses. More than a few lack plumbing essentials. A standout found on Tiny House Listings (which sends email notifications of current offerings) is a Chevy van of unspecified age (at least ten to fifteen years old, per my husband) with a built-in bed selling for $3,000. A more expensive but equally ineligible property was featured on Tiny House Hunters. A Los Angeles area woman with a $70,000 budget was searching for a residence with outside kitchen and bathroom to maximize space available and acoustics to perform sound healing. She opted for a yurt.

Even residences that qualify as real property are challenging to lend on. Some don't comply with zoning regulations or cannot be rebuilt. Small houses on large lots (usually rural) have high land-to-value ratios ineligible for mortgage financing. Properties lacking reasonably similar comparable sales are at best difficult to appraise.

Real estate agents are seldom featured on televised tiny real property transactions, perhaps since low sales prices translate to minuscule commissions. Apparently, asking prices are justified and price negotiations are unnecessary.

That tiny houses represent a growing segment of the housing market is likely but whether this will result in a meaningful market share or have sustainable demand is unknown. Families with children present a challenge and represent a sizable section of homebuyers. An episode of Tiny House Hunters featured a family of six downsizing from over 2500 square feet to 620 square feet, about the size of their former master bedroom. The parents believed the reduction would facilitate togetherness, but I wonder how will they cope with minimal closet space (especially with three daughters) and bulk grocery purchases typical for that family size. If only the family could be revisited three years after purchase.

Earlier campaigns for eco-friendly housing achieved limited success. Berm or earth houses were a quiet trend during the 1970s. These houses were built flush to a hillside, fully or partially underground to maximize energy efficiency. They were at best difficult to appraise since comparable sales were scarce. Appraisers sometimes resorted to dissimilar types of alternative housing or heavily adjusted mainstream housing. Borrowers were predominantly single males, evidently attracted by lower sales prices and utility costs, apparently oblivious to the absence of natural lighting.

Tiny housing presents several issues:

For occupants,

Privacy: Can co-occupants coexist happily with almost no personal space? What happens when one person covets silence and another creates noise, or when musical tastes differ?

Family living: Not surprisingly, the majority of Tiny House Hunters are singles or couples. An advertised episode with a family of seven turned out to be a married couple with four dogs and five college-age children looking for a second home. They ended up selecting a 400-square-foot cottage (equivalent to the size of a hotel room) with sleeping space for all. But even that solution seems short-term. What happens when the children have their own families?

Storage: Design solutions are necessary to soften the compromise of tiny house living. Some are dubious even at the outset. Replacing the traditional rod and hangers in the closet with hooks may work for jeans and T-shirts but what about clothes that require ironing, work clothes or office apparel? Limited kitchen storage precludes bulk buying or prep equipment. Most of us need room to stow hobby supplies, luggage (since travel is now affordable), seasonal and special-event clothing. It's a given that tiny house owners prefer reading books electronically and refrain from buying souvenirs. On- or off-site storage sheds or rental units can be a solution, but can be considered contrary to the intent of a tiny-home lifestyle.

Social compromises: Having a houseguest or even company for dinner is difficult, awkward or uncomfortable, particularly when bathroom privacy is enabled by a curtain rather than a door.

Health concerns: It's hard to stay healthy when living in close quarters with someone with a cold. Best case is it's annoying. More probably germs are transmitted. Some tiny homes lack indoor toilet facilities. Outhouses may not be equipped with sinks nor bathing amenities. Even if they did, the commute is tiresome especially at night, in inclement weather or when someone is not in peak health.

Space challenges: The 6'3" boyfriend of one Tiny House Hunter couldn't fit into the loft sleeping area. Even average sized people might suffer claustrophobia.

Sustained livability: The tiny house movement is in its infancy. Single people and couples should be able to dwell comfortably in less than three bedrooms and two baths (the minimum expectation for most homeowners), but whether a growing American family can thrive long term with 100 square feet per person is as yet undetermined. Most families live in constricted spaces because of economic necessity. Some with greater financial resources predict that the sacrifice in space, belongings and privacy will be offset by togetherness and ethical righteousness. May their optimism continue long-term.

For lenders,

Supported value: To have a credible appraisal, comparable sales should be similar, current and proximate. New small residences can be dissimilar to surrounding residences even when there is similar square footage. The residence also has to be zoning-compliant and appeal to an acceptable segment of buyers.

Rural properties: Although attractive to buyers with back-to-nature leanings, rural properties present complications. With lower population density, comparable selection is difficult. As acreage increases, the value of improvements reduces proportionately, to a greater extent with a tiny house.

Portability: A significant percentage of mass-produced tiny houses are built on wheels. If a house is affixed on the lot, it can be un-affixed and moved. A concise explanation for an early payment default on a manufactured home was "It's gone!" This is not an isolated incident.

Legal non-conforming: Municipalities commonly establish minimum square footages for new construction. That means that new tiny houses will not qualify for permits or older homes, if destroyed, would have to rebuilt with larger square footage unless grandfathered.

Sustained marketability: Smart lenders consider market appeal to mitigate loss in event of foreclosure. Under-improvements have elevated risk similar to over-improvements with the exception of lower loan amounts. The appropriate tactic with less marketable properties is requiring a higher equity position, which may be insurmountable for tiny house buyers motivated by limited savings.

Market share: Only 8% of homes constructed in 2014 had less than 1400 square feet, and tiny houses likely represent a minor proportion of that number. Factoring in that 68% of tiny houses are owned free and clear and others ineligible, the remaining segment may not be worth pursuing.

The sustained foothold for tiny houses is Japan where they are known as narrow houses. The trend started after World War II and continues today. The obvious distinction is Japan's large population and small geographic area. Japan's density is 873 people per square mile, over ten times higher than the United States at 85 per square mile. Azby Brown, author of *The Very Small Home: Japanese Ideas for Living Well in Limited Space* has a second theory: "We are larger people physically than the Japanese, we do tend to need more space, we're less comfortable in some sitting positions, like sitting on the floor, than most Japanese are." Another distinction is that in Japan, narrow houses appear artful while American tiny houses appear utilitarian.

The first home I owned met the Wikipedia definition. It was a 575 square foot condo unit I initially occupied solely and later on with my husband. It had a full kitchen with standard-sized appliances (even a dishwasher) and ample closets. There were defined areas for socializing, dining and sleeping. The unit was fully functional with two occupants, although some possessions had to be stowed in a storage unit. Despite functionality we wanted more space and moved into a detached residence about a thousand square feet larger.

Recent newspaper articles have given the tiny house movement credit for amended rental housing requirements in New York City, allowing less than the previous 400-square-foot minimum. The change was fueled by affordability issues and aided by innovative design features such as a bed converting into a dining room table seating eight. HGTV and DIY continue to air tiny house hunting programming but with less new content. Air time has been shared with beyond the grid living and container homes, which are other manifestations of extreme housing trends. Many of the recent tiny houses featured are portable, not affixed.

Our philosophical guide on a trip to Easter Island informed us that the earliest head statues were small, but became increasingly larger as time progressed. He attributed the growth to our acquisitive nature and continual quest for betterment. Ironically, most housing on Easter Island is modest, thwarted by the island's remote location, lack of resources and need to import nearly all materials and provisions. Our host confirmed that the few two-story houses were isolated to a single hillside location. Away from Easter Island, evidence supporting our guide's theory on statues is easier to find than tiny houses.

CHAPTER 7
VALUATION

Why read the appraisal?

It is tempting to go straight to value. If you do, return to the front page and begin reading. There are shortcuts, particularly when the property is uncomplicated and the appraiser's comments are boilerplate. But the more atypical the property, the more the appraisal bears scrutiny. Even when the property is mainstream and the subject's neighborhood is familiar, you should review the appraisal.

Be aware of the following:

- Technical details such as property type, occupancy, zoning and whether the property is fee simple or leasehold.

- For a purchase, the number of days on market, the difference between the listing and sales prices and whether a real estate agent was involved.

- The value of the subject compared to the predominant value in the area.

- Any negative comments about the subject or the presence of impaired marketability. Also whether photos and the locational map indicate the presence of an undesirable feature.

- The sales prices of the comparables relative to the subject's value.

- Whether the subject is similar to the comparables in terms of the core adjustments—square footage, room count, age and lot size.

- Numerous or few adjustments, and whether individual adjustments seem excessive. (The number and amounts of the adjustments reflect the homogeneity of the neighborhood.)

- Dated comparables, which are less relevant in a declining or escalating market. In less developed areas, dated comparables may be the only sales available.

- On the locational map, if the comparables are on the other side of a geographic divider, e.g., a major thoroughfare or railroad tracks, or if all the comparables are located in another neighborhood.

- The sales history of the subject and the comparables to determine the value trend since purchase of the subject, and whether there is rapid appreciation or depreciation.

- If the floor plan (if provided) has good flow or is awkward. Room additions can be poorly planned, as with tandem bedrooms or bedrooms on a floor without a bathroom.

- In the photos, whether the comparables look superior to the subject and whether the interior views show the need for repair or updating. The condition of furniture and other personal property is inconsequential.

- On a refinance, whether interior photos indicate the subject is vacant, staged or possibly not occupied by the borrower. (Toys may belong to grandchildren.)

- All addenda, in which critical disclosures may be buried.

There is one final question for consideration on owner-occupied or second homes: Is the property a good fit for the borrower?

Major components of the appraisal

Reading the appraisal doesn't mean that the underwriter needs to digest every word on every page and also the visuals. If the underwriter was held responsible for reading every word in a loan file, productivity could fall to less than a file a day. Compromise is not necessary if the underwriter understands which parts of the appraisal are critical.

The **first page** describes the property and the neighborhood. If the area is familiar, only a cursory review is necessary. If comparable sales are located outside neighborhood boundaries or if the neighborhood boundaries seem to be expanded, there should be justification. Worthy of note are whether the property is a leasehold, if predominant value is exceeded and if the property is in accord with zoning. (The usual answers are no, no and yes.) On a refinance, occupancy per the appraisal should correspond with declared occupancy. If on an owner-occupied purchase the property is tenant-occupied, make sure the tenant will vacate so the trust deed's occupancy provision is honored. It is pertinent if the property was not MLS-listed and how many days it took to sell. If the appraiser did not review the sales contract (which occurs rarely), the underwriter should review it thoroughly. If multiple offers result in the sales price exceeding the listing price, days on market should be relatively short unless the offers came in after a price reduction. Read the comments for anything unusual or negative. The underwriter should glance at the end of standardized commentary to see if something interesting was tacked on.

The **market approach** is most valid. The standard number of closed sales is three. When there are less (which almost never occurs), the property may be so distinctive that value cannot be defined and marketability is suspect. Multiple pages of comparables typically correspond with higher value and/or complex properties. Expect fewer adjustments in newer tract neighborhoods and more and larger adjustments with custom homes. Review proximity, ages, lot sizes, square footages, room counts and any large adjustments for the subject and the comparables. Ideally, a property should be compared to sales both larger or otherwise superior and smaller or inferior. This is referred to as "bracketing." Condos preferably should be compared to other condos, and two-story houses to other two story houses. If all comparables are superior or distant, appraised value may be inflated.

The **sales histories** of the subject and the comparables merit review. Substantially increased recent sales prices indicate an unstable market. Rapid appreciation should be supported by details of improvements, preferably not "new paint and floor coverings" which is unspecific and suggests cosmetic upgrades. The details make the difference. Cost and quality differ if flooring is hardwood or laminate, imported tile or vinyl off the roll.

The **cost approach** is most valid in new tract neighborhoods and problematic elsewhere. Data to support land value is seldom available in established areas because lot sales are infrequent. Sale transactions on tear-downs provide insight, although sometimes livable homes are torn down to be replaced by larger structures with contemporary appeal. As depreciation increases, the cost approach becomes less germane. In vintage homes, architectural detail is costly and possibly impossible to replace. Since the cost approach is based on hypothetical figures, it is a less significant (and sometimes optional) component of value assessment.

The **income approach** is employed on one to four unit investment properties and single family rentals. In addition to sale comparables, the appraisal form requires data on nearby rental properties similar in unit count and size, including actual and market rents. On a purchase transaction, the actual income on rental units per the appraisal less a 25% expense factor is used in qualification. On refinances, actual income and expense figures should be used from tax returns.

Since actual rents are not captured in public records and so are obtained from realtors, property managers or landlords, they are considered less reliable. The income approach is not applicable for owner-occupied properties since rental income is not a component of qualifying income.

At some point during ownership, rental income potential may have applicability. Corporate transferees and military households may retain a residence in a location they want to return to after retirement. An owner-occupant in reduced circumstances can retain ownership by moving to lower cost accommodations and using the rental income to cover PITI. An alternative is staying and renting out rooms. Friends rented out a home while the owner (who inherited the house) lived in the guest house and attended law school.

The **value conclusion** includes a dollar amount, a date affecting document expiration and whether the value is as is or subject to.

Addenda take up multiple pages of written text. The majority is standardized verbiage inserted into every appraisal. After learning to recognize what is standardized and what is pertinent to the specific property, the underwriter can breeze through the boilerplate and thoroughly read whatever is left. Often it is meaningful.

The **street address** and **legal description** on the title-work should be consistent with the address on the appraisal, application and loan documents.

Photos provide valuable information. A former appraiser told me he'd rather see the outside of the comparables than the inside of the subject. His point has merit. From exterior photos an underwriter can discern curb appeal, quality of construction and level of maintenance. If the subject appears inferior to the comparables, value may be pushed. The former appraiser's comment did not mean that interior photos are useless. Far from it. They can reveal dysfunctional kitchens, deferred maintenance, improbable occupancy, staged furnishings masking a property's weak points, hoarding with potential health and safety issues, and packed belongings on a cash-out refinance. I once asked an underwriter applicant what she looked for in the appraisal. Her response, "there have to be pictures," immediately disqualified her from consideration. Over the years my position has softened somewhat.

The **sketch** indicates whether the floor plan is functional or not. Poorly functional floor plans are found more frequently in older residences with serial remodels. Attic storage space converted into sleeping space can necessitate traversing stairs to use the bathroom. The configuration of bathrooms and bedrooms bears scrutiny. A bathroom proximate to public areas is preferable so visitors don't have to chose between the children's bathroom or walking through the master bedroom. The older the home (excluding upper-end housing), the greater likelihood bathrooms will not meet current expectations and bedrooms will be smaller. A rectangular house may be manufactured or inexpensive tract housing. Affordability and location should be taken into account; in modestly priced housing or premium urban locations, borrowers may have to compromise.

The **location map** discloses significant geographic influences near the property—a freeway or correctional facility (with negative impact on value), ocean or lake (with positive impact on value). Comparables on the other side of the freeway or down the hill usually indicate a change of neighborhood. The street configuration provides insight. Gridded streets (parallel streets horizontally and vertically) are usually found in urban, older or less expensive neighborhoods. Cul-de-sacs (stubby dead-end streets) are popular in suburban family neighborhoods. Winding streets are more common in suburban or more affluent neighborhoods, and sometimes indicate view properties. Location maps may be tailored to hide adverse influences, what my appraiser friend calls "the three thousand foot view." Online resources should be used if lack of full disclosure is suspected.

Value risk is highest in a depreciating market, since loan-to-value increases as market value declines. However, the converse is not always true. In a rapidly appreciating market, values have the potential of decreasing just as rapidly and may possibly decline to a figure below acquisition price.

You've got to see these photos

> By the time the loan was decisioned, almost everyone had seen the appraisal, at least the interior photos. The appraisal had been passed around through underwriting, operations and sales. Photos revealed that not only the bedrooms were furnished as bedrooms, but other rooms were as well. Video cameras were attached to the ceiling light fixtures. Mirrors were mounted on walls and ceilings. The consensus was that the house was used to film adult videos.
>
> The loan was denied since use was commercial rather than residential and was not in compliance with zoning.
>
> **Lessons: Had the transaction been a purchase rather than a refinance, the loan could be approved assuming owner occupancy was assured. Modifications were temporary and would have vanished by the time the new owners moved in.**

Lessons from appraisers

One-third of my three week underwriting training was spent in appraisers' cars. Little did I know that the training would turn into a career. What prompted the first week was an admission that I didn't know much about appraisals. The next three days were spent with the insightful Joe Bates, the fourth with a respectable appraiser and the fifth with a lazy appraiser. I learned from them all, but Joe taught me the most. Here's what I learned then and since:

1. Concentrate on the structure and its surroundings, not aesthetic appeal. Ignore furniture, decor and paint color. What matters is what remains after the occupant moves out, whether it is unfixable or requires significant cost to fix.

2. The floor plan matters. Is the dining room adjacent to the kitchen? Are the bathrooms well located? Is the master bedroom near to or removed from the other bedrooms? (Close is the choice of young families. Later on, privacy is preferable.)

3. With skillful remodeling, there is no discernible difference between what is original and what was added, and no room has too many doors.

4. The appraiser must report all pertinent findings but not necessarily spotlight them. Read addenda to determine whether verbiage is boilerplate or meaningful.

5. Roofs reflect quality of construction and upkeep. My hierarchy has slate at the top and comp roll (less expensive than composition shingles) at the bottom. Slate roofs occasionally require a few replacement tiles but last forever. Comp shingles differ in quality; the thicker ones last considerably longer.

6. Lazy appraisers short-cut. Photos may disclose condition-related issues unaddressed in the text. With an unusual or complex property, three comparables may be inadequate. (Above average adjustments are the tip-off.) Although lenders cannot pressure for increased value, additional detail or clarification can be requested.

7. Properties can have intangible nuances that less proficient appraisers miss or handle inappropriately. Privacy and view come to mind. My condo unit had a brick exterior and brick walls between units providing insulation, sound-proofing and visual appeal. I briefly worked with a staff appraiser who was so afraid of heights that his view photos for high-rise condos suffered. His view adjustments may have been compromised as well.

8. It is the appraiser's obligation to identify marketability issues, adverse site or external conditions, necessary repairs and lack of functional utility. It is the underwriter's role to determine whether impaired marketability or a structural defect is trivial, a deal-killer or somewhere in the middle.

9. Upper-end properties have less property condition complications.

10. A big house is not necessarily a nice house.

11. If you are concerned or curious, dig deeper. Interior photos in the appraisal and possibly interior photos of comps (available online accessed through the property address) can resolve matters.

12. The insights gained from shadowing appraisers for a week was as valuable as the technical aspects of underwriting. When a loan doesn't perform, the institution doesn't foreclose on a borrower, it forecloses on a property.

The neighborhood you know the best

This is the exercise I used to help trainee underwriters understand the principle of neighborhood boundaries. Class members were instructed to close their eyes and envision the neighborhood they grew up in or the neighborhood they knew the best. They were told to imagine the boundaries separating their neighborhood from adjacent neighborhoods. Boundaries could be man-made (major traffic streets, freeways or railroad tracks) or natural (hills, valleys and waterways). The next step was evaluating whether adjacent neighborhoods were more or less desirable, and why. The final part of the exercise was comparing the interior of their homes to the insides of homes they visited frequently, and recalling what caused them to be more or less livable.

I learned about neighborhoods before high school. My parents moved from a rented apartment to a purchased house and, a few years later, to another house "in a better neighborhood" less than a mile away. The move-up house was slightly larger with a second bath, but was located on a residential traffic street a friend (whose wife grew up on the same street) dubbed "the Castle Heights freeway."

A misunderstood neighborhood comment was from a conversation between two Girl Scout leaders about carpool assignments—"You take the girls who live down the hill and I'll take the ones who live up the hill." At the time, I perceived the up-the-hill leader as a snob since I knew those houses were bigger and nicer. Our house was down the hill. Years later, I figured out her plan was efficient logistically for both leaders.

Learning about appraisal taught me how topography and geographic boundaries affected home prices. Some smaller homes up the hill cost more than some larger homes down the hill.

Location cubed

In my first industry position, I learned that in the flat areas of Beverly Hills, the closer the property to Sunset Boulevard, the higher the land value. Beverly Hills Adjacent (the Los Angeles neighborhood just east of Beverly Hills) and "BHPO" (the hilly Los Angeles streets with Beverly Hills zip codes and mail delivery) benefitted from proximity but not equal pricing. Not surprisingly, multiple West Los Angeles locations have "Beverly" incorporated into their names—Beverly Blvd., Beverly Drive, Beverly Center and so on. Beverlywood, where my parents lived for forty years, was not named randomly.

Every neighborhood has its nuances. What is in it and near it matters. In an industry rife with change, "location, location, location" remains a constant.

Primary appeal

Primary appeal is what motivates a homebuyer to purchase a property for residential use. Primary appeal distinguishes a house with an oversized backyard from a farm. Non-residential primary appeal exists when the outbuilding is larger than the residential structure, or when an urban residence in a transitioning neighborhood becomes outnumbered by higher density residential or commercial properties. For the most part, only a farmer would buy a rural property with most of its value in the acreage, and only a business owner or developer would be interested in buying a property with a workshop dwarfing the residence or the only SFR on the block.

The nurse's house with too many bedrooms

The well-qualified registered nurse was purchasing a primary residence that was not mainstream. The convoluted one-story floor plan indicated a warren of six small bedrooms and five small dens. The house was not large or opulent enough to be called a mansion. This home would appeal to few buyers, and less so to single women with no dependents.

There were other concerns in addition to impaired marketability. The nurse was likely to use the property as a care facility, which could be a zoning violation. Also, the nurse might not be living onsite.

The loan was declined because primary appeal was not as a single family residence. The other reasons were speculative.

Lesson: Some loans have more than core concern. In this case, concerns included limited marketability, potential commercial use and questionable occupancy. Even with an AUS approval, this loan was a decline.

Appreciation since purchase

In addition to current value, a pertinent property consideration is value change. This is a relevant risk test for properties that have resold or are being refinanced with cash proceeds within a few years of purchase.

To determine the percentage of increase, subtract the acquisition price from the current value, and divide the remainder by number of years owned. Then divide the resultant annual appreciation by the original purchase price to obtain the percentage of annual appreciation. If a property owned for three years has appreciated from $100,000 to $130,000, the annual percentage of appreciation is 10%.

The percentage of increase should be viewed relative to average appreciation in the area. If the property was remodeled since the earlier sale transaction, it is easier to justify appreciation exceeding average, assuming that the upgrades truly contributed to value.

Reasons for high appreciation since recent purchase include a below-market sales price, market increases and property improvements. When a flip transaction is suspected, make sure that any renovation went beyond cosmetic. This can be accomplished by checking for permits, through review of the cost breakdown and possibly the property inspection to ensure that the property's internal systems are as sound as the house is attractive. (Under normal circumstances, the inspection functions as a negotiating tool between the buyer and seller, but with a flip or suspect appreciation, it could make a difference on the risk decision.)

For properties owned over an extended period of time, the percentage of annual appreciation is also meaningful. Our house purchased almost twenty-nine years ago has appreciated about 5% annually, factoring in funds spent on capital improvements. This may not seem impressive, but our house was purchased at the top of the market in 1988 and didn't appreciate at all during the first eight or ten years. It did appreciate during its second decade of ownership and depreciated minimally after the meltdown in 2008. Two years ago the Los Angeles Times cited our zip code as one of the five highest in the county for increased value. Despite market vacillations, real estate is usually a rewarding investment over time.

When a property's value has decreased since purchase, the underwriter or appraiser should consider the probability of a continued decline. Further depreciation after a maximum cash-out transaction could result in a monetary loss to the lender in the event of default.

Good neighbors, bad timing

Becka and Rod purchased the first totally rebuilt two story house on the block. It was surrounded by older homes, mostly single story but some with second story additions. They were largely responsible for coalescing three other couples on the block from friendly neighbors into close friends. Their only regret was purchasing at the top of the market in 2007 and being unable to take advantage of lower interest rates. They ended up waiting seven years before other neighborhood rebuilds were available as comparables. Out-of-area comparables were not an obstruction on a 2007 sales transaction where scrutiny of appraisals was relatively infrequent. Luckily, interest rates remained low in 2014 so the owners could finally love their mortgage as much as their neighborhood.

Lessons: Value is more easily supported on a purchase with a fair market sale. Stable neighborhoods evolve gradually, which is a positive unless limited availability of comparables hampers a refinance.

Impaired marketability

Impaired marketability exists when any aspect of a property deters the average buyer. It can range from incurable (close proximity to an environmental hazard site) or easily curable (popcorn ceilings). Cosmetic impaired marketability should not affect the loan decision and may not even merit an appraisal adjustment.

What constitutes impaired marketability is heavily dependent on location. Three bedrooms are above average for urban condominiums and below average for some suburban family neighborhoods. Depending on demographics, a one bedroom condo may be difficult to sell or a desirable alternative to a studio condo. Awkward floor plans are less of a deterrent to buyers in older mid-range tracts where houses may have multiple add-ons, as opposed to upper-end neighborhoods where major remodels entail more cost and professional design.

Location in a coveted neighborhood also affects to what extent impaired marketability is a detriment to sale. An imperfect house in an in-demand location may command a higher sales price than a flawless house in an adjacent neighborhood.

Non-mainstream architecture is more marketable in metropolitan areas. Although most neighborhoods conform to the regional norm (e.g., Western ranch houses or Eastern brick houses) or appear so generic they could be located anywhere, distinct neighborhoods may feature Victorian or eco-friendly or mid-century modern houses. Mature tracts may have renovated homes, some with second story additions, others rebuilt from the ground up and a few in their original state.

When a property lacks features in accord with current tastes, this usually falls into a cosmetic or minor impaired marketability classification. Current preferences are granite countertops, stainless steel appliances, in-home offices, open floor plans and walk-in closets. They will change. If you are in doubt, consider white kitchen appliances, colored kitchen appliances and black kitchen appliances—all highly desirable in previous decades, as were popcorn ceilings.

When thinking about impaired marketability, the underwriter should consider the difference between livability and salability, and also consider affordability as a factor. A family with several children will settle on the largest house in their price range. Most borrowers would prefer two bedrooms over one bedroom, and three bedrooms over two bedrooms. However, economic reality inevitably trumps the wish list. An underwriter's personal taste and affordability should be distinguished from genuine marketability issues. Similarly, appraisers are responsible for objective rather than subjective judgment on properties they appraise.

If the subject property is one-of-a-kind, impaired marketability is probable. When the unusual element is cosmetic, easily curable, has minor impact on livability and / or is addressed with a credible adjustment in the market approach, move on to the next issue.

Impaired marketability combined with a marginal borrower and minimal equity could result in monetary loss in the event of foreclosure.

The refrigerator in the dining room

The East Coast underwriter concluded impaired marketability in the older home with a kitchen so small the refrigerator was in the dining room. The property was in Southern California, and I disagreed with the conclusion for several reasons.

After studying the floor plan I deduced that the kitchen lost square footage when room count increased from two bedrooms and one bath to three bedrooms and two baths. The compromise minimized construction costs; reducing the kitchen slightly allowed utilization of existing plumbing for the new bath. Value and marketability were enhanced despite decreased kitchen size.

Interior photos showed that the refrigerator was not too much of an eyesore. The dining room was located adjacent to the kitchen, and per the appraisal photo, its current use was for informal meals and family activities. Even without the refrigerator, the room was unlikely to be a formal dining room.

I took into account that the sales price of $375,000 would buy a much nicer house where the underwriter lived than in metropolitan Los Angeles, where $375,000 constituted affordable housing. The borrowers and their two children were moving up from a remote and less expensive community. For them, location and room count outweighed the presence of the refrigerator in the dining room.

Lessons:

1. *Appraisal photos give insight to livability.*

2. *Compromise in urban housing is a fact of life. I learned a similar lesson in college during the shared rental of the upper story of a decrepit but furnished Santa Monica house three blocks from the beach and twenty minutes from UCLA. The refrigerator was located outside the kitchen in the hall. Until seniority allowed me a larger room, I made do with a minuscule bedroom accommodating only a single bed, nightstand and small closet. My foldable clothes were in a bureau in the hall. Several years after graduation, the house and detached guest house were razed and replaced by a three-story fifteen-unit condominium.*

Marketability attributes

One way of understanding what contributes to impaired marketability is to review examples.

Exterior impaired marketability

- On a traffic street. Whether this is surmountable or not depends on the amount of traffic and the cachet of the neighborhood. See *Traffic Streets*

- Backing to a freeway, railroad tracks or similar source of noise and exhaust

- Within hearing distance of an airport or smelling distance of some restaurants or livestock, unless you own the farm

- Poor curb appeal, as with evident deferred maintenance or neglected landscaping

- Close proximity to a commercial area where street parking overflows to adjacent streets, or where commercial customers leave litter or make noise

- Adjacent to a school or a bus stop (usually relatively minor)

- Adjacent to a cemetery, or commercial or industrial property (sometimes not minor)

- Adjacent to an environmental hazard site (even worse, and potentially unhealthy)

- Difficult access, such as a dirt road or steep driveway

- No covered parking

- For condos or co-ops, inadequate personal or guest parking

- Outbuildings larger than the residence

- Neighbors with unkempt properties

- Special interest subdivisions, e.g., with an airplane runway and hangars for small plane owners or a clothing-optional community. See *The nudist colony loan*

Interior impaired marketability

- Insufficient bathrooms

- Tandem bedrooms (a bedroom accessible only through another bedroom)

- Too few bedrooms, except in urban locations where location trumps room count

- Too many bedrooms, especially when the bedrooms are small with inadequate bathrooms

- No bathrooms on a floor, except basements or attics used primarily for storage

- Structural modifications for non-residential use such as daycare or hairdressing

- Condominiums without laundry facilities

- Awkward floor plan

- Popcorn ceilings and other passé features

- Any feature in a family-sized house considered hazardous for young children

- Formal dining rooms some buyers perceive as wasted space

Title-related impaired marketability

- Statutory right of redemption. This allows a foreclosure to be nullified within a specified time period upon full payment of arrearages. It is specific to certain locations. Excluded are areas where trust deeds enable non-judicial foreclosure and preclude right of redemption.

- Cloud on title such as an unreleased lien or a lis pendens

- Recorded long-term lease

- Zoning provision requiring mandatory agricultural use

- Overly-restrictive CC&Rs and bylaws

General impaired marketability

- Dated appearance

- Over-improvement or unique property with limited appeal

- Odd or unconventional architecture

- Poor curb appeal

- For condos or co-ops, any structure higher than two stories with no elevator

- Former churches, firehouses, schools or mortuaries converted into residential property.

- When a neighborhood favors conformity over eclecticism, anything considered different or weird.

Marketability considerations

- Is the situation curable, and at what cost?

- Is the property out of sync for the neighborhood?

- Did the appraiser forget to make an adjustment?

- Is there a health or safety issue?

- Are there sufficient and relevant compensating factors?

- Should LTV be reduced?

Geodesic domes, berms and other oddities

Unusual property types require adequately supported value and acceptable marketability. The underwriter should evaluate whether appropriate comparables were provided, taking into account that they may be more dated and distant than mainstream housing. The less similar the comparables, the more questionable value and marketability become.

What is uncommon in some areas may be more accepted elsewhere. There is a community of berm "Earthship" homes in Taos County, New Mexico. These homes are on private roads protected from spectator access; the curious can only drive around the periphery. There are developments of ecologically-forward homes in the Pacific Northwest.

Some believe that such communities will increase in number in the coming years and that alternative housing will become increasingly easier to appraise. Until that time, a confidence level with the property must be established.

See *Tiny houses*

The subjectivity of marketability

Fixer-uppers are desirable because pricing is lower than move-in ready houses, and renovation can be personalized to owner taste. On the other hand, some borrowers willingly pay higher prices to avoid the inconvenience and personal expenditure that go with home improvements.

Corner lots increase privacy with fewer adjacent neighbors, but facing traffic in two directions can be noisy and disruptive.

Urban locations offer convenient access to public transportation, cultural attractions and easily available goods and services. However, the further the distance from city center, the larger the lot sizes and greater the distance from neighbors.

Many property aspects are mixed blessings, double-edged swords. Underwriters should avoid being judgmental and suppress personal taste. Decisioning should utilize the appraiser's analysis, which ideally coincides with what the majority of borrowers see as desirable.

Sustainability

Appraisers' assessments of housing trends are so consistently cited as "stable" and "in-balance" that even diligent underwriters shortcut that section. Although the appraiser cannot be held responsible for predicting what occurs after closing, value trends are a legitimate concern. Sustainability of value (or more accurately, absence of deteriorating value) is more critical to loan performance than sustainability of income or asset base.

Some areas are more susceptible to eroding value—those with inventories of unsold new construction, remote from employment, with downtrending industry and worn neighborhoods where gentrification never occurred.

Lenders may restrict lending in soft markets by implementing more stringent guidelines, typically reduced LTVs. Less prevalent are non-matrix adjustments. Underwriters should refrain from aggressive underwriting in areas where sustained value is questionable. Marginally qualified borrowers with low equity positions are especially vulnerable when equity diminishes.

Starter home, forever home

A forever home is a relatively new concept. It is the opposite of a starter home but some first-time borrowers want their first home be their forever home. If they postpone home purchase until they achieve financial security, amassing a sizable down payment and qualifying with affordable debt ratios, they are justified in not compromising their expectations.

The salient factor is financial maturity. There is no requirement for first-time home buyers to purchase modestly if they qualify for better. But marginally qualified borrowers should consider waiting longer or opting for a shorter-term residence.

Buyer's and seller's markets

In a buyer's market, supply exceeds demand, enabling buyers to negotiate more favorable sale prices and concessions. In a seller's market, demand exceeds supply, forcing buyers to pay more money for less house, fearing prices will continue to rise.

In a buyer's market, dated comparable sales support that the borrower is paying a bargain price for the property. However, if the market continues to slow down, comparables become more scarce. Reduced market sales and loan volume evidence a downward trend.

In a seller's market, housing prices are on an uptrend sometimes to the extent that current sale prices exceed those of most comparables. When this occurs, appraisers rely on time adjustments to produce a current value. These may be viewed with suspicion by lenders unless supported by back-up offers, abbreviated marketing time, equivalent current listing prices and closed sales now obtainable from programs searching public records for the most recently recorded transactions. Trend lines matter, but lenders should be aware that when prices increase quickly, they are apt to decrease.

Most real estate markets are neither buyer's nor seller's markets. They are stable with moderate appreciation.

The all-cash offer

Every aspect of Ashley and Aaron's first home purchase was more painful than it should have been. Aaron had a doctorate from a respected university and a tenure track teaching position at the college level. He and Ashley had saved well over a 20% down payment. Their credit scores were over 800 and their only debt was student loans. Their pre-approval took longer than they anticipated but came though without issue.

Moving forward on a suitable house was not easy. After offering $35,000 over listing price and paying for general and septic inspections, Ashley and Aaron were outbid by an all-cash offer $55,000 over listing price. Almost a year after their home search began, they had made three unsuccessful offers, their first child had been born and they were still renting. All-cash offers enabled other buyers to control the market, sometimes tying up multiple properties and then using the property inspection as an exit strategy.

Then a relative offered family financing below lender rates but above depository rates. This enabled the couple to afford a slightly higher sales price and to offer all cash themselves. They found a house and their offer was accepted despite a matching all-cash bid. The competing buyers even expressed their willingness to increase their offer by $25,000. The

153

difference was a letter written by Ashley about their young family and their hopes for building a future in the home.

Lessons:

1. **A dysfunctional system leads to work-arounds.**

2. **Creative solutions benefitted the borrowers and the relative who stepped up.**

3. **A good replacement for "How can we establish more controls?" is "How did we handle this before the meltdown?"**

Online research

Entering a property address into a search engine usually yields considerable data including square footage, room count, year built, lot size, last sale date and price.

Property information online is partially objective and partially subjective. Not all is accurate. The house next door to ours rebuilt after tear-down a few years ago has current photos but previous square footage and room count.

Value falls into the subjective category. Estimates on our home from two popular sites differ by 7%. Since databases are blind to remodels and upgrades not requiring permits, neither quantified new air conditioning and heating, updated plumbing and electrical, new hardwood flooring, and kitchen and bathroom remodels.

Online research of our property address also revealed my husband's in-home self-employment—a red flag for business use of the property. The type of business suggests whether modification was necessary for non-residential use. Interior photos can give insight. Many residence-based businesses require only telephones (probably non-land lines) and extra electrical outlets.

Front view photos are easily available under the property address or through map sites such as Google Street View. For recently listed properties, interior photos are probably available.

In areas where property data is excluded from public records and in less populated areas, online information can be less comprehensive or, as to value, even less reliable.

The contradictory rental

Zack and Van rented out their house since they intended to return to the city after their children were grown. Online sites were inconsistent. Room count was shown to be 3-2 (industry shorthand for three bedrooms and two bathrooms), 4-2, 4-2.5 and 5-4. Square footage ranged from 2607 to 3100. Parking ranged from one parking space to two parking spaces plus a two car garage.

Inconsistencies in square footage could be caused by the second story addition but more probably by conversion of the detached two-car garage to a sound studio.

A rental site offered the greatest detail. Square footage and room count were the highest, and the extended description cited "picturesque home… spacious kitchen…large master bedroom…designer chandelier…recently remodeled bathroom…creative work space…soundproof acoustic space… artist studio…serene tree-lined street…fantastic neighbors and the coolest landlords you'd ever want."

Descriptions on real estate sites are from visual observation. Public records sometimes are inaccurate. The home page on the rental site referenced two parking spaces and a two-car garage, but the narrative description mentioned the music studio with no reference to parking. The half bath may have been remodeled to a full bath. The art studio could have been converted from an outbuilding used for storage. (The storage shed in our backyard is as soundly constructed as our house.)

The rental site showed the listing rent at $5950 monthly and sold-at rent as $6100. The increase arose from a bidding war between interested tenants. Another site indicated the actual rent as $6000. The Zillow rental estimate was $6567, but increased to $7515 less than an hour later, and then lowered to $6750 the next week. Vacillation occurs because rental income is based on an algorithm tied to fluctuating databases.

Lesson: Online tools are helpful, but users should be cautious about accuracy, both in numbers and adjectives.

See *Online research*

AVMs

Automated valuation models are computer-generated products providing a value estimation and some non-narrative details about the property. Benefits are reduced cost and time efficiency. The limitation is inconsistent reliability, more so for non-mainstream housing and overall during slow real estate markets. In a slow market, an AVM resorted to condo sales to assess our SFR's value.

Until you obtain a comfort level with a specific engine or in a real estate market that is changing direction, AVMs should be tested for reliability. If listed sales are out of the subject's neighborhood or are dissimilar, the value conclusion may be unreliable. Tests are comparing online valuations or the value of the most similar sale to the AVM's value conclusion. Testing is less necessary in homogeneous neighborhoods in a normal sales market.

Some AVMs rely less on neighborhood sales and more on statistical derivations based on property location and value trends.

AVMs typically provide property attributes such as square footage, room breakdown and lot size, and may provide data on local distress sale activity. The latter is invaluable in assessing neighborhood stability, which is key in risk decisioning.

Proponents of AVMs believe drawbacks are offset by the impartiality of databases. My conclusion is that an AVM is a good starting point but cannot replace the work of a capable appraiser.

BPOs

A Broker's Price Opinion is prepared by a local real estate agent rather than a credentialed appraiser. It resembles a short-form exterior-only appraisal, providing a description of the property, comparable sales and value conclusion using public record and Multiple Listing Service data. The benefits are reduced cost compared to a formal appraisal, reduced reading time and at best an assessment by someone knowledgable of the local real estate market. The limitations are less formalized appraisal training and oversight, lower likelihood of the most capable agents accepting assignments for the compensation offered, and the vested interest of the analyst whose primary motivations are securing property listings and closing sales.

Not all states allow BPOs. A few preclude non-licensed individuals from issuing opinions on value, as opposed to price.

BPOs were associated primarily with subprime lending and the REO market. Demand has faded somewhat because of reduced subprime production and the immediate response and minimal expense of AVMs. However, there is continued use by investors (including at least one major player) after loan acquisition to test the credibility of original appraisals, or after default to assess current value.

Remaining economic life

The industry expectation is that remaining economic life exceeds the loan term by at least five years. In real life, acceptably maintained properties likely can be occupied long after their hypothetical expiration dates. A property with thirty-five years remaining would likely have thirty-five years remaining on an appraisal prepared several years later. Many habitable properties are razed and replaced with larger and/or updated structures. Marginal properties in neglected neighborhoods tend to remain marginal unless the neighborhood becomes gentrified, zoning changes allow for alternative use or eminent domain repurposes the area.

A remaining economic life of thirty years or less is a message that the property is in substandard condition.

Actual and effective age

Actual age is taken from public records. Effective age is a condition-based estimate by the appraiser based either on the positive impact of upgrading and ongoing maintenance or the negative impact of neglect and deterioration. Relatively few appraisals cite conditions so poor that effective age exceeds actual age. More likely the appraiser handles this issue by showing actual and effective ages as the same.

Incomparable comparables

Distant, dated or dissimilar comparable sales may be used for a range of reasons, some reflecting negatively on the property and others not:

Negative factors

- Low activity in the local market due to an undesirable location

- Unusual property

- Depressed local economy

- Inflated value through aggressive or inappropriate comp selection

Benign factors

- Low sales activity due to a stable neighborhood with minimal turnover

- Low density population

- Non-homogeneous neighborhood

- Limited availability of financing

Maximum distances and adjustments for comparables are recommendations, not rules. Comparable selection not within normal expectations is commonly justified by "The comparables used are the best available." The underwriter shouldn't assume that distant or dated comparables or above average adjustments reflect negatively on the subject property. The underwriter should assess whether marketability is impaired. If value is in doubt, a review appraisal is advised.

The architect's house

The young architect fell in love with the lot's view, but it took a year and one-half to obtain building permits because of complications with the lot. Plans required tiered retaining walls plus special vegetation to absorb the often intense coastal rainfall. The lot had a stunning water view but the only current access was off a four lane highway sided by a bus lane fronting the property. During peak commuting hours, buses passed at five minute intervals. The small build-able pad allowed only a twelve-hundred square-foot house, and although the planned structure was attractive, there was very limited space for parking.

The request was for 90% single-close financing, and the loan had been denied by two other lenders. Verified reserves barely met the requirement. Comparables had similar views but none had limited accessibility. This was not adjusted for because there were no similar sales, recent or dated. The appraiser did provide extensive narrative.

The loan request was denied. In addition to questionably supported value, other factors were the borrower's employment with the builder constructing the property and no available funds in the event of overruns.

Lessons:

1. *A well-designed house and a desirable view are not sufficient to assure marketability.*

2. *A building permit does not ensure the ability to obtain financing.*

3. *A 90% LTV with a severely defective appraisal could translate to an actual LTV over 100%.*

4. *With access by a private road, the project could be viable.*

Personal property included in sale

Traditionally the value of personal property was deducted from sales price. This inflexible approach has been abandoned for the most part.

The pivotal point is the meaningful value of the personal property. A vacation home with worn furniture and kitchen equipment should be distinguished from a residence with high-end furniture and original art. Used furniture (notwithstanding antiques) and outdoor equipment have minimal resale value even when in respectable condition. With primary and second homes of people relocating, downsizing or moving into care facilities, furnishings may be left behind at the seller's convenience.

If the appraiser refuses to value personal property, an expert can be located online or through an auction house or used furniture store. The expert deserves a fee and should be made aware that the goods are not available for resale. Best case, value should be considered as "minimal resale value" or, if not, with a specific dollar amount reflecting estimated retail value. If the specific dollar amount proportionate to the sales price is meaningful, it should be deducted for an adjusted sales price. If it is relatively negligible, it can be ignored.

Modified use

Some modified use is easily cured; some is not. A garage converted into a family room can be restored for a relatively nominal cost; removing carpet and re-installing a garage door requires minimum time and expense. If a garage has been converted into an unpermitted living unit with kitchen and bathroom, legal use and quality of modifications are germane. Depending on how stringent the municipality is about building permits, even modifications described as being "in a workmanlike manner" may not be sufficiently compliant. If so, the appraiser will stipulate that the value conclusion is subject to permits, and remediation should be signed off by the municipality prior to close.

The more extensive the modification and/or the larger the modified space, the greater effect on marketability. A residence owned by a daycare provider had an addition considerably larger than a large family room. The addition had an exterior door and side-by-side bathrooms, each with a toilet and sink. Although the addition increased gross living area, relatively few buyers would consider its contribution to square footage equal to the residential space. Another consideration is whether non-residential use is acceptable per zoning regulations. The appraiser referenced the addition but did not address the modification's functionality or legality. The loan was submitted to a correspondent investor and was returned to the origi

Acts of nature

Wherever people live there is some potential for natural disaster—lightning storms, floods, hurricanes, tornados, tsunamis, volcanic flow, earthquakes and other weather-related events or geologic instabilities.

The primary determination is whether potential damage is curable or incurable. In my first underwriting position, I was warned about small pockets of homes in Pacific Palisades and Malibu with severe slide danger. A fire-damaged home can be rebuilt, but a home sunk into the earth or slid down the hillside represents a permanent loss to the owner and lender.

Insurance coverage can mitigate the loss in some instances. Flood insurance is mandatory in designated zones. Some areas with dense brush growth or distant from city services are insurable only with state-sponsored coverage. Earthquake insurance is voluntary, probably because major quakes occur infrequently and impact lenders less because of affordable federal rehabilitation loans.

Familiarity with the area makes for better decisioning. Underwriters in Hawaii know that lending is prohibited in certain lava zones. Underwriters in earthquake-prone areas know that minor surface cracks are cosmetic rather than structural, although in rare instances a geologic report is necessary. Despite some ocean-front properties experiencing recurring water damage resulting in stratospheric insurance rates, marketability remains strong and property owners believe that their enjoyment outweighs the possible consequences. Appraisers must be familiar with areas they appraise, not only with regard to comparable sales but also to potential hazards.

Over-improvements

Houses significantly larger or with more amenities and features than average are described as over-improvements. They can be attractive to buyers with large families, those working at home or those seeking higher-end living space.

Over-improved properties may merit loan approval. A larger down payment may be necessary if the sales price is unsupported or if marketability is impaired. The loan amount should be similar to loan amounts on typical neighborhood properties. The result is an owner with a high equity position and a lender likely to be fully repaid.

Depending on the investor, a swimming pool or guesthouse may not be considered an over-improvement, even if no similar comparable is available. Comparables may be unavailable because of a slow market or because similar properties haven't recently sold. For conforming loans, at least one comparable may be necessary. For non-conforming loans, affirmation from the appraiser that the feature does not impair marketability may not be necessary if the adjustment is low or the feature is typical in the area.

See *Unique properties*

Incomplete improvements

Attempts have been made to obtain financing mid-way through remodeling or when purchasing a partially-renovated residence. Even with an "as-is" appraisal, there are several considerations:

- The property must be livable with a functioning kitchen and at least one functioning bathroom.

- Major health and safety issues identified by the appraiser should be rectified prior to close.

- Unpaid contractors, construction workers or other tradespeople involved in renovation or providing materials can obtain mechanic's liens. They exist in every state. Since a mechanic's lien dates to the beginning of a project, a new mortgage loan will be subordinate to it. The choices are delaying closing until the proper amount of time elapses after the notice of completion is recorded or protecting lien priority through a completion or performance bond.

- Occupancy cannot be ignored. Improvements in process requiring owners to live elsewhere must be completed before the occupancy provision in the mortgage is violated. Estimated time to complete should be comfortably shorter than the required occupancy date in case complications arise. If occupancy is in doubt (i.e., a potential rental, flip or tear-down), a credible motivation letter should be obtained, or the loan request should be declined.

FHA 203K financing or a Fannie Mae HomeStyle loan are possibilities, with loan proceeds disbursed during the process and value concluded on the residence after the improvements are complete.

Unpermitted and illegal additions

There is a distinction between **unpermitted** and **illegal additions.**
Unpermitted additions lack municipal monitoring and sign-off. Post-completion permitting may be available but may require partial destruction and reconstruction so below-surface improvements can be examined for soundness. **Illegal additions** violate zoning and have greater potential for mandatory conversion to their previous state. A storage shed likely represents legal use, but its conversion into a car-repair bay with hydraulic lifts likely shifts it into illegal status.

Unpermitted and illegal additions may be tolerated when the local government has stretched financial resources. Flexibility varies by community. A radio call-in dispensing legal advice recently was questioned about undoing a garage conversion several decades old; previous owners had violated the code requiring covered parking. Some municipalities are more flexible on illegal accessory units when a property is owner-occupied or when rental properties are in short supply.

Unpermitted additions should be typical for the neighborhood. Quality should not be inferior to the original structure. Standard appraisal verbiage attests to "acceptable quality completed in a workmanlike manner." The appraiser is responsible for disclosing unpermitted square footage and commenting when it is substandard in any respect. Most investors accept loans on properties with unpermitted additions if the appraiser's comments are favorable.

Deducting unpermitted area from total square footage is illogical and unnecessary. The structure should be assessed for what it is, not as it is permitted.

Staging

Staging is a strategic enhancement of a property's visual appeal to optimize sales price. Deficiencies are minimized by masking both curable and incurable features. This involves eliminating clutter, anything oversized, threadbare or representing personal taste such as photos, plaques, trophies and unattractive objects. Furniture is replaced with smaller pieces to make rooms appear larger, substituting understated contemporary furnishings for obtrusive or dated items, covering worn flooring with area rugs, and changing light fixtures to disguise low ceilings.

Why is this relevant to underwriters? After all, furnishings and cosmetic flaws are not the point of appraisal photos, and appraisers are responsible for disclosing and assessing property limitations.

The ability to recognize a professional or amateur attempt at staging can help mitigate risk such as occupancy fraud. If a house being refinanced is clearly staged or lacks essentials like towels and toilet paper, the owners may have moved out. If the application indicates no dependents, and interior photos show themed bedrooms with stuffed animals and toys, possibilities are tenant occupancy, visiting relatives or an overly-expedited application process.

An accomplished underwriter is observant.

Staging for a teardown

The house next door was being prepared for sale. A young couple had purchased it over six decades earlier and raised their family. By the time we moved in, only the widow and one adult son remained.

The roofing contractor son who left decades ago and his brother who never moved out were aware the house was in disrepair. Everything was clean, but almost nothing had changed. The house was originally built in 1939; the kitchen and bathroom had never been remodeled. The victrola was still in the living room with the dated furniture. The venetian blinds were only partially attached. The only update was a high-quality heavy shake roof thirty years ago.

The plan was to reseed the front lawn, replace the deteriorated garage door, repaint the front of the house a lighter shade to match the rest of the faded exterior and thin out the overgrown foliage. The only interior changes were minimizing clutter. The brothers' mission was curb appeal for a teardown.

FSBOs

FSBO (the acronym for For Sale by Owner pronounced "fizz-bōw") is a sale transaction without a real estate agent or an MLS listing. The seller's benefit is saving on sales commissions. Potential downsides are more numerous—a listing price set without professional expertise, an extended listing period because of no or amateur advertising, uncooperative real estate agents (unless the seller agrees to pay a buyer's broker), a contract that is generic or overly complicated and—for the lender—a higher potential for collusion.

Under certain circumstances, listing may not be necessary. The owners are selling to a tenant or someone they know. Or, with a well-located property in a hot real estate market, buyers scour desirable neighborhoods for available properties.

FSBO transactions should be reviewed carefully. If sales price is well-supported by the appraisal and there are no other red flags, proceed. If the sales price is higher than appraised value and the increased down payment (unless nominal) does not cause the borrower to renegotiate, request a detailed motivation letter from the buyer and review it for credibility. The contract between buyer and seller should always be reviewed.

See *Non-arm's-length relations*

Pocket listings

Pocket listings, also called off-market listings, are not reflected in the Multiple Listing Service. They typically involve high-profile property sellers and luxury properties. Private showings replace open houses. Pocket listings are considered to be market sales, and appraisers are able to access data through personal contacts and public records data available after recordation.

Who overpays

1. In a rapidly appreciating market (i.e., a seller's market), value may appear to be unsupported. Most appraisers avoid time adjustments, usually a sound decision because rapidly escalating markets tend to change direction quickly. So when high appraised value requires aggressive adjustments, a conservative call by the appraiser results in a more prudent lending decision.

2. In fraudulent transactions, collusion between seller and buyer is facilitated by properties with condition and/or marketability issues. Sales of superior properties appear to support inflated value. Be especially wary of flipped properties with cosmetic renovation. See *Flip Transactions*

3. In some cases, convenience outweighs price. Examples would be a buyer wanting to live in close proximity to relatives, employment, a particular school or house of worship. See *Sales price exceeding appraised value*, a subsection of *The purchase contract*

Who buys a bargain

1. A desperate seller is a homebuyer's dream. Real estate listings often use the term "motivated" for sellers who are divorcing, in failing health or have other compelling circumstances. Many but not every listing claiming a motivated seller is attractively priced.

2. Ideally a tenant should receive a below-market price, because the property seller is spared the cost of real estate commissions and making the property market-ready. This is not to say that tenant-borrowers are overpaying when appraised value coincides with sales price. Rather, the tenant is willing to pay market price and the seller is willing to accept it, or appraised value conveniently coincided with sales price.

3. Other non-arm's-length transactions ideally should be below market. With a sale transaction between a buyer and and a relative, godparent or other arm's length relation, there often is benefit for both parties. See *Non-arm's-length transactions*

4. FSBOs have a pricing edge if the seller shares money not spent on real estate commissions with the buyer. But some sellers don't share. See *For Sale by Owner*

5. Buyers are capable of ignoring cosmetic flaws or curable defects. Fixer-uppers are sought after by buyers aware that the cost of renovation sometimes increases market value by several times the investment.

6. Some buyers are unscrupulous. They may convince a naive property seller that the house is worth less than fair market value, then buy it for less, fix it up and sell it for top dollar. There is a blurred ethical line between getting a good deal and taking advantage.

There are two sides of the price/value equation. Although in most cases, sales price reflects fair market value, sometimes is doesn't.

When sales price and market value differ

Whether high or low, in most cases the implications of a sales price inconsistent with appraised value protect the lender. The protection comes from LTV being predicated on the lower of sales price or appraised value. When sales price exceeds appraised value, the borrowers make up the difference in down payment, thus reducing risk by increasing cash equity. When sales price is less than appraised value, equity based on appraised value is higher than the spreadsheet LTV indicates.

Following are potential downsides:

- LTV can err on the high side when sales price exceeds appraised value. This occurs when appraisers, aware that sales price is the best indicator of fair market value, consciously or subconsciously bring in value as close to sales price as they are able.

- When sales price exceeds appraised value, especially when combined with a seller-financed second lien, there is also potential for misrepresented equity because of collusion between buyer and seller.

When there is a minor discrepancy between sales price and appraised value, don't overreact. Most probably there is an innocuous reason such as multiple bids or scarcity of close comparables.

Buyer attraction to new construction

1. Being the first occupant of a house is attractive to many buyers.

2. Buyers like the idea of customizing through options, upgrades and selecting finishings like floor coverings, paint colors and cabinetry styles.

3. New houses often feature contemporary wish-list items like stainless steel appliances, granite countertops and walk-in closets. After time passes, these features will be replaced by a new set of in-demand features.

4. Builder incentIves include lower or waived financing costs and upgrades. Furnishings may be included on model homes. When inventory isn't selling, builders have been known to discount sales prices, offer country club memberships, golf carts and cars.

5. New houses require fewer and less expensive repairs.

6. New tracts target distinct market segments such as young families or empty nesters for buyers looking for a homogeneous neighborhood.

The downside to new construction

1. New homes often entail longer commutes to employment.

2. New homes designed for general appeal may appear generic, bland and impersonal.

3. Builders may leave landscaping to the buyer.

4. Excessively upgraded homes may appraise below sales price.

5. Devotees of older homes believe new homes are built with less durable materials and will not age well.

6. Local shopping may be largely chain stores and franchises. Medical services, sports and cultural venues may require a longer drive.

Pros of older homes

1. Older homes may have sounder workmanship and greater character.

2. Older homes have more exterior appeal because of mature landscaping.

3. Older homes may be closer to urban amenities like theaters and museums.

4. Older neighborhoods offer all kinds of diversity.

5. Updated older homes can provide the best in location and quality of living

Cons of older homes

1. Older homes, unless fully remodeled, may be out of sync with current expectations such as ample bathrooms, larger bedrooms and generous closet space. Space may be dedicated for infrequent needs like formal dining instead of a more useful family room or home office

2. Older homes without updated systems may have inadequate heat and electricity, no air conditioning and poor water pressure.

3. Older homes require costly repairs and upgrading.

4. Older homes in centralized locations have higher cost per square foot.

5. With room additions, floor plans may be awkward.

6. Updated older homes cost more per square foot because of higher land value.

Lender attraction to builder homes

The obvious attraction is volume. Establish a relationship with a builder, especially a national builder, and loans are delivered in clusters. But that is not the only reason.

New construction has no deferred maintenance, no unpermitted additions or awkward floor plans, and far fewer hidden deficiencies and negative appraiser comments. Almost no loans cancel because of home inspection findings.

Appraised value is easily definable. After the first few sales (which are usually closed simultaneously), there are suitable comparables requiring minimal adjustments. The appraisal process is expedited, since builder floor plans replace taping the house.

Builders seldom build tracts that buyers don't want to buy. Buyers are attracted to new homes. They willingly accept the longer commutes and see the distance from the city core as a positive. The houses and the lot sizes are larger, there is an absence of grittiness and the aura of a safe neighborhood.

Buyers of new tract homes have higher credit scores than average. Loan performance is above average as well.

New tract risk

Loans on new construction are not failure-proof. Builder bailouts and failed tracts occur when the supply and demand are imbalanced. However, national builders fare better than regional or local builders because they have the resources to research economic trends and locations before purchasing acreage. Oversupply causes builders to default on construction financing or resort to marginal or straw buyers who subsequently default. Builder remedies are bankruptcy and a new corporate name after the dust settles.

When a seller's market quickly transitions into a buyer's market, an inventory of unsold builder homes is likely. Asking prices reasonable in an appreciating market suddenly seem high. Prospective buyers wait for bargains or the market to bottom. Some developments—more often attached housing or in remote locations—cannot operate successfully with only a fraction of units sold. When builders cannot afford to carry housing inventory, the houses are foreclosed upon and sold by the construction lender for heavily discounted prices, alienating owners who purchased in a healthier market.

Tract builders have been negatively impacted by speculative buyers purchasing for short-term resale or failing to disclose simultaneous purchase of multiple properties. When speculators are unable to resell or find tenants, the result is abandoned properties.

Mature tracts

Housing tracts mature into neighborhoods. The better constructed and located the tract, the more likely the neighborhood will age gracefully. Most houses will be updated and remodeled periodically. I speak from personal experience. Almost three decades ago we moved into a nearly fifty-year-old house. The original tract was two- and three-bedroom, one- and two-bath houses built for working class employees at nearby movie studios. When my husband and I moved in, our house had already been enlarged with a dining room, a third bedroom, a second bath and a family room. Other houses in the area had been remodeled with second stories, or torn down and replaced with new two-story residences.

We are anticipating tear-down of the house next door. This house is a rarity, unchanged in square footage with no updating. My husband predicts that our house, upgraded three times but not enlarged since our purchase, will be considered a tear-down by the time we depart. Since the neighborhood is well-located and well-maintained, houses sell quickly for appreciating prices. Post-meltdown there were minimal foreclosures and short sales.

Not all tracts age gracefully. Those located in still-remote locations tend to suffer, as do more centrally-located tracts with bland architecture and average construction. Those once shiny and new houses steadily deteriorate and decline in desirability. Their best selling point is affordability and their only hope, gentrification.

See *Our first home*

Luxury home appraisals

- Specialized expertise is required to appraise luxury homes. The appraiser must be equipped to identify high-end finishings like built-ins and floor coverings, quantify the percentage of usable lot, select the sales with the most similar attributes and assess privacy and view.

- Target maximum adjustments apply less to non-mainstream housing because custom houses (either as originally built or through decades of remodels) differ from each other. Comparables may be more distant because they are located in less dense and more stable neighborhoods resulting in fewer sales. It may not be realistic to expect similar and close comparables.

- Only three comparables may be indicative of an appraiser with limited experience in this subcategory. Three comparables are adequate if relatively close in location and minimally adjusted.

- A higher than average number of interior photos are standard, since luxury houses have more rooms, amenities and architectural features.

Increasing appraisal expertise

Shadowing an appraiser is well worth the time invested. Perhaps your company or an industry friend can arrange for this. Observe the process and limit questions that obstruct completion of the appraiser's job. Drive-time is the best time to satisfy curiosity.

Another possibility is taking a class or two. Appraisal courses at community colleges or extension programs are common, since it is a broker license requirement. UCLA Extension offerings include Real Estate Appraisal, Investment Properties, Commercial Real Estate and Market Analysis classes.

Walking through weekend open houses is a free alternative. Pay attention to room configuration, sizes and appearance, especially the kitchen and bathrooms, and whether staging was employed. If no prospective buyers are present, ask the realtor about days on market, his/her industry experience and changes made to the house. Make notes on the handout and track the house for the ultimate sales price, noting the difference from listing price and days on market. Start locally and consider expanding beyond. Visiting open houses during vacation is less expensive than a theme park unless you end up buying a second home.

Another free alternative is online research. The Appraisal Foundation's website (appraisalfoundation.org) has comprehensive articles on issues like declining markets and adjustments for concessions. Navigate from *Resources to Courses, Guidance and Q & A Forum*. Bear in mind appraisal sites assume the reader is an appraiser or a consumer. Googling topics of interest works too. Remember that year of publication affects point of view.

Yet another option is watching television. Almost any show about buying, selling, remodeling or flipping is worth sampling. *House Hunters* (the prototype for numerous HGTV spawn) provides education on functionality, marketability, staging, in-demand features and unrealistic expectations. *House Hunters International* also demonstrates how quickly buyers learn to compromise. An array of program options increase expertise in an entertaining manner.

Similarly, *HGTV Magazine* and other shelter publications provide a quiet and portable educational opportunity. Reading is not as resume-worthy as an appraisal class, but any industry-related learning activity adds to professional competency.

Lastly, diligence matters. The more appraisals an underwriter has dissected, the better the next appraisal can be assessed.

What I learned from open houses

1. The listing agent will tell you whether there are one or more bids but not specific dollar amounts. "Generous" translates to over the asking price or, in an extended listing, any offer higher than expected.

2. Asking how long the property has been listed may be answered with an edited response of how long it's been listed at the current asking price.

3. Candor is greater regarding closed deals, listings taken off the market (possibly temporarily) or the agent's personal inability to refinance.

4. Descriptive language used by a real estate agent is dissimilar to an appraiser's or an underwriter's . A bedroom may lack a closet, and a walk-in closet may have no rod for hanging clothes. "It needs finishing," the agent said.

5. Low budget staging can be unimpressive. I walked through a house staged to have three master bedrooms. There were also two identically frayed sisal rugs in the dining room and master bedroom, and a large storage container in the driveway. The house did not sell quickly.

6. Renovation can be selective. Typically, the further you get from the front door, the less the effort at making the property look impressive. One listed home had a living room, dining room and kitchen remodeled as "open concept" while the bedroom had dated mirrored sliding closet doors and a family room with frayed engineered flooring.

7. Listing agents are most willing to chat when there are no potential buyers in the house.

The *House Hunters* formula

The House Hunters prototype features walk-throughs of three properties and a final segment revealing which one was chosen to purchase. More frequently in second home areas, vacation destinations or internationally, the hunters are looking to rent rather than purchase.

Principles explored are location, size, amenities, condition, affordability, suitability for the occupant needs and also unrealistic expectations. Comparing and contrasting properties demonstrates the decision-making process. Does proximity to the ski slopes / employment / restaurants and shopping outweigh a dated kitchen or pricing over budget? How should bedroom complications (too few, too small or with no adjacent bathrooms) be resolved?

The formula relies on two buyers, or one buyer accompanied by a relative or friend offering advice. Differences in opinion can be thought-provoking or annoying. Disagreements are usually resolved with compromise. Insights emerge on functionality and marketability. Knowledge can be gained on locations unless they aren't specified, in which case it's probably Canada.

There are multiple variations based on location (beachfront, Alaska, islands, farms, off the grid), occupancy type, borrower profile (relocating, first time, needing parental financial contribution, lottery winners), property condition (needing renovation) and more. These programs abound on HGTV and DIY. During summer a network property-related miniseries sometimes springs up, usually a renovation competition.

Lessons from *House Hunters*

1. Excluding high-cost metropolitan locations, the minimum desirable room count is three bedrooms and two baths. This lesson came from the first House Hunters episode I ever viewed. The buyer was a geek under twenty, no reference to being in a relationship, but he still wanted three and two.

2. Most couples (or partners or close friends) have differing tastes. Most common are newer/mainstream/contemporary appeal/move-in-ready versus older/unique/vintage appeal/fixer. The first batch likely wins.

3. Too many homebuyers lack the ability to distinguish between imperfections easily curable (e.g., paint color) and functionally flawed. One House Hunter disliked a house because of discarded toilets in the back yard.

4. First-time home buyers are unrealistic. Particularly in established neighborhoods, few starter homes have walk-in closets and gourmet kitchens. We figured out immediately that we could stash clothes in every closet in the house.

5. Buyers of all ages covet whatever features are in vogue currently. It was refreshing and ironic when a couple on Tiny House Hunters found a modest bathroom with a pedestal sink spacious while single House Hunters can be disappointed when the master bath doesn't have dual sinks.

6. Preferences can be illogical. Singles insisting on dual sinks may be planning ahead, but empty-nesters insisting on a split floor plan should take into account that their children no longer live with them

Lessons From *House Hunters International*

1. Housing prices even in third world countries can be shockingly expensive, at least in upper-end neighborhoods where American tastes are more easily satisfied.

2. Prices appear to be non-negotiable.

3. Most couples (or partners or close friends) have differing tastes. Most common abroad are city center versus in the country, and local charm versus modern conveniences.

4. More often in foreign locations, buyers fail to commit in the final segment.

5. Expectations outside the United States are even less realistic than for first-time U.S. home-buyers. The inevitable extra bedroom for visitors usually becomes expendable by the final segment. Minimum square footage and bed- and bathroom updating fall by the wayside even sooner.

6. There is an initial conversation between the hunters and the real estate broker, whose command of English can range from adequate to fluent. The buyers' wish list is often unrealistic. The brokers often grimace and/or comment they will do their best. Borrowing a device from Property Brothers, they may show a property above budget to demonstrate how unaffordable the wish list is.

7. Pricing is simplified. A house hunter relocating from Reykjavik to rural Iceland expressed her maximum budget in American dollars. Currently everyone on House Hunters International expresses his or her budget in American dollars. In previous years, prices were converted to American dollars on a screen overlay. The new approach makes reality television unrealistic.

Nevertheless, it is interesting to learn about housing outside the United States and to observe that many marketability issues apply universally.

Are appraisers an endangered species?

The secondary manager at a consulting gig predicted that appraisals would soon be extinct. What triggered the prediction was Fannie Mae's Collateral Underwriter (CU). Discussing his comment with an industry friend, she responded, "Eventually maybe. It's not as wild a concept as a couple of years ago."

CU reviews the appraisal in an electronic data format and generates a collateral risk score with feedback to the lender. Both GSEs share the Uniform Collateral Data Portal with proprietary risk messages, and FHA and VA are following suit.

CU bounces data in Fannie Mae's property engine against the appraisal and responds specifically to what it views as shortcomings and omissions. It blends the functions of an ultra sophisticated AVM and a review appraisal. Any property database is most effective when and where data is most robust—in an active market in urban and suburban locations.

Other limitations include:

Limited database: To generate a universal appraiser-less assessment, a database would require comprehensive data on properties, including rural properties, those ineligible for GSE financing and unique properties. While Fannie Mae's database is extensive, it is not all-encompassing. It also is exclusive to Fannie Mae.

Inconsistent data: Data from various sources may differ.
See *The contradictory rental*

Condition: Condition is critical to the market approach and requires an interior inspection of the property. The extreme ramification of condition is health and safety issues which affect both risk and liability. A possible solution would be for property inspectors to assess condition, but they would have to be licensed and their observations would have to be communicated to the lender, the borrower and the database.

Unpermitted additions: Room additions are not always reflected on public records, which are sometimes inaccurate in other respects. Public records are also blind to updating and renovations not requiring building permits.
See *The contradictory rental*

Modified usage: Garage conversions represent a significant portion of modified usage. Appraisals have revealed a living room turned beauty salon with shampoo stations, a living room with a pick-up window facilitating cigarette and snack sales, a basement equipped for indoor marijuana farming including an irrigation system, and a suburban house transformed into a pornography studio complete with ceiling-mounted cameras. Excluding the porn house, which could easily be restored to residential use, modifications are permanent, possibly structurally unsound, and could constitute illegal use.

Disaster-related events: Damage from natural disasters like hurricanes and earthquakes is not restricted to easily defined areas. Properties are affected to different degrees, and a property in mediocre condition adjacent to the area may be impacted more than a reinforced house within it. After major disasters, interior inspections are prudent.

Property nuances: Some property aspects can be captured on a grid and others require commentary. Appraisers have differing levels of expertise and greater expertise in some locations than others. An engine capable of quantifying every aspect of every property would be impossible to design.

After AVMs became an industry tool, some predicted that appraisers would soon lose their jobs. AVMs continue to have widespread use. But more often than replacing a full appraisal, they validate value on the subject property, approximate value on a departure residence or estimate loss on a nonperforming loan. Appraiser ranks are thinning as many age, but there is continued need for their services and demand for capable replacements. Natural attrition will likely adjust supply to demand. Data for CU is drawn from the appraisal, and the appraisers most in jeopardy from CU are those who create substandard product.

Describing properties

Positive: well maintained, well preserved, functional floor plan, well configured, marketable, desirable, luxury, exclusive, high end, high quality, high ceilings, gourmet kitchen, professional kitchen, master bathroom, spa bathroom, walk-in closet

Negative: deferred maintenance, awkward floor plan, poorly configured, impaired marketability, dated, outdated, low quality, mediocre quality, small (rooms), popcorn ceilings, obsolete, possible health and safety issue

Neutral: new, newer, contemporary, old, older, tract, custom, over-improvement, unique, amenities, finishings, upgrades, features, renovations, remodel, above grade, below grade,

Exterior/outbuildings: mature landscaping, sparse landscaping, neglected landscaping, garage, detached garage, shed, guesthouse, in-law unit, ohana unit, barn, studio, stable

Locational: urban, suburban, rural, tract neighborhood, eclectic neighborhood, gentrified, adjacent to, backing to, siding to, congested, high density, low density

Comparables: well supported, similar, dissimilar, greater (or lesser) curb appeal, close-by, proximate, distant, current, dated,

Pertinent descriptive verbiage can be found in the appraisal.

CHAPTER 8
TRANSACTIONAL ISSUES

The purchase contract

A purchase contract is a formalized agreement between buyer and seller. It is usually a typed form that varies slightly from brokerage to brokerage, but generic versions are available online. A handwritten purchase contract is as binding as a typed agreement.

Following are some important aspects:

Percentage of ownership: Fragmented ownership is more probable with tenants in common. It is irrelevant to each borrower's liability on the loan. All borrowers are equally responsible for repayment, even with a formal agreement between co-owners establishing percentages of ownership or disparate monthly repayment contributions.

As-Is condition: Two situations cause property sellers to stipulate a property to be sold as is. The first occurs when current owners lack knowledge of the property, which is reasonable after an inheritance. The second is when owners want to limit personal liability because of unpermitted square footage, a structural or contamination problem, or other concern. Under either circumstance, a property inspection before closing is essential. Both the lender and the borrower should have full awareness of property condition. If the borrower has no concern with condition, either the borrower is naive or the property is a tear-down.

Property inspections: Most purchase offers include a provision for property inspection either because the buyer is prudent, or the real estate agent is helpful or wants to avoid potential liability. They are less essential on new construction or on properties purchased as tear-downs. Unless the buyer is related to the seller or is a long-term and savvy tenant, the absence of an inspection provision in a sales contract should serve as a red flag on occupancy or property longevity.

Inspection findings range from critical to trivial. When buyer review and approval of the property inspection is a condition of the purchase contract, the buyer selects items to be remedied at the property seller's expense, disregarding items that are insignificant or postponable. If the seller fails to cooperate, the sale can fall through. Our house was nearly fifty years old when we purchased it, and findings included thirty-some items. We requested that six or eight be fixed, and the seller complied. Depending on the degree of difficulty in finding a replacement buyer, the seller can be more or less accommodating. On an "as is" sale, the seller may be less amendable to correcting deficiencies.

Whether the property inspection is reviewed by the underwriter varies by lender. Some opt to see all property inspection and termite reports, others only case by case when the property appears poorly maintained, and some not at all. Procedures vary by lender and product type. The appraiser has responsibility for assessing property condition although admittedly some property elements, notably functionality of internal systems, are beyond the appraiser's scope. Responsible owners maintain their properties to ensure livability and maximum property value, and prudent borrowers are unlikely to commit to a property in disrepair.

Termite Inspections: Termite inspections are customary when ownership transfers. They are not necessary for new construction. For condominium and co-op units, only the individual unit requires inspection. Typically property sellers pay for corrective work only; they are not responsible for preventive measures. Under most circumstances no reference to a termite inspection in the purchase contract should be considered a red flag. If the property is older, dated or neglected, it may be a tear-down. On refinances, termite inspections should be required only when the appraisal makes reference to potential infestation.
See *Tear-downs*

Sales price exceeding appraised value: A sales price exceeding appraised value is considered a red flag but often is benign. The lender is protected since LTV is based on the lower of sales price or appraised value.
See *When sales price and market value differ* and *Who overpays*

When motivation for overpayment is unclear or there are additional red flags, the underwriter should be wary. A motivation letter may help. Since market value is typically reflected in sales price, appraised value lower than sales price occurs only when a higher figure cannot be supported. When appraised value is inadequately supported, a review product should be ordered. When discomfort persists, loan denial may be justified.

Contributions exceeding closing costs: Until shortly before a sales transaction closes, closing costs can only be estimated. Closing agents preferring to avoid a shortage at close are inclined to overestimate funds. Last-minute requests for additional funds are problematic. But when seller contributions exceed actual closing costs, eligibility for sale is impaired.

The estimated closing statement should be reviewed for padded figures and errors. Before the final closing statement is prepared, if the seller contribution exceeds closing costs, any overage should be applied to a principal pay-down. After the closing statement is issued, a principal pay-down may be possible with a corrected closing statement. If the overage is minimal, it may be considered inconsequential.

Impaired salability is more avoidable with TRID since the originator has responsibility for the closing statement.

Seller contributions negotiated or increased after contract: When the seller contribution increases after the contract is signed, the easy conclusion is a marginal borrower, a desperate seller and possibly a dubious property value. Easy is not always correct. It may be that the borrower is a tough negotiator, or the contribution covers a negotiated repair. Regardless of cause, ramifications for the resultant loan can be lack of salability or pushback from auditors or regulatory authorities. Unless the contribution is clearly justifiable, such as the cost of a repair pending completion, LTV should be derived from an adjusted sales price excluding that portion of the contribution negotiated after contract.

Timing: Extended time between the contract date and the start of the application process can signal inability to obtain financing, especially when accompanied by a delayed closing date.

And/or assigns: When the buyer's name on a purchase contract is followed by "and/or assigns," the original buyer can be replaced and/or additional parties added. This tactic is employed on investment properties or properties represented as primary residences but actually intended for investment. Less frequently, it is used to ensure buyer privacy. A condition of approval should be to eliminate the "and/or assigns" option. If it is not eliminated, the loan origination process may be a waste of time.

See *A gift from the borrower's sibling, a real estate agent, Short sale risk, Sale of personal property* and *Incomplete improvements*

Preliminary title-work

Most of the time a cursory reading of preliminary title-work is adequate, but not always. Prompt review allows time to resolve any complications that could impede closing. Resolution of title issues usually is handled by the closing agent and title company, assuming the cooperation of the borrower and/or seller.

Following are title-related issues:

Changes in title: If names of borrowers differ from those on title, vesting must be amended or conveyed, except when someone is obligated on the loan but not on title. Amending vesting is a standard step on a purchase transaction but is sometimes necessary on a refinance. It may require more than one deed of conveyance. Take the example of a borrower and her former spouse who vested title in the name of their corporation until she was awarded the marital residence in the divorce and returned to her pre-married name. This would require a series of deeds to be drawn and recorded conveying title from the corporation to the husband and wife, then deleting the ex-husband, and finally conveying title from the wife's married name to her previous last name. The steps involved are referred to as chain of title. If none of the parties currently on title will be on title after the new loan transaction, the transaction should be handled as a purchase, with the exception of a business owned by one or more of the people currently on title.

Legal description: A property's legal description should be consistent with the legal description in the appraisal and in loan documents. Any discrepancy should be corrected before loan documents are signed and recorded.

Outstanding deficiency, tax liens and judgments: These items affect lien priority and also give insight to creditworthiness. A borrower may be unaware of an isolated item or feel it is unjustified. However, one sizable or multiple items suggest irresponsibility or lack of resources. (The exception is items proven to belong to another individual. The underwriter should defer judgment when the borrower has a common name.) Outstanding non-mortgage liens should be explained in writing; they are as meaningful as derogatory items on the credit report. If the borrower is unable or unwilling to pay off a non-consensual lien or judgment, continued processing may be futile since subordination is not generally an option.

Open real estate lien(s): These must be paid off, proven to be paid in full or subordinated to assure lien priority. If a lien holder cannot be located, a mortgage can still record. There is an established protocol for setting aside payoff proceeds for lien holders who can't be found.

Bonds and assessments: Bonds or assessments either must be paid off or verified to be non-delinquent prior to close, depending on the municipality. If an obligation is delinquent, a lien could be recorded jeopardizing lender priority.

Fee simple tenancy: This ownership interest includes both the improvements and the land as defined by the legal description. This is the most common form of ownership.

Leasehold tenancy: The borrower owns the improvements but not the lot below. The leasehold agreement discloses the duration of the current lease and the leasehold fee, which should be factored into monthly housing expense. The standard industry requirement is that the lease remains in effect until at least five years after the full loan term. Leasehold tenancy should also be reflected in the appraisal.

Covenants, Conditions and Restrictions: CC&Rs indicate that the subject property is part of a condominium or another type of development able to control aspects of property use, such as a planned unit development (PUD). The borrower should be provided with the most current version of the CC&Rs and any other related documents to review before close. This is commonly handled by the real estate or closing agent, not the lender.

Easements: Easements entitle use of a defined portion of the property by a party other than the owner. Common easements allow access by utility companies or a shared driveway with neighbors. Unlocated easements allow access to the full lot and may interfere with the owner's right of enjoyment. They are generally unacceptable to lenders.

Oil or mineral rights: The first step, which may have occurred years before purchase, is an agreement between an oil or mining company and the owner of land, typically not yet developed. Contractual consent is given to extract resources from below the surface level. Subsequent owners are bound to the terms of the agreement but benefit from income from the continued extraction. If the recorded agreement allows for surface entry, the owner of subterranean rights can drill or excavate from ground level. Unless entry is confined to a distant area of a large lot, this can be disruptive, unattractive and potentially hazardous. In urban or suburban locations, source of entry is typically lateral underground access.

Encroachment: An encroachment is a property improvement such as a fence, room addition or outbuilding extending into an adjacent property. The owner or subsequent owner of the adjacent property has the ability to require that the invasive situation be eliminated, unless approval is formalized into an easement.

Lis pendens: This legal term indicates a dispute sometimes referred to as a "cloud on title" that must be resolved before clear title can be obtained. A lis pendens is filed by someone who presumably has a claim to title.

Life estate: A life estate empowers the recipient continued occupancy for the full term of his or her life. This differs from ownership, since the beneficiary of a life estate, called a life tenant, cannot finance or sell the property. The owner (who typically inherited ownership from the grantor of the life estate, but who may be someone who purchased the property through an arm's length transaction) holds title and may be able to encumber the property, but not as owner occupied. Alternatives to a life estate are handling the issue through a living trust or, in some states, a recorded transfer-upon-death deed.

Other complications: If an item on title-work is not covered above and is not self-explanatory, research online or consult the title officer or closing agent.

Loans, mortgages and deeds of trust

A **loan** is a transfer of funds between two parties and the requirement of repayment. A formal loan agreement is a written contract documenting the loan amount and the terms of repayment.

Mortgages have two parties: The mortgagor (lender) and the mortgagee (borrower). A mortgage differs from a loan since a mortgage is secured by a lien against real property.

Trust deeds have three parties: The trustor (borrower), the trustee (custodian) and the beneficiary (lender). The function of the trustee is to reconvey the lien when full repayment occurs. A deed of trust differs from a mortgage, since a **deed of trust** allows a non-judicial foreclosure.

On an informal basis, all four terms—mortgage, deed of trust, trust deed and loan—are used interchangeably.

Subordination agreements

A subordination agreement allows a new lien in a refinance transaction to replace the position of the lien being paid off. This requires written consent from each lien holder whose position would be improved by payoff of the existing lien. The cooperation of lien holders agreeing to subordination depends on how their position is affected by the change. If property values have appreciated and/or the new first lien is the same amount or lower than the lien being paid off, subordination is more likely, but not guaranteed to be granted. Arrangements are handled by the closing agent.

Equity trades

An equity trade occurs when two parties exchange their established equity positions with each other. When equity positions are unequal, the party deeding over the property with the lower equity pays the difference. Deeds formalizing change of ownership are recorded on both properties. There are three basic scenarios. With the exception of 1031 exchanges, equity trades occur infrequently.

1. **Individual to individual:** Usually one party wants to upsize and the other wants to downsize. The probability of two people or households each simultaneously wanting each others' residence is remote. It is more likely that one party genuinely desires the other's residence and the other party is willing to accommodate for a motivation usually undisclosed, possibly owning a less expensive or more marketable property. Risk considerations are reasonability of occupancy and the equity positions on both properties. Equity is confirmed through value

support, since at least one property is not a market sale. The lender should review both appraisals. If there is suspicion that one property will be a short-term holding, pricing and loan amount should take into account potential early payoff, anticipated costs of sale and the carrying costs.

2. **Individual to builder:** When a builder (or developer) is willing to sell a property in exchange for the buyer's equity in another property, it is reasonable to conclude the builder is unable to find a buyer with ready funds to close. The builder's profit will be decreased by resale expense and cost to carry. Also, unless interim financing or a formal assumption on the property is obtained by the builder, liability for the existing mortgage(s) remains with the borrower. With continuing liability for the borrower and evidence of a desperate builder, loan approval is difficult to justify.

3. **Investor to investor:** This is the most common equity trade transaction, allowing real estate investors to replace holdings in non-concurrent transactions without capital gains liability. The trade transaction does not require simultaneous closings. Proceeds from the earlier transaction are held by an impartial third party until the later transaction closes. The formal designation for this transaction type is a Section 1031 or Starker deferred exchange.

Single-closings and two-closings

Construction financing, also known as construction conversion, is handled in one of two ways:

With a **single-close financing**, one loan covers the construction phase and permanent financing. During the initial phase, interest is variable. The loan balance increases as funds are incrementally disbursed. After the final disbursement, permanent financing begins, possibly with conversion to a fixed interest rate.

With a **two-closing**, interim construction financing is replaced by permanent or take-out financing, with two separate recorded liens. This can be handled by one institution or two different lenders. Commercial financing may be obtained for the construction phase and a long-term mortgage for the second phase. In some locations, the builder arranges and is the responsible party for construction financing, in which case title is conveyed temporarily from the owner to the builder.

During the construction phase, a payment history is typically unavailable since loan balance increases replace monthly payments.

For single-close financing, loan documentation should include a cost breakdown, which should be reviewed for reasonability. Some lenders do not allow a builder to profit on his or her personal residence. Similarly, the cost breakdown for the builder-owner should reflect fixtures and appliances at acquisition cost without markup. Legitimate figures on a client's cost breakdown become padded on the builder's personal residence. Because this type of analysis requires special skills, lenders offering construction financing typically use dedicated underwriters or a construction loan department.

Custom construction intrinsically caters to individual taste. If preferences are too personalized, market appeal is at risk. If new construction located in an established neighborhood is larger and built to current standards, it may be an over-improvement. However, in well located neighborhoods, upgrading dated properties is not an isolated occurrence. Whether a property is over-improved should be evident in the distance of comparable properties and photographs of surrounding residences. Be aware that homes updated and retained by owners are not available as comparable sales, and that stable neighborhoods are a positive factor. See *Good Neighbors, Bad Timing*

If new financing is obtained to retire construction financing, steps must be taken to assure lien priority. Mechanic's liens date back to the beginning of construction so the mortgage should not close until the prescribed period after recording of the notice of completion has elapsed.

Subordinate financing

Secondary liens differ according to the provider of the financing.

Financing through a **business bank** may not be consistent with residential lending expectations. There may be an abbreviated term and fluctuating interest rate. The business bank may consent to compliant financing terms for relationship customers.

Seller financing, especially without a real estate agent's guidance, can be unpredictable. Terms acceptable to both seller and buyer may be unacceptable to the lender. Holders of private party financing can be more difficult to locate than institutional lenders in event of default. Greater risk, however low, is that 80-10-10 financing is in fact 90% financing with a quickly forgiven second lien. This occurs when there is collusion between buyer and seller to avoid the cost of private mortgage insurance.

With seller-carried secondary financing and appraised value unsupported by sales price, either fraud or naivety is in force. A reduction in sales price to appraised value eliminates the need for a second lien. If both parties to the sale accept the restructure, naivety is more likely the case. If the loan cancels, fraud is a good possibility.

Many **private party seconds** are legitimate. Institutional secondary financing can be scarce or expensive, and some property sellers prefer monthly income to lump sum repayment.

Private party financing carried by someone other than the seller is uncommon, and written clarification of the relationship (or lack of same) should be provided. Business or asset managers have been known to arrange secondary financing between clients. Privately arranged financing can be less expensive for the borrower-client and provide a secured investment with good return for the investor-client. A below-market interest rate with any relationship between the financing source and property seller is considered a concession. With non-institutional financing, loan terms should be reviewed, and appraised value should be well supported.

Employer-provided financing may be considered institutional or non-institutional, depending on the size of the employer. Academic institutions, hospitals and businesses may offer second lien financing as a perk for employees and / or in areas where housing prices are high. Full or partial forgiveness may be a component of the financing; this is the equivalent of a recurring bonus, but cannot be used to increase qualifying income. A provision that financing must be repaid (or the interest rate adjusted) if the borrower leaves employment is customary. Due and payable provisions are not acceptable to all investors. For portfolio lenders, considerations are borrower equity (which may increase if forgiveness is bestowed on an annual basis), available resources to repay the lien (or its remaining balance, if incrementally forgiven) and the potential of replacement financing.

If the employer is a small business, a long-term employee may be treated like a family member. If the interest rate is reasonable and the due date allows sufficient time for full payoff, the loan is probably legitimate. If the borrower is employed by a family business, the lien is equivalent to private party financing by a family member.

Secondary financing risk

Which provides better security for the lender—a 90% first lien or an 80% first lien with a 10% subordinate second? The case could be made for either. A 90% loan is protected by private mortgage insurance, although post-meltdown some claims were denied because of flaws in origination. A 90% CLTV first lien is protected by 10% lower exposure and the presence of the second lien holder. The higher the second lien balance, the greater the incentive of the second lien holder to keep the first lien current.

HELOC underwriting

Since interest does not accrue on undisbursed funds, HELOCs are sought after in a number of circumstances such as property improvements, emergency funds, tuition expenses. improvements, an emergency resource or as an alternative to a reverse mortgage. Some borrowers owning free and clear even opt for a HELOC first.

Guidelines for home equity lines of credit are typically matrix-driven. Grids establish minimum credit score, maximum CLTV and DTI, and allowable occupancy and property types. If the loan fits the grid, it is approvable. Pricing is based on loan attributes.

Written support of approval may be abbreviated. There may be little consideration of compensating factors and minimal opportunity for exception consideration. The loan either meets matrix or it doesn't.

Second lien underwriting can be mechanical. Pricing a loan by its attributes is justifiable but risk is no less important than on the first lien. The loan amount is probably smaller but there is higher exposure on a second lien.

HELOC payment qualification is a pertinent issue when underwriting the underlying first lien either on a purchase or refinance transaction. Underwriters should not assume that the second has or will have a fixed interest rate. In a low interest rate environment, the start rate or the payment on the credit report for a refinance may be unrepresentative. If qualification is based on a payment without considering potential for change, borrowers may have affordability issues and limited refinance options.

When property values plummeted after the meltdown, some HELOCs were frozen by the lenders so borrowers could not take additional draws. If the freeze was temporary rather than permanent, lines were unfrozen when value was restored.

HELOC financing was readily available before the meltdown. The industry learned that liberal underwriting guidelines with little consideration for borrower equity resulted in rampant default.

More recently, HELOC programs are apt to be offered by financial institutions—banks, credit unions and brokerage houses—to their customer base. The institutions rely on customer relationships as well as sound origination to assure performance.

LTV, CLTV and HCLTV

Most underwriters understand the relationship between LTV (loan-to-value) and CLTV (combined loan-to-value), but fewer do when HCLTV factors in. The first step is understanding what HCLTV stands for: High or HELOC combined loan-to-value. The latter includes an acronym within an acronym, with HELOC meaning home equity line of credit.

The second step is understanding the difference between the two types of liens commonly used for subordinate financing. A closed-end second is fully disbursed at closing, with the balance declining through amortization. A HELOC has the potential for draws and pay-downs throughout the draw period until the repayment phase begins

A first lien with closed-end second has an LTV and a CLTV. LTV is based on the full amount of the first lien. CLTV represents the full amount of the first lien and the unpaid principal balance of the closed-end second.

With a first lien and a HELOC, in addition to the LTV there is also a CLTV and an HCLTV. The CLTV is based on the unpaid principal balance (i.e., drawn portion) of the HELOC, and HCLTV is based on the maximum draw amount (i.e., the dollar amount shown on the promissory note.) If there also is a closed-end second, its unpaid principal balance would be incorporated into the CLTV.

Since interest does not accrue on undisbursed funds, HELOCs are sought after in a number of circumstances such as property improvements, emergency funds, tuition expenses, and as an emergency resource or alternative to a reverse mortgage. Some borrowers owning free and clear even opt for a HELOC first.

Lease with option to buy

A lease option is a contractual agreement between landlord and tenant giving the tenant the ability but not the obligation to purchase the residence at an established price. It occurs less frequently in an appreciating real estate market.

If current property value exceeds the contractually agreed sale price, the tenant-applicant benefits. If current value is lower, the applicant can make up the difference either with a larger down payment or a lower equity position, or abandon the option to purchase.

Since there is a non-arm's-length relationship between the landlord-property seller and the tenant-buyer, funds to close and the purchase contract should be reviewed closely.

See *Rental credit applied to closing*

Land contracts

When a property seller provides financing for a buyer, the arrangement is formalized with a written agreement referred to as a land contract, contract for deed or land installment contract. The property can be improved or raw land.

This occurs under three general circumstances:

1. The property seller prefers receiving proceeds of sale in extended payments over a lump sum. With private party financing, the repayment term is frequently shorter than thirty or fifteen years. Payments can be based on a long-term amortization but with a shorter-term due date.

2. The buyer cannot obtain institutional financing because of inadequate savings, substandard credit, unstable employment or any other reason lenders deny loans. Blame may be assigned to lending institutions. The cooperative property seller is not necessarily naive. If there is a default, the property can be re-sold possibly at a higher sales price or converted to a rental.

3. The seller is amenable to providing financing, and the buyer is qualified, but there is some complication such as scarce or costly financing or a closing date too soon to obtain an institutional loan.

Refinancing out of a contract for deed, a process sometimes described as conversion, differs from a refinance paying off institutional financing because both parties to the existing contract may be amateurs. Private party financing sometimes occurs when both parties are knowledgable, the borrower is fully qualified and agreement was structured in the best interests of both. However, there also is the possibility of no recorded deed, no title search, no appraisal or other steps standard with mortgage financing—or a sham transaction with the hope that seasoning masks the defect.

The process of underwriting should be thorough, especially in regard to the property and value. Refinancing out of a land contract should be considered a transactional red flag.

Right of first refusal

The right of first refusal is recorded on title to grant a specified entity the option but not the obligation to purchase the property. Before another party can take title, the specified entity must confirm in writing that the right of first refusal is waived. The waiver process is handled by the title company.

Right of first refusal exists under a number of circumstances:

- Tenants, individuals or businesses, enter into the agreement with the property owner in order to avoid termination of tenancy after a change of ownership. This is more common with commercial properties.

- Municipalities have imposed the right of first refusal as a condition of conversion from apartments to condominiums, with right of first refusal recorded on the individual condo units. This tactic was devised at a time when apartment conversions were seen as a threat to affordable housing and gave municipalities the option to purchase units for occupancy by lower-income renters. To date in Los Angeles, the option has not been exercised.

- Builders incorporated the right of first refusal as a preventive measure when speculators aggressively purchased new tract housing. Controls on resale shortly after purchase inhibited the speculators from capitalizing on short-term appreciation, decreased competition for the builders' unsold inventory and ensured more stable communities.

CHAPTER 9
FRAUD

The next manifestation of fraud

Cousin Ron never worked in our industry but still wanted to know what the next wave of mortgage fraud would be. I responded that I don't know yet.

After mulling the topic over, I came to two conclusions. First, it is embarrassing that people outside the industry are aware of mortgage fraud. Second, if anyone could predict the next wave, it could be caught before it started. The industry has instituted controls, and widespread abuses have been curtailed. But many who perpetrate fraud historically are industry-savvy and can devise schemes that will elude scrutiny. Mortgage fraud will continue because it is so profitable.

The traditional key is having underwriters, processors and others involved in origination aware of fraud tactics and red flags. Unfortunately, as underwriting becomes more mechanical and less intuitive, there is reduced chance of pre-closing discovery. This is another repercussion of loan origination turning into process steps. Fraud checklists may be self-defeating; the person who completes the checklist may conclude after sign-off that fraud requires no further thought, not understanding that manifestations of fraud can be file-specific.

There are two better methods of identifying fraud than checklists:

1. **Pattern analysis:** Large institutions implement this on a centralized basis, and smaller shops informally by aware and communicative underwriters. A mentor observed that isolated instances of fraud are unavoidable, but organized fraud can be devastating. Any substantially increased influx of loan applications with one or more similar elements—one location, one loan officer, employees of the same company—should be investigated for commonalities and red flags. A single individual can notice patterns more easily than several. All early-payment and first-year defaults should be reviewed. Organized fraud loans are originated efficiently and likely employ limited borrower profiles, consistent application data, modified statements from a limited number of depositories, etc. Even when fraud is not identified, other patterns of risk may come to light.

2. **Underwriting with thought.**

Industry-driven fraud

"We're getting the down payment from our parents. We don't have to pay them back until we can."

"We've accepted an offer on our house. It's closing three weeks after our purchase so we can finish a few projects, but the lender is requiring a rental agreement."

Similar conversations undoubtedly occur. Industry rules encourage lack of candor because rules are enforced literally. Loans from immediate family members should be distinguished from money borrowed from payday loan companies. Profit and loss statements range from accurate to estimated to conjecture, mattering little since their contents are uniformly ignored (unless profitability is declining, which occurs almost never.) Accuracy is costly for small businesses unequipped to self-prepare.

So how are these situations better handled? We should tread the fine line between guidelines and reasonability. Short-term gift letters should be allowed when family repayment is whenever our child can afford it and also when a departure residence with equity hasn't sold yet. For departure residences under contract, obtain proof of the accepted offer and reserves covering the time until closing. A professional assessment of market rent is a good idea whenever the borrower has less than 20% equity in the departure residence and minimal reserves. P&Ls should be optional for well established and stable businesses.

Borrowers should not be pushed into pointless falsification. Excessive diligence is not good for the mortgage industry.

See *Two documents most likely to be falsified, When a P&L matters more or less,* and *Vacant houses*

Fraud for housing, fraud for profit

The traditional classifications of fraud for housing and fraud for profit should be reconsidered.

Fraud for housing is committed by the borrower and is perceived to be victimless.

The fraud for profit definition references one or multiple transactions by individuals or an organized effort engineered to defraud the lender.

But the line between fraud for housing and fraud for profit is blurred. Fraud for housing can benefit the borrower-occupant with favorable pricing. A forgiven second mortgage results in no private mortgage insurance coverage for the lender, and doctored credit saves the interest rate differential between prime and subprime. Flipping a cosmetically-renovated house with an inflated sales price profits the seller and harms both the buyer and the lender.

Alternative classifications are isolated fraud and organized fraud. Potential repercussions are more significant than the motivation of the borrower. Organized fraud can result in significant financial losses for originators. Fraud prevention should be responsive to what presents the greater threat to our industry.

A benefit of the isolated fraud classification is that investigation focuses on whether the fraud is isolated through the search for similar cases. The search requires analysis, analytics and underwriter education. Underwriters are keenly interested in fraud, so fraud education commands their attention. Discussion should include a description of the loan or loans and the manifestations of misrepresentation. The participants should be encouraged to report any similar manifestations seen previously or in the future.

The unfathomable Florida condo

The new condominium development was in Florida, and borrowers were paying over appraised value for the units. Since the sales contracts were signed two years earlier, property values had declined. This situation not surprisingly occurred early into the meltdown. Why didn't the borrowers back out of the transaction like so many others had done?

Someone noticed a missing addendum referenced in the sales contract and conditioned for it. The addendum required a minimum 20% deposit to reserve the unit and stipulated that the deposit was not refundable if the purchase was cancelled.

The non-refundable deposit provided incentive to go forward with purchase of the condominium units. The borrowers were gambling that property values would resurge and their investment would be a sound one. They were wrong, at least for the next several years.

Lessons: When a transaction doesn't make sense, something is wrong. What is withheld from submission can be critical.

Late-filed returns

Shortly after the meltdown, after noticing that a cluster of loans without final title policies came from one correspondent seller, we discovered that the title company was out of business and the loans had bogus preliminary title-work. Collusion between a former employee of the title company, a real estate salesperson and a loan officer resulted in organized fraud. All borrowers were self-employed with sole proprietorships. Each Schedule C had relatively few deductions and minimal total expenses. The most flagrant was a trucker with no vehicle write-offs. Since the businesses were fabricated, the borrowers qualified easily.

The pertinent commonality was two years' tax returns filed simultaneously close to the time the loan application process started. Transcripts supported the late-filed returns, and social security numbers belonged to individuals with earnings so low they weren't required to file.

Amended returns

The consequence of inflated earnings is increased tax liability. This can be remedied with amended returns filed later. For self-employed individuals, red flags are early filing (since a high percentage of self-employed request extensions), filing two years returns simultaneously or in quick succession, or refund amounts not correlating to the amount shown. Also check for consistency in the filing of the previous year's returns and the net/gross ratio. After loan approval or closing, if the inflated returns were submitted with the loan package to facilitate qualification, transcripts will reveal whether amended returns were refiled.

Flip transactions

A flip occurs when value rapidly appreciates in the abbreviated time between a property's last and current sale. Low acquisition cost is often rationalized by prevalence of foreclosed or abandoned properties. Inflated value is rationalized by the appraiser accepting below-market acquisition and belief that the sales price reflects market pricing and/or a total remodel. Fraud occurs with the representation of complete rehabilitation rather than cosmetic remodeling.

The flip strategy involves generating maximum profit with minimum expense in the shortest period of time. Some flippers are employed in the construction industry or team up with home improvement specialists. All are opportunistic. Since the real estate market is cyclical, they are most active in depressed markets, either nationally or locally.

Flipped properties have visual appeal but possibly deteriorated or outdated heating and plumbing systems, inadequate electricity and/or structural deficiencies. The risk to the lender is that even experienced appraisers may not be able to distinguish between real and superficial improvements, and that naive purchasers assume that a visually appealing property is in equally good condition underneath.

Red flags include the following:

Speed of renovation: Because renovation must be complete before the first open house, relevant time is between the date of acquisition and the date of listing.

Rapid appreciation: This can be calculated by determining the amount of appreciation since purchase and the percentage of a year the property has been owned. Resale 91 days after acquisition with $20,000 in costs and a price increase from $100,000 to $150,000 yields a $30,000 profit on a $120,000 investment, with a 25% return over the three months of ownership. Although $30,000 seems like a reasonable profit, the annualized return of 100% on the flipper's investment probably represents an undeserved reward.

LLC ownership: Flipped properties are often vested as limited liability corporations (LLCs) to shield flippers from post-closing litigation. The LLC name often incorporates the property's street address.

Unstable neighborhoods: Well located houses in decent condition seldom sell for below-market prices. Rapid appreciation is most easily supported when multiple properties in close proximity to the subject are also flip transactions. The sales history of the comparable sales indicates whether the area is stable or a magnet for flippers. When well located houses need updating or suffer from neglect, flippers can profit by bringing those properties up to the standard of the neighborhood. In all cases, a property inspection is essential to ensure that the basic household systems were not neglected.

Out-of-area purchasers: Large-scale flippers can afford to buy radio and TV time (sometimes informercial length) to attract buyers. When depository interest rates are low, real estate presents a tempting investment. Buyers are assured of a remodeled property, a pool of qualified tenants and competent local property management (providing continued income to the LLC property seller under a different company name.) Buyers unfamiliar with the area are blind to neighborhood quality and market pricing. If they do not visit the property, listing and appraisal photos may comprise their only viewing. If they are unfamiliar with appraisals, they may not notice that the $50,000 bargain was recently acquired for $10,000. A 30% down payment on the $50,000 sales price is only $15,000. If positive cash flow doesn't pan out, or costly repairs are necessary, default may be the easy answer.

As-is purchase contract or **no independent third party inspection:** Naive buyers may not differentiate between an appraiser and a property inspector. An inspection probes adequacy of the electrical, plumbing, heating/air conditioning systems, looks for structural deficiencies and assesses health and safety issues with more depth than the appraisal. The inspector climbs a ladder to determine the longevity of the roof and also checks the crawl space. If the property seller will not allow a physical inspection of the property or insists on a certain inspection company, there likely is something to hide.

Distress sale verbiage and generic upgrades: The easiest way to justify rapid appreciation is to portray the prior sale as below-market caused by distress and cured by a full remodel. Some appraisers need little convincing. Be skeptical of non-specific improvements described as a fully renovated kitchen, completely remodeled bathroom, new floor coverings and new fixtures. The interior photos may provide clues to quality. If granite countertops appear thin or are tile instead of slab, the countertops are low-grade. Engineered hardwood is cheaper and less durable than actual hardwood. "Floor coverings" are likely to be laminate or vinyl off a roll. Bathroom appliances should not look like those in a home improvement chainstore sale ad. "Newer" improvements were probably made by the owner previous to the flipper.

A flip transaction and questionable occupancy are an especially risky combination.

Not all flip transactions are purchases. A refinance transaction of a recently acquired property is suspect when financing is provided by a private party or LLC, with a short-term due date or a non-competitive interest rate. If the borrower received 100% financing at purchase, there is no cash equity in the property. Check the acquisition date and the three years sales history in the appraisal. The two spurts of rapid appreciation are possible—the first from the flipper's acquisition until the property's sale, and the second from the new owner's acquisition until the appraisal date. Rapid appreciation is the major manifestation of a flip.

Responsible flippers gravitate to non-marginal properties, and their renovations go beyond the superficial. They do not opt for the least costly upgrades or market to naive buyers. If they discover subsurface mold in the bathroom or deteriorated floorboards in the living room, the contingency fund is tapped for repairs. Opportunistic flippers deliberately don't go beneath the surface.

The double flip

An older home was listed for sale. It most recently had been used as a rental, but the owner thought the time was right to sell. To increase market appeal, new hardwood flooring and two skylights had been installed in the living room. The kitchen and bathrooms remained *dated. The floor plan was awkward because of several additions but the backyard was abundantly landscaped and idyllic. Despite the house's limitations, the $899,000 listing price turned into a $945,000 sales price.*

A few months later the house re-sold for $1,270,000. According to the listing "almost everything had been updated and remodeled."

Six months after resale, workmen started tearing up the small front yard and were still digging two weeks later. Replacement plumbing plus terracing the front yard cost $70,000. The owners said their next project was replacing the 55 year old detached garage. Evidently the "almost everything updated and remodeled" was selective.

Lessons:

1. *Flip transactions occur in all kinds of neighborhoods.*

2. *Appraisers must disclose sales history but cannot be expected to have the same skills as property inspectors.*

3. *Purchase contracts are often subject to loan approval, but appraisal contingencies are less common. Chances are appraisal contingencies are principally used for value support; few buyers know to look for the sales history.*

4. *The difference in higher priced neighborhoods is that new owners may be better equipped financially to cope with unexpected repairs.*

Two documents most likely to be falsified

Early in my career, I was told that there are two items of documentation most likely to be falsified.

Not all **gift letters** tell the truth. Some families would like to gift generously but can't afford to. Because of the familial relationship, a contractual repayment schedule and post-closing lien recordation are unlikely. More probable is an informal arrangement that the gift is repaid when the recipient is able or the property is sold, or will be deducted from a future inheritance. Families are apt to accept extenuating circumstances with tolerance and continued affection. On a worst-case basis, if litigation results (which I have never witnessed) the borrower can use a copy of the gift letter as evidence. Gift letters from non-immediate relatives are suspect. See *Gifted funds.*

Falsified **rental agreements**, usually for the departure residence, may be a function of timing. Tenants willing to delay move-in for sixty or ninety days in advance are scarce. This doesn't mean there won't be a tenant, just not the person who signed the rental agreement. Prime risk considerations are whether the property will attract a tenant and the reasonability of monthly rental income. Tenancy may be a non-issue because the departure residence is being sold. Some guidelines dictate that if its closing isn't prior to or concurrent, debt service must be included in qualifying ratios. This approach is overly conservative if scheduled closing is imminent and probable, with ample reserves, or if quick conversion to a rental is feasible. It is not overly conservative when there is no or minimal equity in the departure residence, in which case proof of the rental check's deposit is prudent.

Phony pay-stubs

The first generation of fake pay-stubs were homemade and crude; one template was easily identifiable because we never saw it used by actual businesses. But when doctored documentation was replaced by stated income, many of us thought phony pay-stubs were extinct. Wrong, now they're available online.

Searching the most accepted way of spelling "pay-stub" (there isn't one), I stumbled on a related search, fake pay stubs, There are multiple sources online: "Inexpensive & authentic fake pay stubs" "Create a pay stub now! Fast & easy" "All calculations done for you" "Price only $4.99 per pay stub." Although the listings tout use for apartment-seekers and car-purchasers, fake pay-stubs could just as easily be submitted as loan documentation. They're not only available, they don't cost much.

The industry has embraced tax transcripts as an effective means of ensuring that verified income is legitimate. The sad fact is that originators are aware of which lenders are more vigilant on validating tax returns. Some send out 4506s on everything. Others order selectively, for example, only with self-employed borrowers, higher LTVs, when an underwriter is skeptical or with new originators. Other smart choices includes cash-out transactions, a random component, and loans from any originator who casually asks about 4506 sampling. Tax transcripts don't work when they're not ordered.

For borrowers who are newly-employed (including second jobs) or with recent sizable bumps in compensation, checking net pay proceeds against depository statements works as well.

Occupancy fraud

A savvy quality control manager said that occupancy fraud is the most difficult fraud to identify. Other fraud can be substantiated prior to closing, but misrepresented intent is difficult to prove. Whichever the case, occupancy on the loan application should not always be accepted at face value.

Occupancy fraud comes in two categories: possible and nearly certain. An example of nearly certain came from a couple who asserted that they and their three children would be moving from a spacious suburban house to a small two-bedroom house in marginal condition. Per the short and un-detailed letter of explanation, the small home was convenient to the children's school and their present residence would be rented out. The letter was unconvincing and the loan request was denied.

Other classifications for occupancy fraud are conscious and unconscious. Money is a motivator. Non-owner pricing is more expensive, and the down payment requirement is higher as well. To maximize profits straw buyers portray occupants, a residence remains vacant until torn down or the investor moves in short-term. There may be serial purchase transactions, each owner-occupied until the next property is purchased. This pattern will be evident in the credit report. The industry is alert to first-time buyers but less to borrowers with multiple recent mortgages held for months, not years. See *Tear-downs*

Examples of unconscious occupancy fraud are purchase of a home that will convert to a primary residence after retirement or for close family to live in. If the future primary residence is used as a second home in the interim, this is not fraud. If retirement is imminent but not within the occupancy provision in the mortgage, this is technically unacceptable.

Only the naive believe that occupancy fraud doesn't occur on refinance transactions. When cash proceeds are sufficient for a down payment, the improved home may be elsewhere. On a rate and term transaction, motivation may be reduced PITI after rental at the most favorable pricing before the tenant moves in. Be wary when a current residence is inadequate for the household size or when loan term increases from fifteen to thirty years. The latter can reflect financial hardship, which differs from occupancy fraud but also elevates risk.

Second home occupancy can evidence misrepresentation in various forms. Examples are intended use as a primary residence following buy and bail, an investment property, or housing for someone with a closer relationship than a tenant. A coworker commented that everyone's first investment property is a second home. Red flags are questionable affordability or a down payment difficult to source. Funds may be gifted from the actual occupant.

When occupancy seems possible but not probable, a good approach is requiring a letter discussing motivation and attesting to occupancy as a primary residence (or second home.) On refinances, use of proceeds should be detailed and credible. If the letter fulfills the criteria, loan approval is warranted. If owner-occupancy remains uncertain and the decision is made to go forward on the loan, a post-closing occupancy inspection can be ordered. This protects the lender and paves the path for repurchase or repricing if the motivation letter was untruthful. Regardless of the results, verifying questionable occupancy via inspection demonstrates originator integrity.

An obscure but thought-provoking occupancy red flag is DTI being too low. People typically want the best house they can afford. They may purchase modestly and upgrade, or have so much financial strength there is no need to spend to capacity. But as demonstrated with the alleged move-down earlier in this topic, people buying considerably below their means may have hidden motivation.

The first step in prevention is discouraging originators and real estate agents from facilitating occupancy misrepresentation. A non-industry friend told me she was closing on a smaller house in her neighborhood as her "long-term residence." I asked whether she had a date in mind, thinking pricing would improve if the move occurred soon. It turned out that during the application conversations, neither of the two prospective direct lenders asked about occupancy. Potential rental income and pricing adds were never discussed. It may be that both loan reps assumed non-owner occupancy without bringing the topic up. However, this seems improbable. So if fraud is identified, whose fault is it?

The coach's second home

The borrower was a college football coach and was purchasing a second home about 25 miles from his residence. Distance was not a deal killer; I had no problem with second homes even closer under the right circumstances. See The tandem tandem bedrooms

But in this case, other circumstances weren't right. The house was older and located in a beach community, but at the opposite end from the ocean. It had four bedrooms and was of average quality with no upgrades. It seemed very much like an investment property. The charming houses in the beach town were close to the ocean. The borrower was applying for the loan without his spouse.

We counter-offered to non-owner. The probability that the coach would be renting out the property to team members was higher than use as a second home. The loan cancelled.

Lesson: Reading the appraisal made the underwriter dubious of second home occupancy. No motivation letter could have helped.

Short sale risk

A short sale takes place when a lender consents to accept no or partial repayment of a lien because of insufficient sale proceeds. Cause(s) are decreased property value from market movement or poor maintenance, extraction of equity during ownership or purchase with no or minimal down payment.

When repayment is allowed to be less than the full amount due, misrepresentation is a possibility particularly when property owners are negotiating with loan servicing. Common tactics are understated property value, embellishment of hardship circumstances and collusion through a non-arm's-length sale. Perpetrators benefit with forgiven debt while the lender absorbs the loss.

The short sale should be reflected in the sales contract because lender permission is required for reduced payoff. On a purchase transaction following a short sale, key points for the originator are as follows:

- The purchase agreement must be complete, including all referenced addenda. Missing pages can reveal side deals providing increased payoff to the seller, personal property included at inflated prices or undisclosed payoff of junior lien holders with funds diverted from the first lienholder.

- Payoffs must be consistent with the amounts specified in the short sale agreement.

- Non-arm's-length relationships should be verified as fully disclosed to the lender(s) and the appraiser.

- On a sale or refinance transaction occurring shortly after a short sale, if value from the previous transaction is shown to be artificially low, bring this to the attention of the previous lender. Although they cannot undo the short sale transaction, they can report it as a fraudulent transaction and alert the licensing authorities.

See *Non-arm's-length transactions,* third paragraph

Manipulated credit

Prospective borrowers adjust their behavior in anticipation of applying for a mortgage. Dinners out are less frequent, shopping sprees are curtailed and cash gifts to pay off an auto loan are requested in lieu of birthday presents. This is not fraud. It is more akin to dressing up for a job interview. Stepped-up financial management can be preparation for responsible home ownership.

Other credit practices fall into the realm of fraud:

Authorized user accounts with a parent, spouse or partner are normal. When there is no relationship between the borrower and the account holder except for a short-term transfer of funds, their sole purpose is to artificially inflate credit scores.

See *Shallow Credit, Pre- and Post-Meltdown*

An account in **disputed status** is not irregular when it is isolated and there is a plausible explanation for the dispute. Questionable integrity is more likely when multiple accounts are disputed simultaneously. Since disputing an account removes that account from scoring consideration, the dispute can be groundless and initiated solely to elevate the score.

Payoff of debt on a major scale is misrepresentation if borrowed funds are not disclosed as a liability. This may not be evident if the source of the borrowed funds does not report, which may be the case with a payday- or private-party loan. If DTI is high and there are older mortgage inquiries not quite old enough to drop off the credit report, it may be worthwhile to directly ask the borrower whether debt was recently consolidated and if so from what source.

Industry collaboration occurs when financial institutions mask credit histories. A creditor may trade off a sanitized credit history in exchange for a borrower paying down arrearages. Late payments may be eliminated or a default labeled as a settled account or a P&L loss.

Credit repair or **credit cleansing** is the most insidious manifestation of manipulated credit. A television commercial from a company pitching credit repair services cites the ability to remove items that are inaccurate and unfair. Inaccurate is justified; unfair is subjective. Cleansing is accomplished by requesting creditors to prove untimely payment or negotiating to remove derogatory data. Flawed credit can be eradicated if the creditor does not respond within the statutory time limit, or if debt payoff is negotiated for an improved account history, thus impairing a lender's ability to distinguish responsible from irresponsible credit usage.

When an originator mentioned she had previously co-owned a credit repair company, I asked her to confirm my understanding of how such companies operated. She did, adding that the business involved a lot of mail and also that derogatory credit was not always their fault.

The fully fabricated loan

This loan originated when stated income was still acceptable and was delivered to the correspondent channel after it was closed. The story of the loan was plausible. The editor-in-chief of a magazine was purchasing a high-end property. He had spotless credit and a hefty down payment. After the early payment default, the full underwriting package including title-work was determined to be bogus. There was no transfer of ownership, and the alleged borrower declared himself the victim of identity theft.

This fraud was immensely profitable. The full loan amount went to the conspirators behind the ghost transaction.

My responsibility was determining what the underwriter missed and minimizing the possibility of recurrence. The task was complicated since the underwriter was one of my favorites. He had been underwriting only a few years, but his talent was already apparent. I scrutinized the fabricated documentation. The only discernible red flag was the name of the magazine. It wasn't familiar, and online research revealed that the magazine was a failed start-up.

I discussed the defaulted loan with the underwriter. He expressed his regret. The conversation was non-accusatory and stressed his lack of culpability. A senior fraud executive called it an air loan and added it was the first he had ever seen.

Lessons: An incident may not be a trend, and not every defaulted loan is the underwriter's fault.

Very scary loans

Years ago before transcripts were used to validate income, a cluster of brokered loans with disturbing similarities was received within several weeks. All the borrowers had common ethnicity, they all lived in lavish high-end homes and, most notably, income was generated from improbably high-paying salaried positions, e.g., office manager for a law firm or administrator for a medical practice earning $400,000 annually. The loans were denied.

I understood the rationale for not pursuing the issue. Since we didn't purchase the loans, we had no potential liability. But my mind kept recalling the similarities, so from home I contacted the FBI. After sharing some of the details, the agent thanked me. There was no follow-up so either there were no findings or the FBI doesn't send thank you notes.

The aforementioned incident came to mind after I reviewed a loan with tax returns that could only be described as irregular. I can't recall ever seeing an attorney's Schedule C deducting substantial (or any) cost of goods, a management company bearing the borrower's initials referenced on partnership returns but not on personal tax returns, plus other original methods of reporting. In my role as consultant, I suggested obtaining transcripts and made management aware of my discomfort with the returns.

When loans are scary, denial isn't enough. For the attorney's loan, the first step is obtaining transcripts and, unless all concerns are addressed satisfactorily, second step is sharing findings with the IRS.

The incomprehensible tax returns

The loan package may have been the thickest I'd ever seen even after doing super-jumbo loans for well over a decade. I worked my way through the pile and assembled a list of additional documentation needed.

To say the borrower's financial holdings were complex is an understatement. Partnership and corporate returns indicated ownership by individuals, corporations and partnerships owned by similarly-named partnerships and corporations. Each shipment of conditions led to another condition list. I never felt I understood the borrower's holdings.

The loan cancelled before the package was ready for investor review, but this is not the end of the story. A year or two later, the applicant was in the headlines for conspiracy and tax fraud.

Lesson: To quote Tim Griffin, "If I don't understand a loan, I don't want to buy it." Thorough review likely caused cancellation. If this loan was submitted when stated income loans were easily available, it would have been approved easily with ownership confirmed through a CPA letter.

Other fraud-related topics

Fraud-related topics in other chapters include *Tax transcripts, The fraud team* and *Fraud reporting and after.*

CHAPTER 10

OTHER RISK CONSIDERATIONS

Underwriting with thought

When I entered the industry, every loan was manually underwritten. Documentation differed too. Paper files contained two applications, the original handwritten and the final typed and signed. VOEs and VODs verified income and assets. Pay-stubs, W-2s and depository statements were favored later on because the GSEs found them more reliable. Tax returns weren't validated. Credit reports were considerably shorter and lacked credit scores. Appraisals were handwritten by staff appraisers and reviews were done by the corporate chief appraiser. Appraisals were about half as thick, and so were most loan files.

Maximum ratios in the earlier years were 25%/33%. When 33%/38% became the norm, traditionalists were uncomfortable. Credit assessment consisted of adding up long-term obligations, requesting written explanations for untimely payments and legal items, and deciding whether explanations (if any) made sense and credit was acceptable.

There were no worksheets for tax returns, rental cash flow, business funds or anything else. My system involved writing down numbers on a college-ruled pad and crossing out the ones I wasn't using. There were no verbal VOEs, balance sheets, use of business account letters and other documentation now considered essential.

Underwriting guidelines fit into a three-ring notebook and changed infrequently. Second liens were seller-carried. An adjustable program was rolled out, but few borrowers were interested.

The act of underwriting involved reading through the loan file, manually calculating ratios and required funds, and making notes on strengths, weaknesses and additional documentation necessary. Loan files were assembled by processors and approved or denied by underwriting managers. Large loans required multiple signatures. Borderline loans were discussed with the manager and sometimes escalated to the manager's manager. Emphasis was on making a prudent decision on the borrower and the property.

Subprime underwriting with thought

The meltdown caused subprime underwriting to be stigmatized. Classic subprime loans served borrowers with substandard credit and owners of cash businesses. Although some loans were fully documented, others verified income with bank statements rather than tax returns. The origination process was similar in most respects to prime, but equity was deeper and pricing was higher.

Classic subprime underwriting differed from prime in several respects— credit quality, the tolerance for higher DTIs and property assessment. Grading classifications ranged from A++ (almost prime eligible) to D (dreadful). Subprime grading actually corresponds with academic assessments, except no one receives an F grade. Subprime underwriters focused on mortgage history, outstanding collections, legal items and credit score. Mortgage history was highly weighted, and although score was a factor, it could be offset by other credit attributes.

Subprime underwriters recognized the importance of the appraisal. They had to be diligent about property condition and deferred maintenance even when it was cosmetic. They did not assume appraised value was reliable. Automated valuations provided due diligence especially on higher LTVs and lower credit grades. The highest risk loans required field reviews.

Subprime underwriting without thought

In the quest for expanding homeownership, relaxed guidelines granted to prime borrowers were extended to subprime borrowers.

Stated programs waived various combinations of income, assets and employment documentation. Minimal or no equity was justified by the belief that property values would increase indefinitely.

Before enhanced subprime, equity supported by a sound appraisal was usually sufficient to make the lender whole in the case of default and yield at least some proceeds to the borrower. Monetary losses increased when equity became optional.

Parallel with prime underwriting, subprime program standards started out prudent but gradually deteriorated. To quote a former subprime manager "the box kept widening." She described the program that allowed 100% financing (an 80% first lien and a 20% second lien) with stated income for borrowers (including wage earners with easily verifiable earnings) as "the worst." Classic subprime underwriting did not cause the meltdown.

Inclusionary lending

Benefits of homeownership include greater neighborhood stability, deductible mortgage interest and probable appreciating property value long-term. People in diverse income brackets deserve their chance at the American dream, and many are qualified.

Lending to low- and moderate-earners can be challenging. Not all of the following factors apply to applicants on inclusionary programs, but some may:

Non-traditional credit: Limited income sometimes results in limited established credit. Low earners have low discretionary spending. Non-traditional credit may be the only option. Rental performance is a key indicator of mortgage performance, but ratings are not always reliable. Providing a chronically delinquent tenant with a positive rental rating is easier than the eviction process, which is why cancelled checks or money order receipts are the reliable choice when the landlord is an individual rather than a property management company. Applicants have strong motivation to keep current on utility bills, especially when weather is intemperate. Not all applicants have checking accounts or debit cards. Verification of vehicle insurance is helpful even if there isn't a monthly payment plan; having coverage supports responsible conduct.

Income: Employment may consist of several positions, either simultaneously or successively. All may be entry level because of limited education, limited job skills or personal complications. The prime consideration should be consistent and sustainable income. Income from public assistance is acceptable as long as it is ongoing, which generally is not the case with temporary disability or unemployment benefits unless employment is seasonal. Inclusive housing programs may allow income sources disallowed on standard programs, such as roommate income.

Savings: Lower earners living paycheck to paycheck are more defendable than higher earners. However, if there is payment shock accompanied by high debt ratios and no history of savings, concern with ability to repay may be legitimate. Changed circumstances can be an acceptable justification with a credible explanation. Sweat equity (acceptable on a limited basis) can provide a suitable alternative to cash equity, and community secondary financing (in some instances forgivable) protects the institutional lender.

Property: The property will be the best house the borrowers can afford. Not enough bedrooms should be considered a very light red flag, if at all.

Compensating factors: Standard expectations may not apply to inclusionary lending. A different yardstick is required. A steadily increasing account balance demonstrates the ability to save. Generating income from one or more or a series of short-term second jobs evidences work ethic. Trade-lines with minimal outstanding balances show responsible use of credit.

Usual and unusual

The majority of loans present minimal challenge. The average transaction has an uncomplicated borrower who is somewhat dull, except to unseasoned underwriters and those capable of finding something interesting in virtually every file.

An approvable loan fitting the John and Mary Buy a House, Johnny Paystub and mainstream property profiles can be classified as **Usual and Good**.

Other classifications are as follows:

Usual and bad: Any cluster of new originations with statistically improbable similar attributes and otherwise undistinguished borrowers is potentially fraudulent. As an example, several unmarried, male borrowers living in Chicago with transportation-related sole proprietorships (truck and limo drivers) were buying second homes in Florida. All were investigated as a group and found to have contrived tax returns and misrepresented funds to close.

Usual, formerly unusual: What is normal for previous generations may not remain normal. Unless there is evidence that changes in behavior result in poor loan performance, expectations of originators should adjust. Pricing adds for non-conforming borrowers with responsible credit usage but a limited number of open trade-lines should be abandoned. The employment histories of Millennials may show longer tenure in entry-level jobs because of economic forces. If their current position is secure, the relatively short term of more responsible employment can be attributed to limited opportunities when they entered the workforce.

Unusual, learning opportunity: When underwriters encounter something unfamiliar, they should not be embarrassed asking someone more experienced for help. An underwriter could work for years without seeing royalty income, a triple net lease or Southern California house with a dugout basement.

Unusual and potentially risky: When something in a loan file appears strange or does not make sense, additional analysis is required and, if not resolved, follow-up and investigation. Concerns may be resolved with online or other research, or written clarification from the borrower. If not, the loan should be suspended or denied.

Compensating factors

When risk is high—despite the presence of an AUS approval—compensating factors may justify approval. They must be meaningful as in the following examples:

- High debt ratios may be offset if qualifying income was conservatively derived, when income is steadily increasing, when additional income is ineligible for qualification or when there are ample reserves.

- Spotty credit may be offset if the lapses occurred in a limited timeframe or under circumstances that no longer exist, or when lapses are verified to be in error or reflect sloppiness on non-critical accounts.

- Limited savings may be offset with a strong equity position, significant cash investment in down payment or property improvements, long-term ownership assuming no pattern of equity erosion, or proven ability to handle a similar debt assuming stable income.

Compensating factors contribute less when LTV is high. The presence of strong reserves is useless when the borrower has little motivation to preserve property ownership.

ThIs book includes no extended list of potential compensating factors as found in some underwriting manuals. This is deliberate. The lists are too often used to select factors that are inapplicable. Some rules-driven underwriters believe that compensating factors have to be on the list to be valid. The best compensating factors are inspired by the loan file.

Character

Freddie Mac preached the Four Cs—Collateral, Credit, Capacity and Character—before the final C became extinct. With technological advances like credit scores and property valuations, consideration of character is viewed as outdated, judgmental and potentially discriminatory.

Loans can be closed without borrower interaction. The case can be made that character is measurable through the credit score and other credit usage (such as delinquent support payments), but there are exceptions. The score is less valid when the borrower has unseasoned or shallow credit. It takes less effort for borrowers not yet living independently to have high credit scores when parents cover living expenses. Delinquent support payments are more justifiable when income involuntarily plummets.

As lending relationships depersonalized, buy and bail transactions and strategic defaults emerged. Borrowers shamelessly diverted funds for down payment on their next home instead of curing the delinquency on their present home. Perhaps "you gave me a bad loan" would have been less prevalent if lender and borrower knew each other.

Stability and integrity can be assessed on documentation other than the credit report. Employment history, savings pattern and choice of property can give insight into borrower strength. I have been known to glance at charitable contributions and dissect reasonability in letters of explanation. Approvals and denials should be supported by facts, but when the decision is difficult, consider character.

Financial management

Over-dependence on credit score can lead to poor decisioning. Borrowers can manipulate scores by paying down accounts, postponing spending, being added as an authorized user, lobbying creditors to increase credit limits, begging creditors to eliminate or soften derogatory histories, and credit cleansing. Financial management differs from credit management and takes into account factors not found on the credit report. The underwriter should evaluate financial management as well as credit management.

In addition to lower credit scores, following are signs of poor financial management:

1. Low or negative net worth not caused by a relevant life event. (Even after this field is deleted from the application it can be easily calculated.) See *Net worth, negative or otherwise*

2. Low equity in a residence or other real estate holdings compared to length of ownership. For example, 60% equity in a residence owned for thirty years, unless substantially renovated, represents respectable equity but less impressive financial management.

3. A pattern of refinances extracting equity. Cash-out to finance major capital improvements or for a medical emergency are valid reasons to refinance, but typically are not recurring events. Serial refinances dated a decade ago or longer may reflect improved financial management skills or, if the subject transaction is a cash-out refinance, the inability to refinance until property values resurged.

4. Inadequate liquidity or retirement savings. Those with assured pensions may be less at risk, but it is conceivable that some government entities (including public utilities) over-promised on pension commitments.

Those with significant equity in real estate investments can, if necessary, generate liquidity by selling a holding or taking out an equity loan.

5. Low month-end checking account balances unless money is being diverted to savings, or savings have been accumulated otherwise. Living paycheck to paycheck doesn't work well for a homeowner.

6. NSF (non-sufficient funds) or overdraft charges

7. Generous co-signing for loved ones combined with inadequate savings or high debt ratios

8. Student loan obligations disproportionate to earnings level or remaining after years of employment. This includes co-signed obligations unless co-borrower has sufficient means to repay without assistance.

9. High debt ratios combined with excessive outstanding consumer debt proportionate to annual income, and/or a wide gap between the housing ratio and the combined debt ratio.

    See *Trended credit*

10. Credit history inappropriate for age. A person who came to financial maturity after the meltdown and has numerous open and balanced accounts is atypical, as is an older person with limited trade-lines.

Before concluding poor financial management because of inadequate savings, make sure that the application reflects all accounts and investments including estimated net worth of business if the business is salable. Review of the appraisal for recent additions, clarification of use of proceeds on previous cash-out transactions and review of tax returns for undisclosed assets may be helpful in decision-making. Such measures may not be necessary on all transactions, but should be considered if there is marginal qualification or a borrower with questionable credit management.

Approaches to quantifying risk

The following concepts quantifying risk have come to prominence and faded away. They are interesting either historically or for potential reconsideration and resurrection.

- **Disposable** or **residual income** refers to qualifying income less housing expense and payments on long-term consumer debt. This was a standard consideration in subprime underwriting and continues to be used in government lending. Since it considers the number of people in a household, it has greater impact on larger families. Disposable income has more validity for borrowers with limited earnings. Higher earners have the ability to cut back on discretionary spending.

- **Layered risk** refers to the overall assessment of risk on an individual loan. If all aspects are positive, its layered risk is low. When there are insufficient strengths to offset weaknesses, layered risk is high. When unacceptable layered risk is identified, specific deficiencies should be spelled out. Otherwise, loan officers and borrowers may not understand why denial is justified.

- At one time underwriters examined **both components** of the **combined debt ratio**—housing expenses and other monthly expenses. As AUS decisioning became prevalent, scrutiny of the housing ratio decreased. This simplified approach merits reconsideration. A borrower's dependence on consumer debt is a valid underwriting consideration, especially when debt is consolidated through a cash-out refinance or is being paid off to facilitate qualification.

- Over the last few decades, the industry has become dependent on **credit scoring** and **AUS decisioning** in making the risk decision. Credit scoring was thought to be predictive until the strategic defaults began. Considering continuing defaults, it is clear that an approval does not guarantee performance. Every loan should be manually underwritten to some extent, taking into account those factors the AUS is incapable of quantifying. See *What the AUS doesn't see*

- **Pride of ownership** is a phrase no longer used by appraisers to describe well-maintained neighborhoods. It was abolished from usage after good pride of ownership too often correlated to non-minority areas. The phrase is valid when not used prejudicially as code. If used to describe a residence, it effectively communicates respect for a property by its owner.

Payment shock

Payment shock is the percentage increase between the current and post-closing housing expenses. With payment shock of 100%, housing expense doubles. The computation has greater applicability for borrowers with high debt ratios, those with spotty credit, first-time home buyers or those on a fixed income. With a history of minimal savings, a borrower may find it difficult to handle a large increase in housing expense. But lifestyle usually changes after purchase of a home. Few houses are lost for a great vacation. Fewer meals out or frivolous purchases are typical but reduced spending may not be sufficient for unanticipated expenses. A former colleague was stunned that his newly constructed house lacked light bulbs.

Payment shock was originally a test on subprime loans. When it was proven to be a valid indicator of loan performance, use expanded. Rationale was stronger when loan files lacked income verification, but has less relevance since DTI gives an accurate assessment of affordability.

Denials justified by high payment shock when DTI is well below maximum can result in turning down low-risk loans. It is less valid for borrowers living under rent control (who should also more easily accumulate a down payment while paying below-market rent) and is incalculable for those living with family. Concern is more justifiable when qualification requires consolidation of debt, or for borrowers with lower credit scores, fluctuating income or scant savings.

Risk factors

Risk factors are one current approach employed in decisioning. Any factor associated with elevated risk is suspect. First time home buyers, cash-out refinances, self-employment, any property type other than a detached single family residence are a sample of what the industry sees as less desirable. However, most individual risk factors—with exceptions such as substandard credit and incurable property deficiencies—should not be taken as deal-breakers. Several risk factors on a loan may be acceptable if the loan on the whole has acceptable risk.

Although self-employed borrowers have a higher incidence of default than salaried borrowers, the longevity of the business and income trend distinguish a viable business from one in jeopardy. An individual self-employed for an extended period with stable income has lower risk than a new hire, or someone employed in a fading industry or at a company aggressively replacing employees with technology.

Consider a self-employed first-time homebuyer purchasing a duplex. Wary underwriters would focus on three of the four types of elevated risk referenced above. Insightful underwriters would note that the borrower's accountancy practice opened six years ago, and rental income on the second unit wasn't needed to qualify. They would also see a 20% down payment, half gifted, a high credit score and a credit history showing paid-off student loans and dated construction job references. Putting the pieces together from date of birth and years of education, they can construe that the borrower worked in construction during college, has skills from current and previous employment aiding in duplex ownership, good affordability and proven money management skills.

An underwriter's role is not to be afraid of risk, but to determine whether risk is balanced by strengths.

Assessing risk in down markets

Fluctuations should be expected in the mortgage industry. Not too long after complaints about endless overtime, volume slows to the point that files are over-processed and overly-scrutinized to fill up the workday. Often when the mortgage industry shifts into low gear, the national economy likely has slowed down as well. So how should risk assessment adjust during an economic downturn?

Recognize that an extended downturn can become a recession. Also recognize that some businesses are more vulnerable than others. Identifying those at higher risk involves two variables—technology and essentiality.

Technology inspires new products and make others obsolete. Cell phones killed the market for pagers and have reduced use of land lines. As technology creates increased efficiencies, staffing numbers may decrease. Once-flourishing companies decline. Longevity for even non-technical businesses is dependent on whether their technology remains current.

Less affected are basic services, some businesses more than others. People can't stop eating or do without essential medical services. Although people may dine out less or opt for less expensive restaurants when they do go out, grocery stores benefit from the increased business. Demand for cosmetic surgery no doubt declines more than non-elective surgery.

When a product or service is discretionary, an economic downturn has a larger impact. Sales of luxury goods slow in down markets when flaunting wealth is less socially acceptable. Personal care appointments are scheduled less frequently, beauty-related expenditures are replaced with drugstore products, and group classes or an exercise video replaces a personal trainer.

People employed in declining industries with transferable job skills have more re-employment options than those with specialized job skills.

Trending matters more in tough times than in good times. While well-qualified borrowers should never be declined, marginal borrowers merit less flexibility.

Occupancy

To lenders, occupancy consists of three buckets: primary residence, second home and investment property. If a loan does not easily fit into the first or second bucket, the default response is the third.

Borrowers may think differently. They consider the home they will move into after retirement as their future primary residence. They believe buying a house for a relative is helping a loved one, not making an investment.

Failure to comply with the industry approach to the three buckets can be motivated by naivety as well as deception. With that disconnect and no fourth bucket labeled "other," analysis is necessary. Consider borrower motivation, probable use of the property and credibility based full file review. A motivation letter may establish a comfort level or confirm misrepresentation. A disconnect caused by naivety could be clarified by explanation. If deception is probable, either deny the loan or counter-offer what is appropriate.

Circumstances not fitting the standard box can occasionally justify classification other than investment property. In such cases, solid substantiation is required.

See *Borrowers can be confused about occupancy* and *Occupancy fraud*

Two primary residences

The borrower was purchasing a single family residence close to his employment. He was renting in the area at the time. What complicated the situation was that the borrower was married, and his wife owner-occupied a home in an adjacent state near her employment. The issue was whether the subject property had to be classified as a second home. I decided not. The property the husband was purchasing was inarguably his primary residence. The residence his wife owned served as his second

215

home when he visited her, and in turn the subject property would serve as her second home when she visited him.

There was no financing on the spouse's residence. If both residences were encumbered, the occupancy issue would be more murky—although my decision would not have changed. This loan was easily approvable.

Lesson: Calling this an owner-occupied transaction makes sense. Make-sense decisioning fell out of favor after the meltdown because too many bad decisions employed this justification, but the cause of meltdown was brain-dead programs, not deficient underwriting.

The commuting owner-occupant

The borrower purchasing a single family residence in Southern California owned another residence being sold so his two sons could live in a better school district. What complicated the situation was that the borrower was employed on another continent and his wife was not on the previous or the current loan. Was the subject property his second home? I decided not. The borrower didn't own any real estate. The apartment he occupied while working was not his primary residence; it was where he slept while doing his job.

The word "domicile" is used more frequently by lawyers than underwriters but is relevant to this situation. Legislators may sleep more nights in their Capital residence than their home district residence, but their domicile is not Washington D.C. After the legislators' terms end and after the borrower's job ends, all will probably move back to what they consider their primary home, which we should consider their primary home as well.

Lesson: Home is where your heart is, or, in this case, the borrower's wife and children.

Equity

A senior risk manager asserted that low loan-to-value as a compensating factor is hard money lending. Here's why his statement was fallacious:

Stability: Accumulated equity combined with long-term ownership and responsible use of credit demonstrate stability.

Motivation: Regardless of the source of financing, the deeper the equity the greater the probability the loan will perform. Equity represents the borrower's nest egg, skin in the game, war chest, stockpile and something to fall back on. Regardless of the cliche selected, equity is likely a major component of a borrower's net worth.

Alternatives: If there is hardship, the property can be sold or refinanced, or a request can be made for temporary forbearance. The owner can move into a less expensive rental and convert the property into a rental. With a solid equity position, positive cash flow is likely, and with write-off of expenses and depreciation, lost income may be replaced.

Equity is a legitimate consideration in both prime and subprime lending. The difference is that it may be the dominant consideration of lower subprime grades and, more so, hard money lending. Borrowers resort to hard money lenders when they cannot qualify for other financing. They probably have substandard credit, unstable income or both. With low overall risk and borrower strength, hard money financing shouldn't be necessary.

Deep equity correlates to timely performance even when borrowers have little or no personal funds committed in purchase. The commitment demonstrated by borrowers who convert hard-earned savings into a down payment extends to gifted and inherited funds, especially when the presence of those funds contributes to deep equity. On loans with lower equity, risk is mitigated by private mortgage insurance or PMI-equivalent coverage on government loans. On non-conforming financing, increasingly higher loan amounts are accompanied by progressively lower LTVs.

It is notable that VA loans have a lower incidence of default than FHA loans even when borrower equity is smaller. This may be attributable to VA's consideration of residual income, the greater sense of loyalty from active or retired military borrowers or the strong support programs available to VA borrowers.

Respect for equity preservation benefits in multiple ways—increased profitability for the lender, less frivolous equity erosion on secured properties, more stable property values in communities—but also when an established customer relationship exists between the lender and the borrower.

Equity, positive or negative

Fannie Mae's Roy Downey said it best: "Equity breeds character." Although many factors are considered in the underwriting process, loan-to-value is the strongest predictor of performance, assuming a sound appraisal.

Positive sources of equity gain include:

Down payment: The most common sources of down payment are personal savings, sale proceeds from a previous residence and gifts (as more fully discussed in the *Assets and Funds to Close* chapter.) Although some advocate that personal savings represents the highest commitment to the property, I believe that any or a combination of the positive sources of equity contribute, and the percentage of equity is more meaningful than the source.

There is benefit to the borrower when sales proceeds are applied to the down payment on the next property. Mortgage payments may be more manageable, capital gains are deferred, and, depending on loan term, loan payoff can be accomplished earlier. The lender benefits from transfer of proceeds and experienced borrowers. The loan has a higher probability of performing.

When borrowers changing residences retain significant proceeds, this should be considered a red flag except in situations such as divorce, when aging borrowers downsize or relocation to a less costly area. Some borrowers opt for a larger mortgage to maximize interest write-offs. If finances permit, a better choice would be a shorter loan term. See *Moving up or down*

Appreciation: Residential real estate provides shelter and over time usually increases in value. Even though our nearly thirty years of ownership has included two extended soft markets, annual appreciation is about 5%.

Property improvements: Most property improvements increase value although not necessarily on a dollar-for-dollar basis. Even when improvements are not fully recaptured by increased value, the improvements demonstrate the owners' commitment to their property.

Increased demand or **Gentrification:** When the least desirable properties in a neighborhood are upgraded, all properties benefit.

Negative sources of equity gain include:

Rapid appreciation: Rapid appreciation is often unsustainable. This is less common when the reason for the appreciation is well supported, such as when a property is upgraded with non-superficial improvements or a community gains a major source of employment.

Manipulated appreciation: Organized fraud becomes more profitable as the number of properties in the scheme increases. Each transfer of ownership becomes a comparable sale to support the value of other properties. Red flags are rapid appreciation on multiple properties in close proximity, especially with common aspects such as short-term ownership, LLC ownership, transfers between a limited number of entities and sale to out-of-area buyers. Opportunistic neighbors uninvolved in the scheme may seek cash-out refinances. When multiple comparables rapidly appreciate over a year or two, the neighborhood may be unstable, and increased values may not be sustained. If valid external factors are identified, steadily increasing values may be more sustainable than manipulated appreciation. See *Flip transactions*

Re-zoning and subsequent redevelopment: Re-zoning from residential to commercial or from single family to multiple family usage can increase value but can have a negative effect on the quality of living for single family ownership. Speculative buyers may profess owner occupancy while their true motivation is profit after quick turnover.

When equity isn't enough

When equity is the sole or overriding compensating factor, the loan merits subprime or hard money pricing. Dodd Frank turned a risk issue into a legislative mandate. Institutional lenders have increased liability when the borrower has irresponsible credit or questionable affordability, even when substantial equity ensures no monetary loss for the lender.

The new employee

The borrower had a mid-700 credit score and over $200,000 reserves. She was requesting $150,000 cash-out on her free and clear residence. LTV was 34%.

The transaction was an employee loan to a recently hired manager at the bank. Short job tenure was not the issue. The concern was the two year gap before re-employment and lack of any commonality between her new and previous positions.

Most of my questions could not be asked. How was this person qualified for hire? Was there an internal recommendation? Had the position been vacant for a very long period of time? What I did know was that her loan request could not be approved. There was no assurance that she was a good fit for the job, or that proceeds would be other than an emergency fund. The borrower was informed her loan request could be reconsidered a year after her hiring date, at which point she would have adequate job stability, and loan approval could be granted without escalation.

Lessons:

1. *Low LTV and high reserves can't cure everything.*

2. *In the brave new world of Dodd Frank, loan approval after an extended employment gap puts the company at risk.*

Equity or credit score?

If given the choice between lending to a borrower with an impressive credit score or with a deep equity position, I would easily opt for the equity position. For average borrowers on average homes in stable markets, a 20% equity position generally provides protection for the lender in the event of default and psychologically for the borrower.

Cash equity should be considered relative to the borrower's income and savings. For a high earner with ample reserves, $100,000 isn't much.

The cash-out spectrum

Cash-out refinances have varying levels of risk. Key determinants are borrower motivation, amount of proceeds relative to equity, loan amount and affordability. Ideally, motivation is explained in an unedited and sufficiently detailed letter of explanation. The higher the proceeds, the more critical the credibility of the letter.

The following list runs from higher to lower risk, for the most part:

Cash-out to **extract maximum equity:** In a depreciating housing market, when a business is prioritized over a borrower's home or when the borrower is desperate for any reason, default has higher potential. The trigger may be economic or personal circumstances. Risk indicators are insistence on maximum cash proceeds, cancellation if proceeds are reduced and an unconvincing motivation letter, such as home improvement when improvements aren't necessary or when proceeds don't correlate with the cost of improvements.

Repetitive **debt consolidation:** Borrowers who refinance periodically to start off with a clean slate rationalize that mortgage rates are substantially lower than credit card rates. Reduced payments also are a magnet for consumers with high outstanding balances. Recurring conversion of short-term unsecured debt into long-term secured debt is poor financial management. When there is insufficient equity to refinance because of serial refinances or down-trending property values, the merry-go-round grinds to a stop. Adjusted spending habits aren't assured even when circumstances don't allow another refinance. The remaining solutions are foreclosure or bankruptcy, which can be as costly to the lender as a foreclosure.

Speculative investment: A speculative investment is any venture verbally guaranteed to be profitable. The borrower should be encouraged to research the investment thoroughly and discuss the probability of profitability with a CPA, financial advisor or other impartial third party.

On an ill-advised investment, loan denial may be later appreciated by the borrowers. Of course, unproven investment income cannot be used in qualification.

Cash-out to be **generous:** Generosity is an admirable trait, but less so when it requires tapping into equity for someone else's down payment, student loan debt or dream wedding. Even when low interest rates allow for inexpensive borrowing, the increased payment amounts and term of repayment may negatively impact the borrower when earnings have decreased. Well-meaning is not always smart.

If cash-out is for **college tuition**, at least one child should be of appropriate age for college. Asking for copies of the admission letter or transcripts is excessive but if there aren't any dependents, feel free to take issue with whoever took the loan application. If tax returns indicate no dependents, be wary of the transaction, unless the borrowers are at grandparent age. Borrowing to provide tuition for a niece or nephew is as suspect as receiving a down payment gifted from a cousin.

Business expansion: If a seasoned business has a proven track record of profitability, cash-out to expand may be a prudent risk. However, a business loan is more appropriate. Using income from an unseasoned source is projected income and therefore unusable.

Cash-out to **fulfill a dream:** The underwriter may be unaware of this circumstance if the borrower is wary about disclosing his or her dream. Tapping into equity to finance a career change, committing a year to volunteering or traveling extensively may be possible if a substantial equity position remains along with sufficient passive income. Some asset dissipation guidelines do not allow refinance proceeds to be factored in. Realistically, loan proceeds will be used prior to liquidation of retirement savings, but return to employment will stave off long-term erosion of funds.

Cash-out for a **medical emergency:** This occurs very rarely—only once in my career. The borrower had rapidly deteriorating eyesight and wanted a specialist not covered by his medical insurance. We not only approved the loan but concurred that it was appropriate for the three-day rescission period to be waived. Circumstances were documented by a compelling letter from the borrower.

Technical cash-out: Technical cash-out occurs when loan proceeds are used to payoff a non-purchase money lien or delinquent property taxes. There is no potential for the borrower to take the money and run, which elevates risk on standard cash-out transactions. When the borrower also commits personal savings to increase the pay-down, risk is even lower.

Slightly more than incidental cash-out: According to generic guidelines, incidental cash-out is (and may forever be) $2,000 or 2% of the loan amount, whichever is less. If a borrower receives $2,500 on a $250,000 loan, should the loan be considered high risk? The loan is correctly classified as a cash-out transaction, but risk is not elevated unless the borrower insisted on receiving that amount of proceeds and LTV is at maximum, possibly indicating financial distress. Cash-out may be instigated by a commissioned loan officer, who convinced the borrower that cash proceeds are free money as long as P&I doesn't increase.

Cash-out for **equity buyout**, as in a divorce or co-owner situation, is not a feel-good transaction but at least it resolves a difficult situation, and use of proceeds is documented with a specific buyout amount.

Cash-out for **home improvement:** Some improvements enhance property value more than others. Online research quantifies percentages of increased value for various improvements. The prototype good example is an additional bathroom for a three-bedroom, one-bath house. A truly bad example was an entertainment industry couple who remodeled to their personal taste by replacing white marble with black marble (or the other way around). Their property value was not increased by the cost of the replacement. Even when value is affected minimally, improvements may enhance livability and enjoyment.

Cash-out for home improvement, in the **ironic** sense: This cover-up is used when proceeds become the down payment on another residence. The borrowers are improving their home, just not the one they're living in now. This is not a half-truth but misrepresentation of occupancy. One method to elicit the truth is to condition for specific improvements being made. If proceeds are substantial, there should be a signed contract or copies of bids. These details in conjunction with interior pictures also can shed light. A motivation letter for cash-out on a tiny one bedroom condo citied plans for a kitchen and balcony remodel. Reviewing photos of an already upgraded kitchen and a crib in the condo's entry hall prompted skepticism. Updated inquiries if the credit report is stale can be helpful too. Insistence on a specific closing date is another tip-off that the borrower is moving out.

Cash-out for home improvement, in the **coached** sense: Cash-out for home improvements is a default answer for loan officers who do not consult with the borrower, believing this response creates a favorable impression.

Cash-out to **sustain lifestyle:** After retiring, borrowers with the foresight to save transition from income-based to asset-based. Common sources are liquid assets, investment accounts, retirement savings and equity in real estate. Refinancing to convert equity into spendable funds is not high risk, as long as a respectable equity position remains. Investment properties being refinanced or purchased preferably should have at least a break-even cash flow, taking depreciation into account. On a primary residence, a reverse mortgage is an alternative.

Cash-out after an **all-cash purchase:** This is the most benign of all cash-out transactions, assuming LTV is based on purchase price or verified improvements since purchase. Also called delayed financing or **asset recapture**, under certain circumstances it may be investor acceptable as a rate and term refinance. The often overlooked strength is that an all-cash purchase requires strong savings—unless funds to purchase were borrowed—which translates to strong reserves after the refinance transaction. Funds borrowed from close relatives who are willing to share their wealth on a temporary basis should be considered a minor but positive compensating factor. Depending on the investor, pricing may be equivalent to a purchase or rate and term refinance.

Final insights:

- Although this section demonstrates the spectrum of cash-out risk, the contributory factor of LTV cannot be ignored.

- If timely repayment is a concern, the solution is a lower loan amount or no refinance at all.

- Larcenous borrowers compose persuasive motivation letters. With a cluster of cash-out requests for medical emergencies, or a borrower with recurring cash-out refinances not supported by improvements cited in the appraisal, beware.

The blind eyes loan

From almost every angle, the loan had acceptable risk. It was a cash-out refinance with LTV below 50%, decent ratios and a high credit score. Proceeds just under $150,000 were stated to be for home improvement. When I asked the processor if she would condition for detailed use of proceeds she said "We never ask for it." Her manager said "The investors never ask for it."

My role was consultant, and no one was receptive to my rule of thumb: If proceeds could cover a down payment on another property, specific use of proceeds should be obtained. Since the borrower was a real estate investor, proceeds could have been the down payment on another property, or the application could be presenting the truth.

The loan officer may have known how proceeds were being used. Most borrowers don't know our rules, and even though this borrower was a real estate investor, income came from two commercial properties acquired many years ago.

Credibility for the loan request rested on the appraisal, which should show whether nearly $150,000 in renovations were needed. But the loan *cancelled before an appraisal was delivered. After curiosity (and location not far from our house) compelled me to look at the property, I concluded no evidence of disrepair. Since the borrower was an older single man, major modifications weren't needed except possibly in preparation to sell.*

Seeing the property clarified why the loan cancelled. The house was on a single-lane, one-way residential street backing and siding to a movie studio. It was a replica Tudor cottage complete with multi-paned windows and slate roof. It probably was originally built for studio use. Because of its distinctive architectural style dissimilar to any other residence in the area and adjacent commercial usage, supporting value would have been difficult at best.

Cancellation was a welcome disposition of a tough loan in multiple respects.

Lessons:

1. *Specific use of proceeds would clarify continued occupancy and potential change in debt service.*

2. *Not requiring specific use of proceeds demonstrates an industrywide preoccupation with minutia in lieu of risk assessment.*

3. *Very few properties are truly unique. Those that are can be impossible to appraise. This property was one of them.*

The return of 100% cash-out?

A radio commercial offering 100% cash-out and loan amounts to $2,000,000 aired in the Los Angeles market over several months. I finally called the lender out of curiosity, not desire to borrow. It turned out that 100% cash-out financing was available only for VA-eligible borrowers, and $2,000,000 cash-out was offered at much lower loan-to-values, either 70% or 50%. I never found out which, because I wasn't willing to wait the ten or fifteen minutes the phone rep said it would take to bring up the program on his computer.

The point is that 100% cash-out financing is available only to a limited borrower base. To my knowledge, history appears not to be repeating itself. For those speculating why VA offers this program, my theories are respectable loan performance, controlled eligibility and borrower loyalty.

85% without mortgage insurance

Considerably less scary than 100% cash-out financing is 85% financing without mortgage insurance. When I first heard about it recently, I was taken aback. However, after debating internally whether it constitutes aggressive lending, I feel relatively comfortable—under the right circumstances.

Considerations are:

- **Break-even point:** Assuming a stable or appreciating real estate market, if default occurs the lender may not take a monetary loss. Paper loss is probable if servicing expenses and missed payments enter into the calculation. If the loan is not brought current, and the time between default and property sale is not extended, the 15% equity position should be adequate.

- **Market share:** Borrowers will be attracted to this program even if pricing is slightly higher than 85% pricing also requiring private mortgage insurance coverage. Loan officers will sell this program enthusiastically as long as adjusted pricing doesn't equal self-insurance. Borrowers would benefit from deductibility.

- **Borrower strength:** It is unknown whether this program allows average borrowers as opposed to requiring well-qualified borrowers. The score threshold may be higher. DTIs may be lower. Verified reserves may be required.

- **Appreciating value:** If the real estate market is steadily appreciating, as the loan seasons the 15% equity position grows. Steady appreciation is integral, since rapid appreciation can reverse quickly.

- **Marketability:** Worst case projections are dependent on how long it takes to dispose of the property. Whether a property is mainstream or non-mainstream could make a difference. A three-bedroom, one-bath house takes longer to sell than a three-bedroom, two-bath house. The appraisal should be reviewed to assess marketability.

- **Customer relationship:** One would think this program would be more attractive to business banks lending to their customer base than originators selling these loans with repurchase exposure.

Asset-based borrowers

Not everyone depends on employment. Some, anticipating retirement, accumulate wealth through diligent saving and sound investments. Others inherit it or win the lottery.

The GSEs allow two approaches to qualifying asset-based borrowers—using averaged investment income from tax returns or their asset dissipation formula. Asset dissipation allows income to be hypothesized from assets divided over a sanctioned number of years.

Both GSE-approved approaches are arguably too conservative. Using investment income ignores the assets that generate the income. Asset dissipation typically assumes the loan will be fully amortized. This is dependent on age, and more probable with a 60-year-old than an 85-year-old borrower.

Some investors will not allow asset dissipation to qualify unless a pattern of withdrawal can be verified before closing. This not only is unrealistic but also a poor risk indicator. Prudent borrowers refrain from depletion of assets until there is a need.

A personal underwriting principle is "You can get fired from a job, but you can't get fired from money." This assumes demonstrated ability to preserve principal.

See *Asset dissipation* and *Windfall assets*

Reserves

Only the naive believe that reserves will be set aside to provide the appropriate number of mortgage payments in times of hardship. Since this at best occurs rarely, why are reserves required?

Reserves are justified conceptually on certain loans, but lender implementation can be excessive. With high LTVs, the lender deserves assurance that the borrower's last dollar was not spent on closing costs. On rental properties, savings should be adequate to cope with repairs, non-paying tenants or vacancy. Inexperienced homebuyers without demonstrated money management skills will benefit from an emergency fund; however, they are the most likely to live from paycheck to paycheck. Some AUS decisions dispense with required reserves, while manual guidelines cite requirements based on occupancy type, transaction type, property type, loan amount, score level and other factors. Irrespective of convoluted formulas, there is no assurance that verified savings will be preserved for mortgage payments.

Reserves were once considered an essential component of creditworthiness. This changed—as so many beliefs did—after the meltdown. In 2009, 71 years after Fannie Mae's inception in 1938, "strategic default" appeared in print. Reserves, low debt ratios and high credit scores could no longer be assumed to ensure loan performance if equity was absent.

Interest and dividend earnings on 1040s provide a more realistic view of ability to save than two months statements. Discounting investment account balances below face value serves little purpose. Scrutiny of large deposits when funds are not required to close is unnecessary and an irritant to borrowers. When there is scant equity and no perceived financial benefit, liquid or retirement savings may not be sacrificed. Problematic properties with equity are more apt to be sold than resuscitated with savings.

After mulling over the necessity for reserves, I came to several conclusions:

1. Loan performance correlates largely to two factors, equity and available funds.

    - Equity + available funds = Loan performs

    - Equity + limited funds = Loan probably performs

    - Limited equity + available funds = Loan may perform

    - Limited equity + limited funds = Higher probability of poor performance

2. Mandatory reserves are easily justifiable under the following limited circumstances: high LTVs, LTVs over 80% with all gifted funds, cash-out refinances except when reimbursement is for verified borrower-financed home improvements, marginal qualifiers and investment property owners either unproven or without applicable skills. Mandatory reserves are less necessary for lower loan-to-values, rate and term refinances, and for seasoned and responsible borrowers.

3. Reserve requirements are effective for disqualifying ill-equipped borrowers such as investment property owners with low cumulative equity or negative cash flow. However, punitive reserve requirements disqualifying all but the super-qualified borrowers should be reconsidered. With considerable cash-out, verifying the absence of hardship circumstances is justified.

4. Correlating reserves to months of PITI is ill-conceived and causes unrealistic expectations. Naive underwriters believe a direct correlation exists; others may erroneously conclude, since the correlative purpose

is improbable, that reserves serve no purpose. Reserves do demonstrate responsible financial management, and inexperienced homeowners may soon understand the benefit of emergency savings.

5. Reserves should correlate to something other than monthly housing expense. Reserves could be tied to fractions or multiples of a month's qualifying income. Changing terminology to replace "reserves" with "emergency funds" would at least add clarity for borrowers.

Reserves on investment properties

Some investors require astounding reserves—twenty-four months or more—on certain investment property loans, those with non-conforming loan amounts or when holdings exceed GSE maximums. Loans on investment properties historically have inferior performance to loans on primary and second homes. Post-meltdown, loans performed even more poorly, resulting in more rigorous reserve requirements. Not all investment properties are high-risk though.

Investment properties easily re-rented after vacancy, with consistently non-negative cash flow and low maintenance expenses should be distinguished from units with unstable tenancy, problematic tenant replacement, inconsistent or negative cash flow and habitability issues. Reserves are critical on troublesome properties despite the equity position, because of maintenance costs and to keep the lender current. Non-troublesome properties pay for themselves. Reserves are also critical on seasonal rentals and student housing since cash flow is not consistent throughout the year. What actually protects lenders on troublesome properties is equity. If there is equity, the properties will be put up for sale, not given to the lender.

Despite six months or considerably higher reserves on each investment property, in the event of hardship, savings would likely be applied based on equity position. High reserve requirements demonstrate financial strength and effectively redirect deficient borrowers to other lenders. A more effective control would be denying credit to borrowers with limited equity.

The departing employee

This loan was escalated because the branch where the borrower was employed was being acquired by another bank. The only proof of the employment transition was an offer letter. That was the most surmountable of the complications.

The borrower's fiancé/co-borrower was recently employed as a sales manager. He had a high base salary with a relatively small incentive component. In addition to their separate residences, the borrowers each owned an investment property.

Here's what made the loan inadvisable: All four properties, the two current rentals and the two departure residences being converted into rentals, had shallow equity and negative cash flow. The co-borrower could qualify on base salary, but sales positions with high bases are secure only when the new hire performs well.

We questioned why the borrowers entered into the purchase contract while both were transitioning in employment. We were told they had no concerns with their decision. This response did not add to our comfort level, and the loan request was denied.

Lesson: Sometimes the problem isn't the rule violation but the layers of risk surrounding it.

Net worth, negative and otherwise

Net worth is easily calculated by subtracting liabilities from assets. Despite elimination as a field on the loan application, net worth remains a valid risk consideration at least for some borrowers.

Likely to have negative net worth are first-time buyers, those with considerable student loan debt and those who purchased real estate at the top of the market. For many in these categories, negative net worth is either a life stage or the result of economic forces.

Negative net worth under other circumstances should be evaluated on case by case, but may be difficult to excuse. Equity conversion through cash-out refinances, upside-down real estate investments caused by aggressive acquisition, inability to curtail spending and pursuing an expensive education despite a low-paying career goal all reflect poor financial management. If applicants qualify marginally when moving up in value or withdrawing equity, negative net worth can be a legitimate obstacle to approval.

The final example of negative net worth is entirely preventable. Understated liquid and retirement savings can result in loan denial. Full disclosure can justify approval of difficult loans. This is not to be confused with massaging a bad loan to give the illusion of a good loan. To the contrary, by providing a comprehensive loan application, the loan officer enables the underwriter to see the complete financial picture and compose a defendable decision.

See *Asset-based borrowers*

Flexibility

Some loans merit flexibility; others do not. Whether flexibility should be allowed should be based on a combination of attributes, likelihood of timely performance and loan program.

Lower loan-to-value and high credit score are not enough. Flexibility requires more than a spreadsheet understanding of the loan. The loan must make sense, which requires underwriting with thought.

Salability and potential exposure if the loan does not perform have to be taken into account. Government loan programs have minimal flexibility because the highest degree of latitude is incorporated into qualification tolerances. Conforming programs have greater flexibility, and there may be potential for overlays to be waived or a GSE single-loan variance. Greater latitude may be possible on non-conforming programs because with deeper equity positions, more discretionary income and stronger reserves, flexibility is justifiable.

Borrower wealth does not justify latitude. Sustainability of both income and assets are critical. Wealthy borrowers less likely to merit flexibility are entertainers and athletes.

A loan with strong merit deserves better than denial.

Qualified borrowers, despite not qualifying

An attorney applied for a non-conforming 65% purchase money loan. Because he switched law firms less than a year earlier, the underwriter excluded his bonus from qualification. His retired father was added on the loan to reduce ratios, but occupant ratios exceeded Fannie Mae's guidelines. The cure was changing occupancy to non-owner which required an additional 5% down. The loan was escalated, since non-owner occupied guidelines didn't allow asset dissipation.

The borrowers didn't understand why a 35% down payment wasn't sufficient. They also didn't understand why an owner-occupied property was being classified as investment property.

The borrowers had a better grasp of risk than the underwriter. Fannie Mae restrictions (since nullified) were excessive on a non-conforming loan with a 35% down payment, all from the occupying borrower, and a high likelihood of continuing bonus. The transaction was clearly owner-

occupied and there was no reason to disallow asset dissipation on the father's $6,000,000 of verified liquid assets.

See *One size fits most*

Lesson: Rigid adherence to rules can obstruct approval of a low-risk loan.

Loan term as a reflection of creditworthiness

Underwriters generally view loan term as a reflection of creditworthiness. A 15-year fixed rate loan evidences a prudent borrower with long-term vision; a 5-year adjustable does not. A fixed rate borrower is superior to an adjustable rate borrower.

These conclusions are sometimes unjustified. The best choice depends on individual circumstances. An anticipated relocation or an upcoming empty nest may not be addressed in the file.

My husband and I made an unconventional decision on our personal residence. Our goal was unencumbered ownership as soon as we could afford it. We started with a 30-year fixed loan, refinanced to a 15-year fixed loan and eventually converted to a 3/1 ARM which was paid off in two years. Early payoff was possible because beginning with the 15-year loan, we consistently paid more than the 15-year payment even through the 3/1 ARM years.

Traditionally the average life of loan is 5 to 7 years. Pre-meltdown, the span reduced to 3 to 5 years. In any case, very few 30-year loans are repaid over 30 years.

Borrowers with low debt ratios or a refinance after several years ownership may appreciate learning about loan term options besides the obvious ones. Terms of 20- or 25-years should be offered if 15-year payments are too high. Borrowers attracted to 30-year loans because of higher and longer interest deductions should be urged to check with their tax advisor. Borrowers could be grateful to discuss something other than additional conditions.

Permanent financing

Permanent financing is sought after completion of construction and after an all-cash purchase. Each circumstance has distinct risk considerations:

Post-construction: Construction financing is short-term and more expensive than permanent financing. For take-out financing, value should be assessed in two respects, appraised value and cost. Spot construction is intrinsically one-of-a-kind, which makes the appraisal process more complex and subjective. With permanent financing, the cost approach is at least as relevant as the market approach. Cash equity in the property is a relevant consideration. Barring complications, the calculation is simple—the borrower's cash investment divided by the total of cash-in plus financing on land and improvements. Complications come from gifted land, land owned so long its acquisition price is not representative or when new construction replaces a teardown. There are methods of factoring in these elements. Original land cost can be enhanced by a factor representing annualized percentage of appreciation, and the value of the demolished improvement can be subtracted from acquisition cost—or the ratio calculation can be dispensed with if the owner's cash investment and value appear adequate to ensure commitment to the property.

If the borrower is a builder applying for owner-occupied financing, additional issues should be considered:

- If the property was listed for sale, what was the listing price(s) and how long was the listing?

- Is the property appropriate for the builder's household size, or is owner-occupancy an expedient solution to repay construction financing?

- Did construction financing include funds over the amount necessary for materials, labor and to pay third parties, i.e., unused contingency allowances and builder profits? If so, monthly payments will repay money disbursed to the borrower and potentially included in qualifying income.

- Does the appraisal acknowledge that the builder is the borrower?

These questions address intent to occupy, borrower equity and value. The answers indicate acceptable or unacceptable risk.

All-cash purchase: An all-cash purchase usually indicates financial strength or tenant occupancy. To determine which, borrowers requesting permanent financing should address why they closed without long-term financing and the source of the funds used. The usual response on the first issue is an emergency situation for the seller or buyer, or a competitive seller's market. The most desirable responses on the second issue are personal savings, a temporary loan from close relatives or an unsecured bank loan. Credibility on this type of transaction is critical because all-cash transactions occur frequently on investment properties. But sometimes an all-cash purchase is the only option after loan denial(s)—which may not be clear from the inquiry letter. The appraisal should support value well and identify any property concerns. If the property is older, if deferred maintenance is evident or if the contract references an "as is" sale, a property inspection is essential.

Proceeds from permanent financing on an all-cash purchase should be distinguished from a cash-out refinance where the underwriter is unsure of the actual use of funds. Proceeds of the loan will replenish savings or short-term financing, and the borrower will benefit from the mortgage deduction.

For either circumstance, the property should be occupied before permanent financing is obtained. Vacancy can indicate lack of owner-occupancy or the inability to find a qualified tenant. If occupancy is non-owner, additionally ensure that the borrower has a true cash equity position in the property, and cash flow is at least break-even.

Non-occupying co-borrowers

Non-occupying co-borrowers may be annoying to underwriters since qualifying takes more effort. Some believe occupying borrowers who cannot qualify on their own intrinsically have high risk. With both GSEs allowing blended ratios, investor choice is simplified. However, investor requirements on non-conforming loans may perpetuate maximum occupying borrower ratios. Whether owner-occupied ratios are justified on all non-occupying co-borrower transactions is debatable.

There are risk issues that outweigh the annoyance issue. The statistics on co-signers (not limited to real estate loans, which invalidates the findings to some extent) are alarming. Thirty-eight percent of co-signers end up taking full responsibility on payments. Their credit scores and personal relationships with the co-borrower suffer too. This information is provided to make the point that, despite Fannie Mae's alignment with Freddie Mac, there is additional risk when a co-borrower lives elsewhere.

Mitigating variants are the percentage of equity and potential income of the occupying borrower. It is preferable that the occupying borrower has capacity to be self-supporting in the future, but not essential with a large enough down payment. Any significant equity position averts default.

The counter-point is that when all parties qualify marginally, non-occupying co-borrowers add little strength to the loan.

Non-arm's-length transactions

Underwriters are taught to consider non-arm's-length transactions with caution. This position is well justified in some situations.

In a non-tainted parent to adult child sale transaction, all parties benefit. The parents avoid real estate commission. Frequently, the child pays a bargain price and the lender has a stronger equity position than the LTV indicates. The adult child should have realistic expectations of livability and property condition, and a familiar neighborhood.

A tainted parent to adult child transfer is exemplified by an unsupportable sales price or a questionably supported appraisal. Motivations are the appearance of a deep equity position and excessive proceeds to the property seller.

There is another possibility of malfeasance. Lenders have unwittingly consented to short sales where parents with financial problems sell to their son-in-law, or to another relative with a different last name. The relationship is not disclosed nor is the intent of the in-laws to remain in the home. The lender absorbs a reduction in principal with minimally improved chance of repayment.

Non-arm's-length transactions also have potential for collusion between unrelated individuals, an owner selling to a tenant or an employer selling to an employee. An inflated price can result in an 80% LTV that is actually 90% or 100%, with inflated proceeds to the seller and immediate default by the buyer. There is also the potential that tenancy is long-term and the tenant improved the property with mutual expectation of future purchase, or that during an extended working relationship the employer transitioned to mentor and finally to "like family."

With any non-arm's-length transaction, the underwriter should closely examine the integrity of the deal starting with value and occupancy, the nature and length of the relationship, and also scrutinize whether funds to close are acceptably sourced. If the sales price is well supported, gifts of equity may be acceptable depending on loan-to-value and relationship. Gifts of equity need not be considered a risk factor but the covert transfer of funds between parties is. The appraisal must include acknowledgement of the non-arm's length relationship.

My conclusion on non-arm's-length transactions is that there are three possibilities. Reminiscent of the Three Little Bears, the sales price is either too high, too low or just right. The underwriter should be confident which of the three applies.

Unrelated co-borrowers

Long-term commitment is a positive factor in lending. Unrelated co-borrowers differ from partners, spouses, family members, lifelong friends or long-term co-occupants. Their ties are casual—apartment sharers planning to each occupy one unit of a duplex or three couples buying a ski chalet together. These arrangements work until priorities change.

One co-owner of the duplex marries. After the couple has children, they want to convert equity into a down payment on a single family home with more privacy, bedrooms and backyard.

One couple sharing ownership of the ski chalet decides they'd rather spend their vacations by the ocean, but there are no candidates to buy out their one-third interest.

Co-ownership does not always work out. Owners can end up with differing needs or unequal benefit.

Resolution depends on assets, motivation and most of all equity position. With sufficient equity, the remaining owner(s) can refinance to buyout the departing co-owners. They also can mutually agree to sell the property or be forced to sell if the exiting co-owners exercise their right of partition. With limited equity, the options are buyout financed out-of-pocket or default.

With unrelated co-borrowers, equity should be assessed by each entity's proportionate ownership interest. With 95% financing on the duplex, each party's initial buy-in is 2. 5%. With 90% financing on the ski chalet, the initial buy-in is 3.33% per couple. Long-term ownership and an appreciating real estate market increase equity, but discontent sometimes arises quickly.

Some lenders limit the number of borrowers, possibly due to origination system limitations. Depending on the system, this may be self-imposed. Even before the meltdown loans with several borrowers were considered higher risk. The lower the entity's ownership interest, the higher the risk.

Moving up or down

Common motivations for moving up in value are:

- Increase in household size

- Increased income and/or affordability

- Stabilized employment or seasoned self-employment

- Relocation to a more expensive housing market

- Desire for a superior house in size and/or quality

- In-home work space or other personal need

Common motivations for moving down in value are:

- Decreased income

- Divorce

- Other hardship circumstances

- Motivation to convert equity into spendable funds

- Empty nest

- Desire for a simplified lifestyle

- Relocation to a less expensive housing market

Minor differences in property value may be insignificant. Risk indicators are move-downs accompanied by declining income (which may further decline) or move-ups with questionable stability or occupancy. Less concerning is higher ratios with upward trending income. Those outside the industry (which includes most borrowers) base affordability on current earnings. Qualifying income should not be pushed, but higher ratios impact risk less when there is appreciating income.

See *Entrepreneurial types*

First-time home buyers

Every borrower starts out as a first-time home buyer. The event is so widespread that the industry uses the acronym FTHB as shorthand. First-time home buyers lack experience in repaying a mortgage and their loans admittedly perform less favorably than loans to seasoned homeowners. However, they should not be condemned as a group. It is up to the underwriter to evaluate qualification without a mortgage history.

The more limited the documentation, the less valid the loan decision. This lesson led to contraction of reduced-doc and no-doc programs. With FTHBs, complete reliance on the AUS decision leaves too much to chance. Consideration of intangibles that the AUS is incapable of weighing is essential. A reliable rental history is important, as is an analysis of the length and depth of established credit. Other considerations are stability of employment, consistency of income, and sufficiency of reserves. If affordability is at issue, consider whether the borrower has a pattern of savings or the absence of payment shock. Non-credit related issues are reasonability of commute and property condition. Why property condition? Though some originators minimize underwriter involvement with the appraisal, a FTHB may be poorly equipped to assess the cost of upkeep. Maintenance is less of a burden on newer residences, those with consistently conscientious owners, and newer attached condominiums or those with acceptable reserves.

Depending on the extent of shaky credit, unstable income and scant reserves, the right decision may be to deny the loan. Not everyone is ready to be a homeowner.

See *What AUS doesn't see*

No primary housing expense

Appropriate circumstances for having no housing expense are living with family members for convenience, because of traditional values, to accumulate a down payment or after relocation. Long-time close friends, godparents or relatives may allow guest occupancy on a shorter-term basis,

A dubious circumstance is a borrower with good earnings and credit whose spouse is solely responsible for mortgage expense. There is justification if the borrower's spouse owned the residence solely before marriage or if the spouse's family provided the down payment. In either instance, the spouse has legitimate motivation to maintain the residence as a non-marital asset. But in most marriages both spouses contribute to household expenses, and even long-term unmarried cohabitants share living costs. Unless there is a legitimate motivation, the assertion of rent-free cohabitation may be a strategy to qualify with reduced housing expense, to finance an increased number of investment properties or, for lenders who calculate payment shock, to evade that calculation.

Married sole and separate

Situational: Typical motivations for one spouse vesting solely are the non-borrowing spouse's employment (unseasoned, not documentable or unprofitable), credit (excessive, non-existent or substandard) or ownership issues (pre-marital asset, preservation of inherited funds or number of properties owned.)

Legal: It is ironic that legislation originally enacted to allow a married woman to purchase property without her husband's permission or ownership interest turned into a strategic tool used by married couples to circumvent maximum numbers of properties owned. However, loan denial cannot be justified because of a non-borrowing spouse even in community property states. In short, a loan cannot be denied based on marital status. There are legitimate legal motivations such as when property was acquired before marriage or acquired with inherited funds.

Risk: Likelihood of default is higher on a loan with one borrower. This includes married individuals borrowing without their spouses. It is not discriminatory to view a loan with a sole borrower with caution, and aggressive qualification should not be allowed.

Philosophical: Those of us guided by the story of the loan cannot help speculating on the reason for married sole and separate vesting. Documentation sometimes assists. Joint tax returns reveal spousal income and alimony payments. When motivation is discernible, it cannot affect the loan decision.

Pregnancy and gender bias

The *Los Angeles Times* recently reported that Wells Fargo's mortgage unit paid a $5-million settlement to U.S. Department of Housing and Urban Development "over allegations that the lender discriminated against women who were pregnant or had recently given birth and were on maternity leave."

The issue could be used as a debate topic, pitting statistical research on the incidence of default of those not returning to work against gender-based discrimination, with a side issue of political correctness.

Although there is some risk from discontinued employment, the traditional practice of excluding a parent's income when she or he is on maternity leave has become unacceptable. Equally unacceptable is deriving qualifying income for employed or self-employed parents including periods of decreased earnings pre- or post-childbirth.

Undeniably a fraction of parents do not return to employment, but most continue because their income is necessary to support the family. Alternatives to default are tapping into savings (possibly not reflected on the application), receiving financial assistance from family, or transitioning to part-time and/or home-based employment.

The percentage of default, which I believe is low, is irrelevant since compliance is not optional.

As to repurchase exposure, the originator should be protected from investor claims of negligent underwriting when full income is used in qualification despite a borrower being on parental leave. The defense is simple—compliance with federal guidance not to discriminate in matters concerning parental leave.

Caveat: The final word on this issue should be from your legal counsel.

Aged-related spending

As an adult transitions from student to wage-earner to homeowner, discretionary spending usually increases proportionately to income, pausing when homeownership increases housing expense. Similarly, after retirement, decreased spending accompanies reduced income. Payment shock for homebuyers can mirror earnings shock for retirees, depending on financial management skills, particularly accrued savings.

Discretionary spending patterns change in response to life events. Most homeowners-to-be become more financially responsible before the purchase contract is signed. They save funds to close and for the inevitable move-in must-haves. First-time borrowers not self-motivated to reduce debt will be lectured by their real estate agent, the pre-qualifier and relatives. Most likely there will be additional changes in spending habits as proposed housing costs turn into reality. Priorities change with added responsibilities.

Underwriters who think that their role involves dissecting the borrower's spending patterns on depository statements don't understand that for responsible borrowers, spending habits adjust.

Age discrimination

1. Underwriters cannot discriminate because of a borrower's age.

2. Underwriters must be alert to red flags.

These two contradictory sentences create situations where an underwriter cannot make a decision without disregarding one or the other.

People exhibit similar but not uniform behavior during the progressive stages of their lives. Underwriters should be able to make assessments relative to those phases. Retirement savings of $25,000 are impressive for a 25-year old but not for a 65-year old. A 50-year old with a successful career rarely switches fields voluntarily unless retirement resources are ample. What appeals in a forever home may differ forty years later.

A loan on a multi-story house being purchased by early retirees should not be automatically denied, but some doubt should register when a five bedroom, three bath house with no bedrooms on ground level is being purchased by an 88-year old. Possibly he or she is extraordinarily agile. Possibly there is the intent for multigenerational housing with a plan to repurpose the den and adjacent half bath into a bedroom suite complete with walk-in shower. Clarification of intended occupancy should be handled with an open mind, but credibility is essential, and the borrower should be personally involved.

Housing fads

Out-of-date features may have minimal impact on value. Whether a refrigerator has a white, colored or stainless steel exterior has no bearing on its ability to cool and freeze. The efficiency of a lighting fixture is dependent on the shape and wattage of the bulbs, not whether the fixture is visual appealing. In-demand items expedite sale and enhance value, but fashions go out of fashion and are replaced by the next wave of in-demand items.

Structural limitations such as inadequate bathrooms or tiny bedrooms should be distinguished from curable cosmetic flaws. Expectations that older homes meet contemporary preferences are unrealistic. And after a full remodel there may be incompatibility between a house's interior and exterior.

Appeal is subjective and usually a relatively minor component of value. More important are location, lot size, square footage, room count (especially number of bedrooms and bathrooms) and overall condition. What contributes to livability is sound construction and internal systems (electricity, plumbing, etc.), diligent upkeep, a functional floor plan and location. Everything other than locational factors can be cured through remodeling.

Rapid appreciation in hot locations

I was pleased last year that our house was in one of Los Angeles's hottest ten zip codes and and equally pleased this year that it's not. One year's reign was sufficient. Hot isn't necessarily good for an extended period of time. When property values rise quickly there is potential to deflate.

Deflation is not a certainty. Over my underwriting career I witnessed very rapid appreciation in three second home areas popular with Southern California borrowers—Santa Fe, New Mexico and Aspen and Vail, Colorado. All show continuing demand although not as high as in their peak years. While they heated up, Palm Springs cooled down but resurged later when mid-century modern became fashionable again.

Second home popularity is tied somewhat to trendiness. Location and economic forces play a larger role in primary residences. Demand is driven by increased employment opportunities; added housing stock in turn attracts employers. Rapid appreciation also can be fraud-driven, although more likely within a limited area rather than an entire community.

In a heated market, be especially wary of flips, cosmetic remodels, marginal borrowers, questionable occupancy and long-term residents seeking maximum cash-out. Stable borrowers with a significant cash commitment for down payment are more likely to stay the course.

Tear-downs

A teardown is a property purchased with the intention to construct a new residence on the lot. Red flags are a run-down or outdated property, no termite and property inspections in the purchase contract; a borrower who works in construction or property development or is a real estate investor; a maximum cash-out refinance shortly after purchase (which can also occur after cosmetic renovation and inability to sell) and questionable occupancy or a possible straw buyer. Appraisal red flags are low depreciated value of improvements in the cost approach and visual clues of deferred maintenance in exterior and interior photos, particularly the street view. Online resources such as the street view feature of Google Maps may be helpful too, especially when the street view photo in the appraisal offers limited insight. Highest and best use could be a tip-off, but too often that field is automatically checked "yes" by appraisers. Not all deficient properties are tear-downs; many will continue to be occupied by the owner or tenants. Conversely some properties in good condition may be torn down and replaced with larger and more contemporary residences.

Investors seek mortgage financing because it is more favorably priced than construction financing and there are no troublesome lender inspections. If financial resources are inadequate, the lender can be left with an incomplete replacement residence or an empty lot. Payoff of the mortgage is likely when the owner pays off construction financing.

See *Occupancy fraud*

Second homes

Second homes serve a variety of purposes. Many but not all getaway residences provide their owners with a relaxing atmosphere, the traditional profile of a second home. Locations providing proximity to urban amenities or proximity to family members are other legitimate choices. A change of environment has become an acceptable motivation for second home usage.

With expansion of the traditional second-home definition, the issue arises of how an originator can protect against second home pricing on a property intended for investment property usage. If the borrower owns no investment properties, the subject property is appropriate in size for the borrower's family or extended family and a credible motivation letter is provided, the benefit of the doubt should be allowed on purchase transactions. On refinance transactions, Schedule E will confirm the presence or absence of rental activity. Second home occupancy may be justifiable when gross rental income validates limited rental usage. Short-term rental income should be determinable through online research and a written statement from a local rental agent. Credible written substantiation is necessary because short-term rental income in sought-after areas like some beach communities or event locations may be equivalent to long-term rental income in other areas.

Some second homes are purchased as future retirement homes. The indicator is usually the age of the borrower—middle age and older. These homes may be located in popular locations like Florida or Arizona or wherever property values are reasonable relative to the borrower's income. Single story residences are typical but not exclusively. Downsizing in square footage and value often occurs, but less frequently in recent years. Not downsizing is an acceptable choice with abundant reserves, a substantial amount of equity in the present residence and/or the probability of a generous pension. If current affordability is not an issue and the borrower has potential for near-future continued employment, consider that retirement savings may not be fully disclosed or the borrower can down-size later if affordability becomes a problem.

A rule of thumb for second-home expense is to quantify annual debt service and compare to hypothesized vacation costs including transportation. Affordability should be relative to what the borrower earns, not the underwriter.

See *Second homes in non-second home areas*

First time home buyers buying second homes

There are situations when purchasing a primary residence is not viable. The borrower may work for a company where periodic transfers are the norm or may be contemplating a relocation. Affordability can obstruct buying in high-cost areas. Individuals purchase houses because they aspire to be homeowners, want benefit from appreciating values and mortgage interest deductions, and may plan to eventually retire to or relocate to the area where the second home is located.

The borrower's current housing and employment should be analyzed. Employment allowIng working from home is a positive favor.

Second home purchases by FTHBs have higher potential for fraud than owner-occupied transactions. The borrower may be a straw buyer or the property could be intended for use as a rental. The size and room count of the subject property should be reconciled with the size of the borrower's household. Be skeptical of those who are living rent-free; this may be a qualification strategy. A motivation letter could be helpful, but only a convincingly credible letter is sufficient to offset questionable occupancy in terms of suitability and proximity.

See *No primary housing expense*

The dubious second home purchase

The closed loan was a purchase money transaction on a second home. The borrower was a young single man living and renting in a high cost area. The property was a four bedroom, three bath residence 700 miles from his employment. Both locations had similar temperate climates, and the second home was in a suburban neighborhood.

I concluded that the property could be anything but a second home. Either he was relocating, the house would be tenant-occupied at least for the near future or he was purchasing for family. There was some chance the applicant's intentions were aboveboard, that he was steps away from changing employment and possibly expanding his household. In that case,

he would be accepting more onerous loan terms for what would soon be
an owner-occupied property. But that wasn't disclosed in the application
package, and the cost of debt service on the property plus commuting
expense were unrealistic for a second home.

Because occupancy as represented was doubtful and the file did not
include a motivation letter, the loan was denied.

Lesson: Occupancy in most cases can be accepted at face value but not always.

See *Occupancy fraud*

Second homes, three phases

There have been three phases of second-home ownership in the course of my underwriting career. Initially second-home owners ranged from financially comfortable to very wealthy. The next phase occurred during our industry's ugly years when a far wider range of borrowers purchased second homes usually under stated income programs for quick resale or longer-term rental. Most recently, second-home purchasers fall into three categories: those who are close to retirement, those clearly able to afford two residences, and those with questionable motivation.

For the questionable group the second home may be used as a rental, a replacement home for a primary residence if there is no equity or as a primary residence for someone else, most likely adult children unable to qualify themselves. Even when motivation is unselfish such as housing for loved ones, this constitutes occupancy misrepresentation.

Second-home purchases justify a higher degree of skepticism than other transactions. The equity position in the borrower's primary residence should be confirmed. A second home close to the primary residence or lacking any second-home attribute justifies a credible letter of explanation. Affordability should be questioned when debt ratios are high or when the down payment is not from the borrower's personal savings. The donor of the gift may be the next occupant.

Second homes in non-second home areas

The expectation that a second home must be near a lake, ocean, ski lift, hiking trail or similar recreational amenity is unrealistic. There are other acceptable situations. A small condo unit located near the borrower's employment may be purchased as a second home to avoid a long commute. An urban second home may be the choice of people who prefer museums, theaters and shopping to outdoor activities.

Some skepticism is appropriate when the stated purpose of a second home is "to be near family." The true purpose may be housing for family. Consider whether the room count of the second home is appropriate for the borrower's household size—including grown children and grandchildren.

On purchases, request a motivation letter and ensure that it is credible. On refinances, obtain tax returns confirming the absence of rental activity.

See *Kiddie condos*

Retirement homes

This topic does not address care facilities, but how to differentiate between properties likely to be owner-occupied and straw buyer situations.

Retirement residences should be manageable. They should be easy to maintain inside and outside as well as appropriate for aging borrowers with (or cognizant of the possibility of) mobility limitations. Common choices are single level residences and condos on the first floor or reachable by an elevator. Those who disparaged condominiums in their earlier years may grow to appreciate simplified living and a built-in social set. The property should be affordable. Ideally mortgage debt should be fully or nearly paid off by time of retirement, but this is not always realistic. High LTV, high DTI, unimpressive reserves and a borrower not yet adjusted to reduced retirement income can be an explosive combination.

Borrowers at the upper end of middle age may disagree with the last paragraph and have a valid case. Transitional housing may be appropriate for those in their sixties or even older. For example, a friend's parents contracted to purchase a home on an island accessible by a ferry during limited hours. It was the perfect retirement home, they told their son. How many stories, I asked. Two. Are there bedrooms on the lower floor? I don't believe so. What happens if one of them trips or has a stroke? I don't think they thought of that. Later on he learned there was a first-floor bedroom, and the island dwellers rely on their volunteer fire department, three helicopter pads and medevac coverage for emergencies. His parents are content but at some point may move to a less remote location.

Multi-generational housing may be the ideal solution for younger families seeking homeownership and their elders' diminishing ability to live independently. This is common in many cultures. But what if the

245

elders prefer early dinner and other family members aren't hungry or home yet, or have restricted diets or different palates? What happens when grandparents relish quiet and grandchildren are noisy? Compatibility depends on the size and configuration of the house, the temperaments and flexibility of the occupants, and financial resources as well. Lennar Homes has found a viable market for their Next Gen Dual Living Situations, conventional homes plus private suites of approximately 500 to 700 square feet with cooking and laundry facilities.

It is not the lender's role to predict whether living arrangements will work out. Sincere and credible intentions should be respected. Not every plan for cohabitation succeeds but failures occur in all age groups sometimes not resulting in default. As always, equity position and market trend play a role.

Retirement homes revisited

A Los Angeles Times article in early 2015 featured a Merrill Lynch survey revealing "almost a third of baby boomers and their elders are choosing to buy larger homes in retirement." My immediate conclusion was many were idiots. But the article qualified the respondents' choice to their last move, which could have occurred prior to retirement. The survey also indicated that 85% wanted to receive extended healthcare in their own homes, 10% preferred assisted-living institutions and only 4% would want to live with family members, and that respondents in the survey "were primarily motivated by a desire to house visiting family members."

Here are my conclusions:

1. Some of the respondents, who were fifty years or older, could be relocating from higher cost locations. They could be moving up from 500 square feet to 750 square feet.

2. Some moved to more affordable locations where lateral moves in value allow for greater square footage.

3. Some wanted space for visiting family and perhaps future caregivers.

4. A few were straw-buyer transactions.

5. Some of them were idiots.

Overlays

An overlay is a more restrictive version of an investor guideline. A common overlay is increasing an investor's minimum credit score. Overlays are applied because major investors, including the GSEs, FHA and VA, reach out to a wide spectrum of borrowers while originators want to control losses from poorly performing loans and repurchases.

In some companies, written guidelines delineate all overlays. At least select originators—notably sales management, those empowered to grant exceptions and senior level underwriters—should be able to identify overlays embedded into investor guidelines. There may be loans that violate an overlay but have strong overall merit. Loans that are salable and have acceptable risk merit approval.

Fannie Mae and Freddie Mac

For much of my underwriting career I though of Fannie Mae and Freddie Mac as fraternal twins, the girl larger and more friendly and the boy more distant at first. This may be the result of re-re-branding both organizations. They started as Federal National Mortgage Association and Federal Home Loan Mortgage Association, transitioned to FNMA and FHLMC and finally to Fannie and Freddie, like aunts and uncles who allow the grown-up you to call them by their first names.

After we attained a comfort level with Fannie and Freddie, they distanced themselves. When loans that originated under relaxed standards started defaulting, Fannie Mae and Freddie Mac moved into defensive mode. They tightened on high LTVs and low credit scores, discouraged investor loans and lost sympathy with poorly-behaving borrowers. Further down the road, they required repurchase of loans with attributes clearly forecasting unacceptable risk.

Their defensive mode was difficult, but reasonability finally returned. Guidelines resembled those published during the sanity era with perceptive improvements. Fannie recognized savings at full value, finally adopted Freddie's blended ratio approach for non-occupying co-borrowers, and stopped being punitive on typically discretionary non-reimbursed business expenses. Freddie dropped the two-year rental management requirement and rent loss insurance coverage. Perhaps the most promising change is Fannie's revised tax return worksheet that underwriters have the option of disregarding as long as qualifying income is detailed sufficiently to justify the sources. The GSEs are back to resembling the relatives you want to be related to.

FHA and VA versus conventional lending

GSE-centric underwriters don't understand why FHA and VA programs willingly allow approval to high risk borrowers. They're even worse than subprime, some say. Relative to conventional loans, government programs allow higher debt ratios, lower credit scores and lower equity—and in combination. An industry friend refers to government underwriting as compliance underwriting, where dotting the i's and crossing the t's is more essential than loan quality.

Primary motivation for government programs is expanding ownership to all who are able and keeping the United States housing market active and healthy. As long as loans are originated in accord with guidelines, FHA and VA assume responsibility.

VA loans provide tangible demonstration of national gratitude for military service. Elimination of down payment offsets low compensation during service. VA loans out-perform FHA loans that have higher equity positions. Very possibly the loyalty between the military and Veteran's Administration results in superior performance.

Many FHA loans unlikely to perform per spreadsheet attributes in fact perform. High ratios may be offset by unusable or undisclosed income. Low credit scores may be impacted by limited credit experience, and derogatory credit may be attributable to helping out loved ones.

Successful government origination requires non-aggressive qualification. Flexibility on exceedingly liberal guidelines is excessively helpful. Justification for flexibility without a substantial equity position or other strong compensating factors is not warranted.

See *How to underwrite high risk loans*

What the AUS doesn't see

1. Questionable occupancy

2. Employment stability

3. Declining, unstable or unsustainable income

4. Whether qualifying income is unduly conservative or overly optimistic

5. Whether established credit is consistent with the borrower profile

6. Derogatory credit that creditor(s) suppressed, deleted because of technicalities in the dispute process, and other manifestations of

doctored credit

7. Whether the borrower is co-vested on verified accounts, and whether all funds are acceptably sourced

8. Whether the borrower has financial management skills

9. Whether the property has marketability issues

10. Whether the property has condition issues

11. Whether the property has health and safety issues

12. Whether the application appears sufficiently complete and accurate

13. Title and purchase contract issues

14. Inconsistencies and red flags

15. Whether the story of the loan is plausible

16. Fraud

This list is not comprehensive. The naive assumption that an AUS Accept decision guarantees performance has been proven invalid. The best decisions are made by a balance of rules and judgment.

AUS: pros and cons

I haven't wavered from believing that an AUS decision is better than a good underwriter on a bad day. I believe that AUS decisioning is predictive and even-handed at least for conforming product, and that smart minds continually work to make it better. Appropriate decisions are issued on the vast majority of loans, assuming input is accurate.

An AUS decision is limited by what it can't quantify, the subtleties of a loan that may give insight into intangibles like occupancy and integrity.

Unquestionably AUS decisioning has dumbed down the underwriter population—and senior management blind to AUS limitations. I remember describing a scary loan to my manager. (I was a first vice president and he was a senior vice president at the time.) He ended the conversation after I answered his only question, affirming there was an AUS Accept. Inexperienced or less assertive underwriters could construe that an AUS approval outweighs all other concerns.

Some of the post-AUS generation of underwriters are ill-equipped to manually underwrite. They see the AUS as the decision-maker and their role as ensuring complete and thorough documentation. I believe these tasks better align with a processor's job description. Underwriters should have the ability and authority to evaluate risk.

AUS decisioning will never be better than a good underwriter on a good or even average day.

Manual underwriting

Currently most loans are AUS underwritten. To ensure quality all loans including those with an AUS approval should be manually reviewed. Considerations should be the intangibles—stability, sustainability of income, creditworthiness, livability, whether occupancy is probable and whether fraud is improbable. The points in "What the AUS doesn't see" merit consideration.

The story of the loan matters. If the loan falls into the John and Mary Buy a House category, the manual review process should not take long. With salaried borrowers, responsible credit, affordability, traceable funds and a mainstream property, approval is a simple decision.

Manual underwriting restores underwriters to their original role— making good risk decisions. If there is concern with time necessary for analysis, it should be understood that the time spent in thinking is probably equivalent to the needless effort wasted in completing unnecessary worksheets and attending to superfluous documentation.

One size fits most

"One size fits all" isn't true for retail apparel or in the mortgage industry. Standardized guidelines across all loan amounts can be viewed as efficient simplification. Eliminating exceptions seems like an effective way of controlling risk. Neither is true.

One size shouldn't fit all when non-conforming guidelines align to conforming guidelines for consistency's sake. The average conforming loan has a lower equity position and fewer complicating factors. More inexperienced borrowers apply for conforming loans. A higher percentage of non-conforming borrowers are self-employed. Self-employed conforming borrowers generally have less complex tax returns. Non-conforming loans have a higher probability of corporate and partnership returns, trusts, alimony, income that is inconsistent, sheltered or deferred, and other infrequently-encountered circumstances. Non-conforming borrowers use business funds more often and have lesser need to liquidate investment or retirement savings.

Higher-end properties are more complex than mainstream properties. They have more and higher adjustments but typically have fewer condition issues. Non-mainstream properties in conforming areas have more impaired marketability than non-mainstream properties in non-conforming price brackets.

Eligibility for exception consideration should be extended on a broad basis. This does not mean that exception approval should be granted indiscriminately. Exception loans require thorough analysis and strong compensating factors. Exception underwriters must be both experienced and insightful; many competent underwriters lack the vision to assess exceptions. However, some loans out of accord with written guidelines have acceptable or even reduced risk.

Uniform guidelines and a limited tolerance for exceptions exclude worthy loans from approval.

Erroneous assumptions

1. Assuming that assets not on the application don't exist.

2. Believing there is only one correct figure for qualifying income.

3. Thinking that calculating qualifying income to the cent or DTI to two decimal places is a good use of time and reflects a high degree of competency.

4. Believing that the most conservative approach to qualifying income is always the best.

5. Believing that borrowers have limited ability to determine what they can afford, not taking into account that qualifying income may be a historic average or exclude other sources such as unseasoned income that will continue.

6. Accepting every letter of explanation at face value.

7. Disbelieving every letter of explanation.

8. Not distinguishing between declining income and fluctuating income.

9. Not recognizing that wealthy people may strategically minimize taxable income.

10. Believing that use of business funds is intrinsically risky, and that without an underwriter's detailed analysis, a business could easily fail.

11. Believing knowledge of the score replaces reading the credit report,

and knowledge of property value replaces reading the appraisal.

12. Believing that loans on atypical properties should not be approved.

13. Believing that the AUS approval ensures an acceptable risk. The more complex the transaction, the more thorough the manual evaluation should be.

CHAPTER 11
DECISIONING

The best figure for qualifying income

Those convinced that there is one correct figure for qualifying income value precision over judgment. Qualifying income is easier to calculate for borrowers who are salaried or work regular schedules, but even then there can be differences in how a partial month is quantified. The craft of underwriting comes into play when dealing with a borrower who has multiple components of income or irregular earnings.

For most borrowers, there is more than one defendable approach for qualifying income. However, valid approaches generally fall within a close range. Overly aggressive income qualification is a disservice to the borrower and lender. Overly conservative income qualification may cause a qualified borrower to be denied financing. Those focused on calculating qualifying income with exactitude may miss more relevant issues.

Testing qualifying income

Testing income requires calculating more than one approach and deciding which is the most appropriate. For salaried borrowers, test the previous year's W-2 earnings against year-to-date earnings. If current earnings are reasonably consistent with the previous year, using current base is supportable. The lower figure need not be used if the difference is a moderate increase in base pay. For employed borrowers with variable income, separately average both prior year's W-2s and current year-to-date to establish a trend line. With an appreciating trend, a twelve-month average of the most recent full year should be supportable, assuming appreciation is moderate and the year-to-date figure is at least consistent with the previous year.

Significantly increased income should be analyzed. Likely causes are a promotion or increased incentive pay, but the increase must be credibly supported and sustainable. A higher year-to-date average can be attributable to an annual bonus received during the early part of the year or seasonal overtime. Moving out of a trainee position (which also applies to a medical resident now fully credentialed) or into a management position generally justifies a larger bump in salary than standard step promotions.

Unseasoned employment complicates income testing and may present a stability issue. Income from previous employment is inapplicable unless the compensation level is dependent on personal effort such as auto sales or dental hygiene. Under normal circumstances, if the borrower has been employed for long enough to ensure a good fit, use base pay or average on-the-job income. A moderately increased earnings level is normal; most people who voluntarily change jobs do so for greater earnings potential. Questionable qualification more commonly occurs when job titles, functions or industry changes abruptly.

Averaging commission, bonus and overtime income requires consideration of seasonality, which varies from industry to industry. Sales of barbecues and Christmas trees peak at opposite times of the year; self-employed accountants generate considerably higher income during tax season. Averaging over two full years is the universally most acceptable approach.

For self-employed borrowers, see the *Reliability* section of *Evaluating Schedule Cs*.

Approaches to qualifying income

- Sources of income can be averaged over different periods of time when there is reasonable justification.

- Interest and dividend income should not be averaged over two years if earnings in the more current year are lower than the previous year, indicating deterioration of assets or reduced yield, or if all the assets were used to close. Income from retirement accounts should not be used in qualification unless the borrower is of retirement age.

- Income from capital gains is generally acceptable with a two-year pattern for the GSEs and a three year pattern for FHA, assuming remaining assets to assure continuing income. VA does not specify a time frame.

- Deriving rental income from Schedule E is preferable to taking 75% of gross rent less debt service. Unless there are extraordinary circumstances, real numbers are better than hypothetical numbers. Rental income from the most recent tax return year is usually most indicative of current rental income and expenses.

- When income is declining, use the more recent year. If the downtrend is severe, consider loan denial unless there is credible evidence that the trend has ended. See *Declining income*

- When a borrower's annual income is irregular, the most valid approach may be to average for longer than two years. The reason for the erratic pattern may help determine the number of years averaged. The most dated year should not have the highest income.

- Using a profit and loss statement to derive qualifying income is generally unacceptable. It is more defendable with documented gross income, a consistent net/gross ratio and CPA-written substantiation of increased profitability. If the loan is not originated for the portfolio, make sure the investor agrees with the rationale prior to close.

- If auto expenses are written off as a business expense, only the non-business portion need be included in debt service

- The best source of qualifying income for salaried borrowers or those receiving pension or social security benefits is not tax returns.

- If debt ratios don't work and there is alimony expense, see whether it is investor-acceptable to decrease alimony from income instead of using it as a debt. See *When alimony payments ruin ratios*

When income needn't be averaged

Some underwriters average out of habit. Averaging is not always necessary. For example:

- Use current base when the borrower is salaried with no evidence of instability or potential decline.

- For a seasoned hourly employee with an apparently consistent workweek, test year-to-date or previous year earnings to assure minimum seasonal fluctuation.

- Social security benefits or pensions for retirees need not be averaged. For annuity income, duration should be verified.

- For an applicant with base pay plus incentive earnings or overtime, only non-base income need be averaged. When base and incentive earnings are frequently readjusted, this approach has less value.

- In a normal real estate market, the most current full year average usually reflects the most current level of rental income and expenses, unless there are vacancy or disrepair issues.

- When there is declining income, the method of calculation should be considered in conjunction with the cause of the decline and whether it will continue, as well as the borrower's options if there is a continued decline. If risk is offset by deep equity and significant reserves, a one-year average from the most current tax year may be justified depending on the transaction type, i.e., not a cash-out refinance.

Ten thoughts on qualifying self-employed borrowers

1. Although self-employment is a risk factor, risk is relative to the profession, the term of self-employment and the stability of the income.

2. Tax returns don't have to be intimidating. Learn which numbers are relevant to the underwriting process and ignore the rest.

3. Start with all sources of potential qualifying income and eliminate those you can't use.

4. Unusable income may be used as a compensating factor.

5. Consider the trend.

6. Consider reliability.

7. For atypical situations, consider the best fit between the investor and borrower.

8. If the investor doesn't have a mandatory format, use any source of income that can be justified.

9. The easiest approach to justify is cash flow, as long as the business can afford the cash flow.

10. Aggressive qualifying income must be accompanied by strong compensating factors, one of which should be significant equity.

Debt ratios

Debt ratios reflect affordability. High debt ratios usually indicate questionable affordability. There may be exceptions. A low debt ratio with unstable income may be problematic, while a high debt ratio with ample liquidity is less challenging.

To personalize the impact of debt ratios, calculate increasing monthly obligations based on various percentages of your own personal gross income (e.g., 35%, 40%, 45% and 50%) and consider whether that level of obligations based on spendable income is feasible or too high to handle.

Many factors can offset high ratios—ample reserves, conservative qualifying income or additional income sources undisclosed or disregarded.

What is considered affordable varies by the time of origination. Pre-meltdown, equity loan programs allowed 45% DTI with standard pricing, 50% DTI with added pricing and up to 55% DTI on a restricted basis with higher added pricing. At the beginning of my career, target ratio thresholds started out as 25%/33%, increased to 30%/38%, and increased gradually until they skyrocketed. Post-meltdown, 43% became the Dodd-Frank standard.

Two sets of ratios

My version of creative underwriting is far removed from inflating income or recasting a letter of explanation. It has to do with presenting facts effectively and a good loan in its best light.

The standard industry approach to qualifying self-employed income is a two-year average. When a loan has identifiable strengths but an unimpressive DTI, calculate a second set of ratios using a less conservative approach to income. Potential rationales for approval could be an upward trend of profitability, decreasing or discretionary expenses, and DTI based on the more recent year being several points lower than a longer average.

When high ratios matter more or less

More Critical:

- questionable or unproven financial management skills

- fixed income combined with minimal reserves

- limited earning years combined with unimpressive savings

- above-average number of dependents

- at-risk employment or income combined with non-transferable skills

- unstable economy or declining real estate market

- wide gap between housing expenses and combined debt ratio (i.e., heavy credit user)

- rapid acquisition of real estate, cars or other possessions especially when combined with low reserves and property not in prime condition (instant investors, more common pre-meltdown)

Less Critical:

- appreciating income

- DTI calculated on a conservative basis or excluding unusable income

- proven ability to handle commensurate housing expense assuming income is stable and will continue

- proven financial management skills including respectable reserves

- ample reserves in tandem with equity

- cash business or discretionary business write-offs, e.g., travel, entertainment

- generous relatives with resources, as evidenced by a large gift toward down payment

The gifted child

The borrower was in her early thirties purchasing a condo in an upper-end neighborhood. Affordability was enabled by the 50% down payment. The borrower had stable employment, a high credit score and verified savings over twice gross annual salary, but could not qualify without help.

In the numerous lists of compensating factors, none to my knowledge mentions parents with considerable financial resources. Loving support extends past loan closing. In the event of hardship, parents will likely continue protecting their child and their investment. Even if they do not, equity would motivate property sale rather than loan default. Either circumstance is unlikely. The motivation for parental benevolence is protecting the child by ensuring affordability, which protects the lender as well.

*Lesson: **Financially secure and generous parents (or grandparents) are a silent compensating factor.***

Interest and dividend income to qualify

The GSEs mandated averaging interest and dividend earnings over two years on verified funds not required to close the loan. This was necessitated by contriving originators who previously used a 1/36 portion of verified reserves in superficial compliance with the three-year continuing income requirement. The tactic increased income but represented engineered qualification since only non-creditworthy borrowers would exhaust accumulated savings over the next three year period.

Averaging interest and dividend income is problematic in more than one respect. Qualification is more difficult when interest rates are low and is questionably sustainable when interest rates are high. The approach also fails to take into account principal, which may be unrealistic for asset-based borrowers. Asset dissipation is a better approach for those borrowers.

When interest and dividends are used to qualify, there also may be a pattern of recurring capital gains, which is typical for borrowers with significant investment income. Borrowers must have sufficient remaining assets to perpetuate capital gain income.

When alimony payments ruin ratios

All support obligations needn't be treated the same way. Alimony is tax-exempt, while child support is not. An approach aiding qualification is deducting the alimony payment from qualifying income instead of including it as a debt. This reduces the impact of the alimony payment on debt ratios. This approach is accepted by some investors (typically on non-conforming programs) and is justifiable—equivalent to grossing up non-taxable income.

259

Paying off debt to qualify

Paying off debt to qualify was more prevalent pre-meltdown when numerous borrowers relied on converted equity to pay off credit cards and auto loans, sometimes repeatedly. Since prudent spending has become more widespread, the underwriter's task is simplified somewhat. Debt consolidation likely increased on purchases as tolerance for higher ratios has decreased. In any case, underwriters should be aware of what type of debt is more likely to recur.

The answer is revolving debt. A borrower is less likely to cut back on shopping, dining out and getaways than to purchase a car or take on other installment debt.

On loan requests requiring revolving debt consolidation, an explanation for the cause of the debt may shed light. One-time events such as wedding expenses or property upgrades are less likely to recur. Property upgrades have the benefit of increasing property value to a greater or lesser extent, or sometimes not at all. Property maintenance may not enhance property value but prevents value erosion. Random spending is more difficult to curtail, especially when the borrower's concept of normal matches the underwriter's concept of excessive.

The life event

The borrowers were making a lateral move, selling their condo and buying a similarly-valued detached house. Their year-old child would soon be able to enjoy a backyard. The sole roadblock was the wife's income. She was a self-employed therapist, and during the time she was confined to bed rest and tending the new baby, her income had declined substantially.

But income was consistent prior to when the pregnancy-related complications began and in the profit and loss statement covering the most recent nine months. Based on a before and after average, the loan was approvable.

Lesson: To be equitable to new parents, time periods used to derive income need not be consecutive. This principle can be applicable to other life circumstances as well

See *Pregnancy and gender bias*

Representative income

The industry standard for averaging income is two years unless a shorter term is permitted through AUS approval. An alternative non-consecutive period can be justified if earnings have been disrupted by a relatively short-term life event. Averaging two years or longer is preferable, and less than eighteen months is chancy. Resumed income should extend at least six months; longer is preferable. Income after the event should be relatively consistent with income before, not higher unless the more recent period is documented by tax returns and transcripts. (If this documentation is unavailable, average income before the event and include the P&L to demonstrate improved income.) Third party documentation, if available, plus a written explanation of the life event should be provided.

Use of representative income is appropriate under limited circumstances. The applicable source of income should be seasoned and sustainable. The borrower should have at least twenty percent equity in the property. Although significant savings are desirable, this may be unrealistic since savings might have been depleted while income was interrupted. Credit quality should not have deteriorated. Cash proceeds may be necessary to consolidate debt, but substantial cash-in-hand elevates risk.

If the loan is being originated for sale, do not assume an investor will concur with this non-traditional approach. It may be helpful to compare the situation with a leave of absence followed by return to the workforce for a salaried borrower. The investor's comfort level should correlate to the length of the combined time periods.

The graphic design library

The graphic designer grew up in the Midwest with no inclination for cheating on tax returns. Having taken two semesters of college-level accounting (as recommended by his MBA father), he was also aware that deductions range from overly aggressive to overly conservative.

After the designer turned freelancer, built-in book shelves were installed covering most of the wall space of his large in-home office. As his business grew, the shelves of the design library filled.

Some strategy was involved in writing off the cost of the books. The designer and his underwriter wife recognized that deductions appearing excessive could result in an IRS audit. When his wife discovered another potential expense category in a borrower's returns, she called him from the office. Both agreed that "Research" was a viable alternative to "Books and

Periodicals."

Lesson: Accounting and underwriting are both fields where there is an element of craft, which should not be confused with creativity.

Expenses

Expense write-offs decrease taxable income and consequently qualifying income. For conforming loans, there is increased flexibility on non-reimbursed employee expenses, reflecting Agency recognition that deductions can be optional for the employee. For self-employed non-conforming borrowers, there is less flexibility. In assessing risk, it can be worthwhile to consider not only net income but evaluate some categories of expenses:

Start-up expenses: New businesses have expenses that are partially or entirely non-recurring. This encompasses tangibles (furnishings and office equipment) and also non-tangibles such as legal and marketing costs. Newer businesses require scrutiny because of higher risk than seasoned businesses, but start-up costs merit some flexibility. This is a circumstance where first and second year tax returns and a credible P&L should be trended. With increasing per-month profitability over three earnings periods (not necessarily twelve months each), net/gross ratios may increase because of healthy growth and decreased start-up expenses, not because of an inflated P&L. If the P&L shows a credible increase in profitability, consider disregarding the initial year's tax return in qualification.

Discretionary expenses: Not all expenses are equal. Some are essential, and some are not. Discretionary expenses can be predictable, especially with higher write-offs for travel, entertainment and also continuing education, mandatory in some professions including medicine and public accountancy, and often conducted at travel destinations. When discretionary expenses have been identified, the critical decision is how to handle them. Adding them back would probably be considered overly-aggressive; however, citing them as a compensating factor for higher ratios or presenting a second set of ratios is not. See *Two sets of ratios*

Non-recurring expenses: The GSE's have allowed exclusion of non-recurring expenses, usually capital improvements, on investment properties. There undoubtedly are parallel situations that are not property-related. If excluded from qualifying income, justify in writing.

Non-cash expenses: Don't forget depletion and amortization, appreciation's less prominent siblings.

Counter-offers

Counter-offers are too often overlooked as an alternative to denial. Under some circumstances a lower loan-to-value, reduced cash-out (e.g., enough to consolidate debt but less cash-in-hand) or a different loan term could make a difficult deal approvable.

Years ago at the end of a long day, I wanted to deny a loan because debt ratios were too high. A short conversation followed. "Anne, how about moving it from fifteen years to thirty?" "Great idea, Doug."

Marginal loans meeting guidelines

Denying a loan that is borderline in several respects but meets standard guidelines takes effort to justify. "Layered risk" does not communicate clearly to the borrower and would likely be vigorously contested by the loan officer. A detailed explanation such as "combination of high LTV, recent untimely credit and barely adequate reserves" provides specific rationale.

An AUS Accept decision on the loan complicates matters. If there is a significant negative factor not quantifiable in the AUS decision (such as poor employment stability, an unconvincing letter of explanation or a neglected property), denial is more easily justified. With an AUS Accept, a minor concern and documentation in full compliance with the AUS decision, approval may be justified.

Manipulated qualification

Manipulated or engineered qualification occurs when an AUS approval cannot be obtained using standard underwriting practices. Borrowers are urged to pay down debt and underwriters are pressured to increase qualifying income. Whether this is acceptable depends on the amount of effort required and whether misrepresentation is necessary. On a loan with merit, using a less conservative approach to qualifying income or paying off a debt or two is not a compromise.

Examples of manipulated qualification are:

1. Using qualifying income investors would find unsupportable.

2. Understating housing expense or non-mortgage debt.

3. Disputing legitimately derogatory credit to elevate the score, or using

rapid re-score to determine how many derogatory accounts should be disputed and how much debt consolidated to make the loan work.

4. Adding the borrower to a relative's depository account or representing borrowed funds as gifted.

5. Coaching letters of explanation. They should state the truth, not an edited version structured by an originator.

6. Cancelling the loan and applying elsewhere for a new start, which includes fresh documentation. Not all mortgage inquiries arise from searching for the lowest interest rate.

These efforts can result in a transaction bearing scant resemblance to the original and requiring so many AUS versions the investor is alerted.

The days when appraisers could be begged to increase appraised value are over. Suspect income documentation can be sussed out through transcripts or testing net pay against depository statements. Improved loan quality requires integrity in origination.

There is a difference between presenting an acceptable loan in its best light and massaging a bad loan until it becomes approvable. This topic is not part of the "Fraud" chapter because it is not a black-and-white issue.

Smart loans on tough properties

Examples of challenging properties are over-improvements or houses with impaired marketability. An equitable solution is reduction of LTV to the level that the lender is made whole without financial loss in the event of default. For example, with a $650,000 over-improvement in a neighborhood of $500,000 properties, a safe level of financing for the lender would be a loan amount of approximately $400,000. The calculation should take into account potential servicing charges and fees (e.g., late charges, lapsed payments and foreclosure costs) and to a lesser extent the strength and stability of the borrower. When marketability is severely impaired, the potential of extended lapsed payments before an interested buyer steps in could preclude loan approval.

The qualification enigma

The processor asked me to review tax returns to explain how a loan she couldn't qualify was acceptable to the underwriter and purchased by an investor. The borrower was a 43-year-old doctor moving up from a $750,000 condo to a $1,750,000 detached residence. He also owned two residential rentals and two parcels of farmland. All properties were unencumbered and his net worth was just under $4,000,000.

After reviewing the tax returns, I identified four potential sources of additional income:

1. Two Schedule E investments had losses carried over.
2. A third Schedule E investment had a loss labeled PAL (passive activity loss).
3. A Schedule E rental added in the more current year, farmland on large acreage, yielded rental income several times higher than the smaller agricultural acreage.
4. The application showed salaried income at $75,000 annually, higher than either tax return year.

My conclusions were:

1. Losses carried over occurred in years previous to the year considered in qualification. Therefore, they can be disregarded. (An alternative term is losses carried forward.)
2. Passive losses on investment may be non-cash losses. Business returns would be required to verify this.
3. The fourth rental property increased Schedule E profitability considerably. If both pieces of farmland generate continuing income, the earlier year would be non-representative, and an average for the more current year could be used in qualification. (This loan was originated when two year averages on rental income were standard.)
4. Move-up could correlate to a move-up in compensation. A $75,000 annual salary is representative for a medical resident or a post-doctoral researcher. After 37 years of education, the doctor deserved a major bump in compensation.

Lessons:

1. **Transferring numbers from tax returns onto tax return worksheets makes a mechanical process out of what should be a mental exercise. Understanding the borrower as represented in the loan application is the first step in qualification.**

2. **Accurate data on years of education helped solve qualification on this loan. With that field deleted, when income appears too low as well as excessive, additional research is warranted.**

3. **Asking the underwriter directly could have resulted in immediate enlightenment for the processor and increased skill in making complex loans work.**

CHAPTER 12

THE MELTDOWN AND AFTER

Learning from our mistakes

The overriding lesson from the meltdown is that abandoning prudent lending to facilitate homeownership was a terrible idea.

Remedies have caused harm as well. Undisclosed obligations have resulted in aggressive scrutiny of expenditures. Inability to repay on stated income loans has resulted in over-documenting income and inflexibility on debt-to-income ratios. Self-limited credit for qualified borrowers has resulted in arbitrary trade-line restrictions or pricing adds. Farfetched rationales employed to justify repurchases have been applied to new originations. Restrictions on projected income do not distinguish between commissions for a new salesperson and a retiree's social security benefits.

Institutions, legislators and regulatory agencies have failed to recognize that the cure can be as bad as the disease.

See *Intense scrutiny of depository statements; Shallow credit, pre- and post-meltdown;* and *Projected income.*

What really led to the meltdown

A change in attitude by Fannie Mae foreshadowed the meltdown. Their focus on single-loan variances (their term for exceptions) changed from the merits of the loan to whether the borrower or the property location was underserved. The shift from loan quality to inclusiveness impacted the American economy and international economy as well.

Fannie Mae's attitudinal change reflected the government's direction to broaden homeownership. The initiative was well-meaning, but implementation led to disaster. Relaxing risk controls was a horrific decision. Irresponsible credit usage became acceptable under subprime guidelines. Unverifiable or inadequate income was cured by stated programs. Inability or unwillingness to provide down payment was no longer an impediment. (Recommended reading on this topic is Gretchen

267

Mortenson and Joshua Rosner's Reckless Endangerment, an informative and readable book.)

The government's direction was embraced by the mortgage industry and facilitated by Wall Street which provided voluminous funds for investment. Pleasing the regulators and generating profits were a tempting combination. Mortgage instruments facilitating qualification were created. Some were modifications of programs with successful performance histories. Three- and five-year ARMs joined seven- and ten-year ARMs on the adjustable menu. Teaser rates inched lower and lower. Negative amortizing loans—initially the preference of financially sophisticated borrowers—became the choice of borrowers who didn't or couldn't read; more than a few were unaware they could end up owing more than they borrowed.

Economic consequences were magnified by over-dependence on AUS decisioning. Some originators sincerely believed that automation replaced risk evaluation. AUS engines make good decisions most of the time, but not always. The quality of decision falls when matrices expand and verifications are waived. In some companies underwriters were replaced by "funderwriters," a blended position with judgment taking third place to high production and timely closing. When the anointed risk engines granted loan approval and underwriters disagreed, underwriters often lost the battle.

Government's well-intended motivation of expanding homeownership was matched by the industry's motivation of greed. Management eagerness to please the regulators and justify their own increased compensation were embraced by front-line originators who realized that with aggressive qualification, their compensation would expand commensurately. Origination mindset disintegrated from tolerant flexibility to uncontrolled abandon.

The enthusiastic purchase by institutional investors of progressively increasing numbers of securitized loans fueled origination volume. It is questionable whether their due diligence entailed reviewing spreadsheets or sampling loan files. If so, disappointment with loan quality should have surfaced much sooner, eliminating the need for subsequent litigation after rampant defaults.

As an industry, we were too acquiescent. What started out as expanded flexibility ended up with complete erosion of standards. Not all originators chose to participate. Enthusiasm was regional but the most reluctant originators were located in stable areas with relatively low loan volume.

Although finger-pointers designated major lenders as scapegoats for the meltdown, there is a longer list of responsible parties:

- government officials sacrificing prudent lending in the interest of expanded home ownership

- regulators who didn't regulate

- borrowers misrepresenting employment, earnings, assets, property holdings and occupancy

- borrowers who failed to read their loan applications before signing

- GSE management diverting profits into bonuses more appropriately retained for future loss reserves

- developers believing the fevered appetite for homeownership would perpetuate

- real estate agents, mortgage brokers and loan originators who coached borrowers in perpetrating fraud or facilitated the act in their name

- everyone who believed that housing prices would continue to appreciate indefinitely

See *The geography of home ownership*

The table-mate's daughter's loan

At an event with assigned tables, my opening comments included my mortgage banking career. The man across the table responded that the industry "was still screwed up." When I requested an example, he responded that his daughter while in law school (which turned out to be in 2006) wanted to buy a condo. After committIng to buy one unit, she found another unit in the same project she wanted even more. She ended up buying both with first liens and "second liens for the down payment" from the same national lender. The man said there was no way his daughter could qualify for either loan since she was in law school. He added that she still owned both units as rentals, and there had never been a default.

The most tactful response I could come up with was "You've given me a lot to think about." The truth would have been inappropriate dinner conversation.

His points:

1. *The lender should have known the daughter was unqualified.*
2. *The lender was lucky to be repaid.*

My points:

1. *The daughter had to be complicit. She could not qualify without misrepresentation, and a first-year law student should know better.*

269

2. *Both loans continue performing because the units were a sound investment.*

Lessons:

1. *The lender should have been aware of simultaneous applications. Lack of controls resulted in 100% financing on two units if the borrower's father's statement about lack of down payment was correct. Misrepresented employment and income are certain, and occupancy misrepresentation is probable.*

2. *The borrower is as responsible as the lender.*

The geography of the meltdown

Until recently I believed the the meltdown was concentrated in "the five ugly states"—Arizona, California, Florida, Nevada and Michigan. Michigan's dynamics were intensified by economic dependence on the auto industry. In the four other states, supply and demand simply went completely out of whack.

I stand corrected.

The meltdown was concentrated in eight states, the four sand states (California, Florida, Arizona and Nevada) and the four rust-belt states (Michigan, Ohio, Illinois and Indiana.) Between 1999 and 2004, rust-belt states had even higher loss severities than sand states. Severity is measured by the percentage of unpaid principal balance lost at the time of default. Between 2011 and 2013, six of the eight most affected states had not only recovered but had severity ratings below 1999 to 2004 levels. The exceptions were Michigan and to a lesser extent Arizona.

A second group of states was impacted significantly. Severity rates for Idaho, Maryland, Mississippi, Montana, Oregon, Utah, Virginia, Washington, Wyoming and Washington DC more than doubled at the peak of the meltdown (2007 to 2008) from the years preceding it (1999 to 2004).

Every state was adversely impacted to some extent. The average percentage increase in defaults between pre-meltdown and peak was 61%. Curiously, the lowest differential belongs to Indiana; this was due to high severity before the meltdown, not strong recovery since.

Statistical analysis was provided by *Loss Severity on Residential Mortgages* (February 2015) authored by Laurie Goodman and Jun Zhu of the Urban Institute using data provided by Freddie Mac covering 1999 through 2013.

The geography of homeownership

It seems logical that homeownership would be prevalent in developed countries and a high standard of living would correlate to a high percentage of homeownership. This is untrue. Wikipedia lists the percentages for 46 countries at 10-year intervals and some of the results are baffling. In 2012, the United States (64.5%) and the United Kingdom (64.6%) placed 38th and 37th out of 48 countries, and Canada (67.6%) placed 32nd. The top five spots are held by Romania (95.6%), Lithuania (92.2%), Slovakia (90.5%), Singapore (90.3%) and China (90%). The lowest rated of the 46 are Austria (57.3%), South Korea (54.2%), Germany (53.3%), Hong Kong (51.0%) and Switzerland (44%). Since 1960, the United States rose gradually with some peaks and valleys from 62.1% to a high of 69% in 2004.

Renting is not necessarily a negative. Positives are flexibility, no maintenance expenses, no long-term indebtedness and easy ability to relocate. Rent-control enables below-market housing expense; it also facilitates the renters' ability to save or squander. Non-homeownership is a smart or tempting financial decision for many people.

Not all tenants should be classified as stymied homeowners. Those with the motivation and the ability to repay should be encouraged toward homeownership. Needless obstacles should be removed. The others should not be considered failures.

Comments on the source material:

1. The 46 countries are located in North America, South America (Brazil only), Europe and Asia plus Australia and New Zealand. Choice appears to be countries with available data.

2. Figures for countries at the high end of the list may be inaccurate, less so Singapore.

The British test

I believed that England suffered from the economic consequences of the meltdown, but did not participate in its creation. I was set straight by Phil, a Manchester resident, who explained that in the quest for continually accelerating loan volume, England's compromises mirrored those of the country they colonized.

Phil's college training was in accountancy, but after analyzing his clients' financials he switched to the garment industry. In his early sixties, Phil and his wife Michelle decided to scale down their business and extract equity from long-held investment properties. Despite predicting their values would be under-estimated, Phil did not anticipate further problems. Loan qualification was considerably more difficult since the meltdown, but it was justified by decades of financial responsibility, good personal net worth, substantial remaining equity, positive cash flow, desirable locations, ongoing upkeep and stable tenancy. But Phil was unaware of the British industry test used to support full repayment, the borrower's age at the end of amortization. Phil would be in his eighty-seventh year, which exceeded the maximum for loan qualification.

The test is being reconsidered. A maximum number may be raised because of widespread complaints of ageism. Phil and Michelle are hopeful.

Some American mortgage executives would view the British test as a brilliant method of controlling risk, but unfortunately impossible to implement in the States since it is discriminatory and illegal.

How the meltdown affected exceptions

When exceptions were granted on aggressive lending programs, loans predictably failed to perform. Blame placed on the easy availability of exceptions was more accurately the fault of expanded program parameters.

Years later exceptions remain under close scrutiny. What is not considered is that the nature of exceptions has changed. A typical pre-meltdown exception was LTV 5% over maximum, sometimes accompanied by a credit score 8 points below minimum. Current exceptions are more often waiving an overlay or an internal guideline. Matrix exceptions are infrequent.

Those afraid of exceptions may attempt to impose eligibility criteria for exception submission. Curtailing exception requests on a blanket basis (all cash-out refinances, every investment property or credit scores under a certain level) is a bad strategy. This tactic defies the purpose of exception underwriting—to allow approval for loans with too much merit to deny. The more effective control is to insist on strong compensating factors and high probability of timely performance.

The triple exception

Six borrowers applied for a 17% purchase money loan on an investment property, a charming Southern house selling for $1,325,000. Two borrowers were retired; their only contribution was the $1,100,000 down payment in a 1031 exchange account. The other four borrowers were their two daughters and their husbands. One husband was a named partner in a law firm with 30 years tenure. The other husband was a physician *and wealth management customer of the lender. The two younger couples had combined earnings of $1,000,000 annually, more than enough to qualify. The lawyer was willing to provide personal tax returns and K-1s but didn't understand why full partnership returns were required. Other complications were that the lender limited the number of borrowers to four (except on refinance transactions where the bank held the existing lien), and investment properties were ineligible for exception consideration.*

I encouraged the sales manager to send the loan over. There was no possibility it wouldn't perform and I suspected there wouldn't be a tenant in the property. The sales manager confirmed intended use was as a second home for the daughters and their families when they visit the parents, who live about an hour away.

Sadly this loan cancelled before the exception was submitted. The borrowers decided to pay cash for the property—probably because of excessive documentation requests.

Lesson: Requesting additional documentation is an effective tactic for making marginal loans disappear. The tactic should be avoided on strong loans.

The disease and the cure

The rampant imposition of rules after the meltdown was as well-intended as extending home ownership. In the process, judgment skills were suppressed. Mechanical underwriting was accompanied by disengaged brains. The emphasis changed from decision-making to data-entry. Unflinching adherence to rules rendered underwriters not only dumbed down but numbed out. Many of the best went to work for portfolio lenders or retired. When no one was left to answer questions, underwriters stopped asking.

The near-future retiree

The loan was a 45% purchase transaction on a second home with an 820 score, a 15-year loan term and a 14% DTI. Funds for down payment were proceeds of sale of the borrower's residence, and DTI was calculated from retirement benefits from the borrower's lengthy service as a senior-level government employee. The borrower provided written explanation that he would be living rent-free with relatives for a period to be determined. It was apparent he was retiring at an unspecified date.

This loan was ultimately lost because there was no established

273

retirement date or verified receipt of retirement income. Neither mattered,
since the borrower could qualify on current or retirement income and was
content with second-home pricing.

Lesson: Controls implemented to protect borrowers can work to their
disadvantage.

The Dodd Frank remedy

One repercussion of the meltdown was the Dodd Frank legislation.
When irresponsible governance in the mortgage industry surfaced,
Congress passed the Dodd Frank bill to correct the situation. It had good
intent, but legislators couldn't recognize that underwriting based on
stringent rules can be a disservice to qualified borrowers. Flexibility is
allowed on non-compliant loans classified as ATR (ability to repay), but
originators have additional loss exposure so borrowers pay higher costs for
what is categorized as increased risk.

Ability to repay is not a new concept. The phrase "the desire and ability
to repay" is engraved in my memory from the very first underwriting
manual I read. The 43% threshold resulted in inequitable implementation.
Fannie Mae, Freddie Mac, FHA and VA could exceed that threshold for a
limited period of time under a provision dubbed "Temp QM." Under Temp
QM, FHA loans allow DTIs over 50% at 96.5% LTV with a minimum 580
credit score and minimal reserves. Meanwhile the GSEs have ratcheted
down to 45%, even when accompanied by substantial equity, an exemplary
credit score and impressive reserves.

Profit and loss statements have been an industry anomaly for
decades. Traditionally P&Ls were required but ignored when it came to
qualification. With AUS underwriting, P&Ls were optional on numerous
loans. With Dodd Frank, they are mandatory for all self-employed
borrowers and ignored unless they reduce qualifying income, which occurs
infrequently.

The industry has been punished for bad decision-making. Good parents
know that penalties should not be permanent. Dodd Frank should be
revoked or substantially amended. No doubt some lenders will continue
enforcing even its most purposeless precepts.

Why 43% shouldn't be viewed in isolation

Dodd Frank's debt ratio message is that 42.9% represents responsible decisioning and 43.1% represents irresponsible decisioning. The exception is AUS-blessed loans, possibly temporarily if Dodd Frank continues in force. In the interim, it is inequitable that lenders have limited exposure on AUS-approved government loans with inarguably high risk, but no safe harbor for lower-risk loans with stronger ability to repay.

Higher DTI does not predict poor loan performance when accompanied by high equity, ample reserves or conservatively-derived qualifying income. The 43% threshold penalizes creditworthy borrowers, either with loan denial or inflated pricing.

Empowerment versus rules, a fairy tale

Once upon a time underwriters were empowered to make good decisions and occasionally break a rule or two. This was taken for granted until a period of insanity reigned. Some people believe the reign of insanity was cured by the institution of very tight rules. Others believe a new version of insanity prevails, and in order for the industry's story to end happily ever after, additional evolution is necessary.

Good decisioning requires a balance of rules and judgment. The rules that led to the meltdown were so relaxed that they weren't rules at all. After the meltdown, rules were restored with a vengeance. The forces in power believed the more rules and less empowerment, the safer the industry is. Exceptions were believed to embody empowerment, and a double exception was assumed to be near-fatal. The forces in charge viewed rules as sacrosanct and didn't consider their effect on individual loans because they never looked at individual loans.

Under some circumstances rules matter less. Those of us who have reviewed thousands of loans look forward to the day when worthy loans aren't denied, when over-documentation and excessive conditioning are forgotten, and when the balance between rules and judgment is restored.

Encouraging bad behavior?

Cousin Gail's friends were angry. The couple wanted to buy a retirement house, sell their current residence, quit work and retire—in that order. They never anticipated not qualifying for a mortgage.

Before Dodd Frank, some lender would have qualified them on verified imminent retirement earnings while offsetting debt service on their current home with market rent. Ability to repay would be taken into account without the legislated mandate of Ability to Repay.

Without compromising the truth, the couple's best course currently would be purchasing their retirement home for cash and obtaining permanent financing after their primary residence sold and retirement income started.

Compromising the truth (which they were unwilling to do) would offer several alternatives. The most deceptive would be a cash-out refinance on the current home without disclosing pending retirement or purchase of another home. Somewhat less deceptive would be purchasing the retirement home as a second home, assuming they could qualify with both payments, and occupancy as a second home was convincing.

Cousin Gail's friends are not marginal in any respect. They likely would be exemplary borrowers unless they went for the all-cash purchase and decided a mortgage isn't worth the hassle.

Lesson: Years before the meltdown, make-sense loans required overall merit. The level of quality deteriorated incrementally, and by the meltdown make-sense decisions were synonymous with compromised quality. The original concept is worthy of reconsideration.

Three eras in recent industry history

Long before the meltdown: **Sanity**
Leading up to the meltdown: **Chaos**
As a result of the meltdown: **Rigidity**

Opportunistic origination

The borrowers were a married couple, both physicians. A national bank assessed them a quarter point add to fee for inadequate established credit on a jumbo purchase transaction. Inadequate credit consisted of one spouse's single personal trade-line, a seasoned revolving account with a $10,000 high credit limit from another national bank. It was opened when she completed her medical training. Her other two trade-lines were authorized user accounts with her husband. LTV was 70%, the lower of the two borrowers' scores was 775, DTI was below 35%, and reserves of approximately $350,000 were ironically on deposit with the lender. The $10,000 high credit limit evidenced creditor confidence and evidently met her needs. Although a quarter point seems relatively inconsequential, it was a costly charge on a jumbo loan with minimal risk. See *Normal credit usage* and *Shallow credit, pre- and post-meltdown*

This story is not an anomaly. Originators have used Dodd Frank constraints plus outdated standards of normalcy to their financial advantage. Niche lenders created special programs targeted for non-QM eligible borrowers. DTI over 43%, less than two years' employment, and the self-employed unable to qualify on a two-year historic average evidently justify premium pricing despite offsetting strengths.

Regulators and consequently auditors view added pricing as legitimate. Performance far exceeds originations during the era of insanity as well as current FHA originations. Risk-based pricing has gone awry.

Cleaning up the mess

Managing employees tasked with reviewing post-meltdown buyback requests was an eye-opener. My underwriting point of view had to be adjusted, since minimizing loan repurchases required defending rather than identifying risk. My teams reviewed loan files to determine whether default was caused by the loan attributes (which investors were aware of before purchase from the spreadsheet) or deficient origination.

On more than a minority of loans, the investors submitted evidence of blatant misrepresentation. Incomes were doubled and tripled, job titles were inflated and other sources of income were fabricated. Every time I visit Costco I recall the borrower who was represented as a marketing executive who was really a tire installer. Rental properties weren't disclosed; some borrowers omitted ten or more. My conclusion some borrowers were as culpable for the meltdown as some originators.

Additional insight was gained years afterward at a party. Chatting with a friend's friend, I mentioned having worked in the mortgage industry. She had a friend who worked in the industry too. She explained that her friend worked for a national lender but left the industry because she was uncomfortable with what she was doing. She further explained that the friend's responsibilities included making up applications and other paperwork. This shocked me. I naively had believed borrowers were coached, but not that lenders—or their rogue employees—executed the fabrication. Another casual conversation with an industry acquaintance revealed that one of her co-workers had the ability to modify decisioned loans in their company's computer system. Conditions were waived, and denials were turned into approvals.

Cleaning up the industry is more effective from the inside than the outside. Looking at defaulted loans for close to a year was a lesson in origination gone wrong.

Who isn't responsible

Underwriters. If anyone had asked us, we would have told them too much flexibility isn't good for the industry or for borrowers.

Can it happen again?

I had a conversation about the meltdown with an Ivy League-educated businessman. He predicted that it could recur. I am more optimistic.

His case was supported by a business plan he explored. Energy auditing was effective for businesses, and it might work for homeowners as well. Customer benefits were energy preservation and cost savings. The white paper had been presented to business partners and financial backers, and the response was encouraging. Bankers were enthusiastic. Not only could they provide financing for the homeowners, but they could bundle and sell off the loans. These conversations occurred in 2012 and 2013, several years after the meltdown. As far as the businessman was concerned, the bankers' enthusiasm could be history repeating itself.

The mortgage industry is cyclical in multiple respects. Winters are quieter than summers, interest rates ratchet up and inch down, housing prices appreciate and decline. All are inevitable. What is not inevitable is erosion of quality standards. As long as the industry evaluates borrower credit and affordability, sources funds and verifies equity—that is, does not compromise the underwriting process—the meltdown should not recur.

Appraisal post-meltdown

Very possibly the most effective post-meltdown improvements were implemented in appraisal. Over the last decade, appraisal quality has vastly improved. This is a result of better automated tools, more stringent appraisal and quality control requirements, shared databases identifying appraisers with unacceptable work, and mortgage industry acceptance and understanding. Those with inferior work have been culled out and are continually being culled out as a result of the process.

Most of the content in the previous paragraph was suggested by a close industry friend. She was a senior manager in subprime before the meltdown, transitioned to prime after the meltdown and in the last few years worked on a temporary basis (her choice, so she could have summers off) for a business bank with a predominantly entertainment industry clientele. Her span of expertise from troubled to financially complex borrowers is impressive.

I shared her thoughts with another industry friend, a senior manager in the appraisal industry. He agreed, commenting that appraisal quality has improved because of increased technology, pre-delivery quality control, online access to more data services and especially since the implementation of Fannie Mae's Collateral Underwriter.

The improved system is not perfect. Appraisals have become considerably more costly, turn-time can be excessive, appraisal assignments are not always matched to appraiser competency, the most skilled appraisers are retiring, and accreditation requires too much formal education and too rigorous on-the-job training. But these issues should be surmountable without impairing appraisal quality and integrity.

If only the mortgage industry adjusted as well.

How to fix what's broken

Nullifying Dodd Frank will not cure the industry but is a good first step. The mindset of originators, especially excessively risk-adverse major banks, needs to be re-calibrated. Next steps are as follows:

1. Realize that rigidity can be as harmful as excessive flexibility.

2. Emphasize judgment skills in underwriter training. Time can be reallocated from process step training.

3. Share "the why" with everyone involved in origination.

4. Recognize that property review is essential to risk assessment. A hand's-off policy for underwriters is justified regarding requests for value increases but not for clarifications about the property.

5. Ensure that appraisal management companies understand that disallowing lenders to select the appraiser does not require random assignment of appraisers. Appraiser assignment should correlate with depth of experience, geographic expertise and competency in atypical property types.

6. Leverage the experience of mature and insightful underwriters before they retire. They can bridge the knowledge gap exacerbated by AUS decisioning, stated programs and subprime programs.

7. Retrain loan officers on the value of a complete application. Reinforce that it is not optional.

8. Allow underwriters to choose between a tax return worksheet and an analysis customized for the borrower's particular circumstances.

9. Dispense with mandatory usage of business fund spreadsheets, investment property analysis forms, salaried and self-employed borrower worksheets and the like. A seasoned underwriter unable to assess use of business funds without a worksheet deserves a change in job title. A short written commentary should suffice.

10. Dispense with the "one size fits all" approach to guidelines. Conforming and non-conforming loans have some overlap but different borrower and property profiles. Either assign underwriters by product, or identify underwriters capable of handling more than one set of guidelines.

11. Remove the stigma from exceptions.

12. Recognize that borrowers are negatively impacted by changes intended to prevent recurrence of the meltdown. Qualified borrowers are excluded from homeownership or pay premium pricing. Those who qualify undergo a needlessly tortuous origination process. If expanded homeownership remains a goal, emphasis should be shifted to innovative lending programs such as the Wealth Building Home Loan, a 15-year loan with no down payment and a reduced P&I payment enabled by the borrower's contribution for a multi-year buy-down.

CHAPTER 13

BORROWERS

Borrowers are not idiots

Early into underwriting, I observed that the vast majority of borrowers are not idiots. Despite exposure to a wider range of borrowers and property locations, the conviction has not changed.

Most borrowers know what they can afford. A 38% DTI may be too high for some while a 44% DTI may be within easy grasp for others. This depends on the strata of income and how discretionary income is spent. It is also dependent on how qualifying income is calculated. Averaging historic income and worst-casing debt can make good borrowers appear risky. Guidelines should not be abandoned, but what appears questionably affordable to some may be no problem for the borrower.

Relatively few borrowers bankrupt their businesses to come up with a down payment. Excluding cash-out transactions, borrowers refinance to reduce their payment or repayment term.

The unabridged version of "the borrower is not an idiot" is "borrowers know what they can afford unless they are stupid or larcenous." The underwriter has to distinguish the difference. Stupidity is demonstrated by poor credit and financial management. Larceny translates to fraudulent loans.

Unless there are concerns with ability to repay or integrity, or minimal equity, the borrower deserves the benefit of the doubt.

Borrower behavior post-meltdown

Borrower behavior has changed as much as the mortgage industry has. Manifestations include restrained credit usage, older first-time home-buyers, more prudent purchase of second homes and investment properties, and fewer debt consolidation and cash-out refinances.

A June 2015 New York Times article headlined "After an Era of Ups and Downs, Home Prices Return to Sanity" highlighted a married couple purchasing in Florida. They created spreadsheets determining what they could afford, compared the cost of renting versus buying even incorporating HOA fees into their calculations, and ended up purchasing for $23,000 less than the $215,000 prior-approved amount. These borrowers appear more diligent than most, but today's borrower is considerably more responsible than the typical borrower a decade ago.

Borrowers who lost our respect with the meltdown have re-earned our respect since.

Honoring the borrower

Behind every loan application is at least one human being. The industry's responsibility to the borrower includes:

1. Ensure that the borrower's voice is represented in the loan file, notably on letters of explanation.

2. Ensure that there is benefit to the borrower. On a refinance, a lower interest rate or reduced payment is inadequate justification. Remaining loan term and cost of origination matter also. Borrowers may be unaware that prolonged payments thwart the ultimate goal of full repayment.

3. Discuss affordability with marginal borrowers. Additional information, possibly an imminent promotion or a roommate sharing expenses, may offset concerns. Before any discussion, review the file to see whether income was conservatively derived, will soon be increasing or if unusable income exists.

4. Take into account that the borrower is probably unfamiliar with industry jargon. Acronyms enable time-efficient communication with co-workers, but most borrowers have no clue what DTI stands for. Even "reserves" understood in other contexts can flummox them.

5. Be prepared to explain paperwork sent to the borrower from disclosures to the appraisal. Some borrowers will want to understand; most won't. (The closing agent usually handles closing documents.)

6. Do not hesitate to hand off questions you are unable to answer competently. If workload allows, listen to the correct answer so your expertise increases.

7. If there are complaints about too much paperwork, feel free to share that many (but not all) of the rigors result from government controls. If this results in complaints to a senator or congressperson, so much the better.

8. Borrowers' personal circumstances do not always fit the box. Escalate

when appropriate. A solution equitable to the borrower and the lender may be found.

9. Listen well. The borrower deserves it. If you are distracted, admit it, apologize and try your best to concentrate on the repeat. The borrower's time is important too.

10. Express gratitude. Borrowers are asked to supply piles of documentation and multiple written explanations, and share personal data much of which they consider private and unnecessary. Thank them for cooperating even when they do it grudgingly.

There may be overlap between loan officer and underwriter responsibilities. Loan officers are usually more involved in major events such as taking the application and congratulating the borrower after the loan is approved, leaving the underwriter or processor to follow up on the details. Unless you are lucky enough to have a hands-on loan officer, some of the responsibility in dealing with the borrower will fall into your lap. Direct communication with the borrower generally results in a better loan file.

Rapport with the borrower

I could never be a bus driver. I couldn't handle not knowing about the passengers and why they were traveling. I prefer continuing relationships and believe there is value in personalizing even transitory ones, especially with borrowers.

There are many benefits. Questions can be answered, conditions can be explained and insecurities dealt with. Knowledge we take for granted is foreign to borrowers. A short but accurate explanation of "the why" can make the difference between ending up with a well-packaged salable loan rather than a cancellation.

The ultimate goal is making the borrower experience as painless as possible without compromising loan quality. The side benefits are, in corporate jargon, elevating the customer experience and making your own day more fulfilling.

Borrowers don't know our rules

Since borrowers don't know our rules, they typically don't compromise the truth on source of down payment, additional properties owned and support obligations. They may forget to disclose a co-signed loan if their brother and sister-in-law make the payments, but on the whole they give unedited disclosure.

Edited disclosure occurs with borrowers working in the industry, in affiliated fields like real estate or real estate investment, or with close relatives or friends who do. Those denied on previous applications are aware of why they didn't qualify. Lack of candor can also be caused by an abbreviated application interview, flagrant coaching or larceny as discussed in "Borrowers are not idiots"

Since the vast majority of borrowers don't work in the industry, haven't been denied financing and aren't criminals, it makes sense to treat them with trust and respect—unless they show they're not deserving.

Borrowers can be annoying

When borrowers are annoying, bear with them. What we do every day is a major life event for them. Most have limited understanding of our industry. The origination process is stressful, and the overkill and bureaucracy is frustrating even to us.

Why bear with them? If you have ever become involved in a relative's or friend's transaction, you know that pressure might have caused that person to act atypically at some point. Most borrowers are not full-time jerks. If they are confrontational or abusive, you needn't put up with it but if they appear slow to understand or ask a lot of questions, try to be patient. Consider bringing in help since hearing answers from another voice sometimes does the trick. Or tell the borrower "Let me see what I can do for you" and then work on it, a little or longer depending on the merits of the issue.

Good loan officers see themselves as service employees. Underwriters seldom think of themselves in that light, but we are.

Borrowers can be confused about occupancy

Owner occupancy type is not always clearcut, especially for a borrower. Parents purchase a university-adjacent condo for their child, or successive children in my in-law's case. A small home down the block can be acquired for an aging relative, or the house next door as an overflow annex or for increased privacy. Any of these situations will be perceived by the borrower to be more of a primary residence than an investment property.

Some borrowers have more than one second home, and others rent out their second homes intermittently to offset some of the expense. Their owners consider them to be second homes, but investors may or may not agree.

Depending on the investor, residences occupied by elderly parents or challenged adult children may be priced as primary residences. Prior to the meltdown, the GSEs allowed condo units occupied by college-aged children ("kiddy condos") to be priced as second homes. A second second home is not designated a third home. Occupancy inconsistent with industry definitions is not always fraud.

Stages of financial life

Growing up and then older is a continuing process. Long past childhood, changes in behavior often surface at predictable age ranges. Homebuyers in their seventies are more apt to downsize than to be first-time home buyers. When downsizing occurs with middle-aged borrowers, the cause is more likely divorce or a failing business than desire for less bedrooms or the inability to climb stairs.

Life stages are accompanied by financial stages. During the first decades of adulthood, borrowers are income-based. During the last few decades, borrowers are on fixed incomes, savings-poor or asset-based.

Younger borrowers traditionally purchased a starter house, but the newer trend is a "forever house." This can be a good choice if debt ratios are not excessive and the borrowers are not spendthrifts. Older borrowers may covet a long-postponed dream home. This can be a prudent choice if income is sustainable.

At some point, many borrowers with reduced earnings and substantial equity convert equity to subsidize income. Financing can be conventional cash-out refinance, a reverse mortgage or a purchase money lien on a down-sized residence. Tapping into equity after retirement is a better life decision than periodic extraction of equity while still income-based.

The best non-answer

Even after years in the mortgage industry, there were questions I couldn't answer. The realm of origination is complex even for smart people. Deferring to specialized expertise differs from incompetency. Those aware of their areas of proficiency should have no problem admitting their limitations.

The best response to a question you can't answer is an honest "I don't know." The follow-up should be "but please let me research it" or "but let me find you someone who does."

The real cause of default

Borrowers who are asked why their loans defaulted usually reply starting with a personal pronoun: "I lost my job." "My spouse died." "Our sandwich shop lost most of its customers after the plant closed." The easy conclusion is that foreclosures are caused by life events.

The borrower's point of view omits the accompanying factor, lack of equity. With equity, the property could be sold and the borrower would benefit from sale proceeds.

Real estate commissions and seller-paid closing costs are just under 10%, so the break-even point for a seller is 10% equity, assuming loan payments are current. Borrowers in distress lack savings to bring the loan current or equity to make the lender whole. Foreclosures have higher probability with a low down payment and during the earlier years of ownership. Market forces can impact value positively or negatively, but generally the longer the term of ownership the more value increases. Property owners maximize equity through good upkeep and property improvements, and negatively impact equity through property neglect and cash-out.

A combination of personal and equity-related circumstances leads to default. Personal circumstances usually cannot be anticipated but marginal qualification is identifiable. Flexibility in approval should be reserved for instances when the lender is not at risk for loss.

The defaulted borrower who lied

Loan servicing notes said default occurred because the borrower couldn't afford the payments. That didn't make sense. The borrower was a retired teacher with a pension and several hundred thousand dollars in reserves.

The subject property was a nondescript older Las Vegas condo unit. Value at time of default was $100,000 below acquisition price. Maybe living in Las Vegas didn't meet his expectations, or he decided to upgrade to a nicer property at a distressed price.

Lessons:

1. *At every stage loans have to make sense. Borrowers don't always tell the truth, whether in origination or in default.*

2. *This loan was my first encounter with strategic default, but I didn't realize it at the time. The term hadn't reached prominence yet.*

Borrowers can decide not to borrow

Word of mouth is a powerful force. Stymied or frustrated borrowers share their experience with anyone who will listen. Some complain that loans were denied for vague or nonsensical reasons. The luckier ones complain about endless requests for documentation and explanations, and often delayed closing.

The audiences of these unhappy borrowers already have mixed feelings about our industry. The taint has not disappeared. Millennials, the generation that should be buying homes, had their career plans and other life visions derailed from repercussions of the meltdown. Inability to find suitable employment was sometimes resolved by a return to school and increased student loan burden. These factors may account for Millennials' reluctance to sign up for thirty years of additional debt, especially when the alternatives—continued renting or living with family—are bearable.

Some originators seem to be deliberately discouraging volume—closing sites, vigorously adding restrictions, and denying not just marginal but worthy loans. Greed has been replaced by fear for lenders and borrowers alike.

Restrained use of consumer credit usage is positive. Not buying a home, opting for a tiny house or obtaining financing from relatives or crowdfunding bodes poorly for the mortgage industry.

See *The all-cash offer*

Some applicants shouldn't be borrowers

Three types of applicants unworthy to be borrowers are the ineligible, untruthful and unqualified. A fourth and less obvious category is those who take too much effort to qualify, not because of complexity but because they are marginal. Expending extraordinary effort for questionably qualified applicants is not doing them any favor.

CHAPTER 14

UNDERWRITERS

The underwriter toolbox

I personally could not underwrite a loan, or review a loan someone else underwrote, without a mechanical pencil, a thin-lined legal pad, Post-its, an HP12-C and an eraser. Virtually all of this equipment has been obsoleted by technology. Nevertheless when I am writing or consulting, all are close by. Some of the equipment has been obsoleted by technology. Nevertheless when I am writing or consulting, all are close by. The act of writing helps engrave a loan in my mind and facilitate decision-making.

What technology hasn't changed are the intangibles that make a good underwriter:

1. Curiosity

2. Backbone

3. Understanding of the why behind the rules

4. The ability to weigh risk

5. The ability to discern between fact and fiction

The tangibles are personal taste; the intangibles are essential.

Underwriting, etymologically

According to an etymological dictionary (which explains words' original meanings), underwriting—from the root words, under and writing—references the signature at the bottom of an insurance or shipping policy accepting potential liability.

Loan underwriters evaluate risk with the goal that future liability is avoided. This applies less to government and affordable housing loans, but even on those programs judgment skills come into play on income qualification and credibility. Risk evaluation differs from AUS input, which is clerical in nature.

The underwriter's job description

An underwriter's core responsibility has more complexity than just ensuring qualification. Those who believe that the underwriter's role is making sure the loan fits guidelines are only partially correct.

Admittedly, making sure loans comply with guidelines is a major component of the underwriter's role. But there are two other components—ensuring that the loan is salable or portfolio-appropriate, and determining which loans have a strong probability of performing. There are loans fully within guidelines that don't merit approval and loans not fitting the mold that present acceptable risk. I think of the latter group as "bet my paycheck" (that it will perform) loans.

Worrisome loans should be denied when there is concrete rationale for denial. Depending on the investor and the mortgage market, a non-performing loan meeting guidelines may turn into a repurchase for the originator. Worthy loans should be championed, which may require that they be strengthened with additional documentation, or considered for counter-offer or an exception.

The underwriter's job involves using intelligence, experience, command of guidelines and command of risk in making responsible loan decisions.

The why

Journeyman underwriters know the rules. Insightful underwriters understand "the why" behind the rules. Understanding the why enables better decisioning.

Projected income for a newly-hired commissioned car salesman differs from projected income for a newly-hired college professor. Even without a pay-stub, the college professor's salary and term of employment are stipulated in a contract. An industry that allows a borrower employed for three weeks because there is a pay-stub should be equally accepting of a borrower who has a contract for employment.

Going back to the newly-hired car salesperson, if that person changes dealerships in the same area, earnings are more predictable than for someone previously working in retail sales. If that car salesperson earned four months commissions consistent with previous earnings and was requesting a rate and term refinance, risk would be different than for a cash-out. If he had two late mortgage payments in the past few years, consistency of income would be outweighed by problematic credit. If the letter of explanation blamed delayed commission checks, the real issue would be variable income combined with inadequate reserves.

Those who see underwriting as an exercise in risk and probability usually take pleasure in and are valued for their work. Those who do not may never graduate from journeyman status.

The best way to learn the whys is to ask questions (try your manager or well-seasoned underwriters) and mull over the answers on the way home.

Online research

Considerable information is available by looking up a property address. This is helpful before the appraisal is available and, when there is a departure residence, to see whether the borrower is moving up or down. Be aware that property-specific data is not always accurate. See *The Contradictory Rental*

Other online information can also help with random concerns such as clarifying a business's function, substantiating questionable income, or figuring out the distance between a primary residence and employment or between primary and second homes. When there is potential for fraud or doubts about occupancy, online research is a good starting point.

Online research is helpful under other circumstances too. When I was managing what I called a "clean up the mess" team after the meltdown, we had weekly teleconferences discussing repurchases loan by loan. The crux was whether the loan was originated responsibly, or misrepresentation was apparent. An attorney participating on the calls occasionally came up with pertinent insights from online research, like "This borrower's in prison for mortgage fraud."

Foreign documentation

When the down payment is proceeds of sale from an inherited dacha in Russia, there should be no expectation of a closing statement. If a borrower generates income from minority share of a rum factory in Barbados, conditioning for a W-2, a K-1 or a 1099 will be fruitless. Conditioning for U.S. forms used to report income, pay taxes and transfer ownership is unrealistic. It cannot be assumed that other countries share similar processes or forms.

The better way of obtaining documentation, instead of citing forms, is requesting verification of earnings or retirement benefits for a specified year, or proof of proceeds from the sale of property at a specified address. If the borrower is a United States citizen who has been working outside the country, income can be verified through U.S. tax returns (assuming the level of earnings requires filing) although earnings are tax-exempt.

Expectations should differ according to where the documentation is coming from. The smaller and more remote the country, the less likely equivalents are available. Written confirmation from the employer or depository or, for transfers of property, a written statement from an attorney, a mayor or other local dignitary may be the best substitute, along with proof of deposit of check or wire transfer.

See *Challenges in verifying funds to close, Offshore funds* and *International credit reports*

The craft of conditioning

Bright children learn early that how a question is asked influences how it is answered. For the most part, the bad versions of conditions below address legitimate concerns or omissions. However, they appear intrusive, rude and judgmental. The better phrased conditions show improvement but should be tailored for the specifics of the loan.

Bad: Is this your entire life savings?

Better: Please provide documentation supporting additional sources of liquid or retirement assets to aid qualification.

Why: The assets on the application may be incomplete, possibly based on the mistaken belief that more than required reserves have no benefit. On a borderline loan, asset strength can justify loan approval. Requesting additional documentation is kinder than denying a loan for inadequate compensating factors.

See *When reserves matter more*

Bad: How did you accumulate $56,000 in consumer debt?

Better: Provide a detailed statement explaining $56,000 in outstanding balances on revolving accounts relative to high credit limits of $62,000.

Why: High non-mortgage debt can reflect questionable financial management. But the figure should be considered relative to the borrower's income and other obligations. Debt of $56,000 is high for someone dependent on social security benefits, but less concerning for someone with high earnings. Trended credit can give insight to the typical level of debt. If high utilization is consistent, the source of debt (unrestrained spending, as opposed to something purposeful like property improvements or medical expenses) should be part of the evaluation.

See *Trended credit*

Bad: Why do you owe $300,000 on a home purchased for $80,000 twenty years ago?

Better: Please clarify whether current mortgage debt is the result of property improvements or other expenditures. If there were property improvements, provide details on what was done and the approximate cost. Backup documentation may be requested.

Why: The elimination of Improvements Made Since Purchase leaves a gap in risk assessment. Knowing whether refinance proceeds were spent wisely or frivolously is key in assessing money management skills. Property improvements (but not timing or cost) should be supported by the appraisal. Whether backup documentation is requested depends on the magnitude of refinance proceeds and credibility of the explanation.

Bad: Why does the P&L show considerably higher profits than tax returns?

Better: Clarify increased gross income and decreased overhead as reflected in the year-to-date P&L. Verification of gross income is (or may be) required.

Why: Trending income is critical with a newer business or when the most recent tax-year shows a decline. Some possibilities are fluctuating income, improved efficiency or an inflated P&L. With a newer business, start-up expenses may be complete while the customer base continues expanding or (giving the borrower the benefit of the doubt) the P&L could be optimistically estimated. If credibility of the P&L is established, higher ratios, more than a two-year average or, under justified circumstances, less than a two-year average may be acceptable.

See *Fluctuating income*

Bad: How are you really going to spend loan proceeds?

Better: Please provide details of planned property improvements of approximately $124,000. Current residence is a high-rise condominium. Provide contractor bids or signed contract.

Why: Actual intent may be for the down payment on another residence. Although a signed contract is unusual before closing, several bids are customary with a high-cost remodel—unless the homeowner has personal experience with the contractor's work, in which case the property might already be upgraded and/or is a flip.

Bad: Are you really going to live there?

Better: Please clarify motivation for occupancy. The property being purchased is further from employment and considerably smaller than your current residence.

Why: Occupancy fraud is difficult to prove because implementation occurs after closing. It is more likely when the current residence is being retained. Life stage and household size are valid considerations. The condition should present specific concerns, and the borrower's response should be specific as well.

See *Occupancy fraud*

Bad: Why did you wait until you were 39 before establishing credit?

Better: Please clarify why your two oldest trade-lines were opened two years ago.

Why: The situation can be innocuous, embarrassing for the borrower or spark red flags. It may be that the borrower relocated from another country, was previously incarcerated or has sanitized credit. Whatever the circumstance, the majority of borrowers establish credit not long after becoming adults. Clues from documentation may eliminate need for a written explanation.

Bad: How much did you win in the lottery and how much is left?

Better: Please clarify net lottery proceeds, use of winnings and remaining funds.

Why: The explanation will give insight into financial management skills. The explanation could support approval or denial if qualification is marginal. If the borrower qualifies easily, it's intrusive.

Composing conditions is a learnable art. Each condition should communicate clearly to the borrower and its purpose should be explained if not apparent. Be brief whenever possible. Several overly-detailed conditions give the impression of excessive conditioning.

The relativity of conditioning

Only the most naive underwriters (and loan officers convinced that any additional conditioning is unnecessary) believe the AUS conditions comprise a complete list of what is needed. Conditioning can be selective. To decide which are essential, each should be considered relative to the specific loan.

Detailed use of cash-out is not necessary if proceeds are a few thousand dollars. The more substantial the proceeds, the more detailed use of funds should be. Marital settlement agreements should not be required from every divorced borrower. Once sufficient funds to close and reserves are sourced, additional funds should not be questioned.

Conditioning involves assessing the loan strength. If borrowers clearly qualify, move on. If qualification is less clear, decide what additional documentation would strengthen (or kill) the loan, and ask for it.

The purpose of conditioning is not protecting the underwriter. "I had a loan once where I didn't ask for..." is not acceptable rationale unless there is a direct connection with the loan. No prizes are awarded for the highest number of conditions.

The borrower fed up with condition requests

The borrower had contracted to buy after walking through a model house. The house was nearly complete, and his loan had been in process for six months. It was a second home purchase with LTV below 60%. The application indicated that income came from a partnership and the down payment was in a business account. There were 60 documents in the virtual income and asset folder, the borrower had already provided updated asset statements and was losing patience with requests for more.

Twelve minutes into reviewing the documentation, I concluded that what we had was sufficient. The borrower owned 95% of the partnership and its sole holding was a $10,000,000 brokerage account. Income was generated from interest, dividends and capital gains. The current partnership return was on extension, but a year-end statement verified portfolio value was within $100,000 of the value on the latest filed partnership return.

What took longer than twelve minutes was composing written justification for waiving the documentation customarily required for partnerships and use of business funds. Both the partnership and the business account were atypical. The current brokerage statement made a profit and loss statement redundant. No analysis was necessary of the business's ability to remain profitable after withdrawal of funds to close. The borrower's impressive asset base covered the down payment and eliminated any concern of affordability; there was adequate documentation supporting that conclusion.

Lessons: Standard documentation isn't always necessary documentation. Additional documentation doesn't always make a better loan.

Killing with conditions

Killing with conditions is a legitimate strategy for marginal or inadequately packaged loans. It involves compiling a list of every item necessary to make the loan closable. Probability of closing need not be high, and fulfilling the conditions can be a chore.

The loan may be cancelled and placed elsewhere. The originator may learn that difficult loans require diligent packaging, or to direct them to another lender with lower standards and/or higher pricing. Or, the loan may be abandoned if the intent in submission was proving that the loan could not be approved. Or, as a result of the underwriter's and the originator's efforts, the loan may work.

Killing with conditions is preferable to waking up in the middle of the night wondering why you rejected a potentially decent loan or accepted a flawed one.

File review

My routine was to review in what I consider to be basic loan file order: application, credit report, assets, income, appraisal, title and purchase contract. My first district manager always looked at the appraisal first, consistent with his belief that "it all rests on the property." There is no right or wrong. What is essential is a routine followed consistently so nothing is overlooked.

The imaging system affects the efficiency of file review. The best systems leverage the expertise of underwriters in the design process. The worst have poor functionality, like Income and Assets in the same folder or folders in alphabetical order, which makes more sense for systems used infrequently. Although some foresee a paperless future, others (typically very seasoned underwriters) print out core documentation to highlight and notate. This is not wasted effort if printing is selective—the application, major components of the appraisal and key tax return schedules. For some, highlighting aids in retention and pattern identification, and note-taking expedites write-up while reducing oversights.

Method and intensity of file review depend on the reviewer's role. Line underwriters review everything. Second signers audit for accuracy and valid decision-making. Investor review ranges from cursory to thorough. Exception review concentrates on key documents and anything prompted by the nature of the exception. When a role changes, the method of review probably should change as well.

Errors occur when an underwriter is preoccupied with one facet of a file and devotes less attention the rest, or when a loan is initially denied and then resurrected without complete review.

Cover letters – the why

Hired as the sole underwriter for the start-up mortgage group, I wrote a cover letter for each loan file. As we expanded to several states, the practice continued. Cover letters contributed to our divisional success and the respect institutional investors gave us.

A friend shared that in his new place of employment every loan file has two cover letters, one from the loan officer and the other from the underwriter. Is this overkill? I don't think so. Loan officers can provide insights and clarifications gained from borrower interaction. A detailed and convincing letter from the loan officer can motivate the underwriter to help structure and approve a loan that otherwise might be denied.

In the process of formulating a cover letter, the underwriter must evaluate the loan in every aspect and as a whole. A cover letter's purpose is to present the loan in its best light to the reader—second signers, management, auditors, the investor, loan servicer, or whoever is reviewing the file after close. It should personalize the borrowers, emphasize strengths, present convincing compensating factors for weaknesses, reference pertinent letters of explanation and justify the loan decision.

A cover-letter equivalent on a denial is not a bad idea. Justification of denial may turn out to be as worthwhile as justifying an approval.

Cover letters – the how

A standardized template ensures that standard points are covered, but the format should be adaptable to what needs to be explained. One possibility is:

- Paragraph 1: Loan attributes

- Paragraph 2: A short description of the property, including any complicating factors

- Paragraph 3+: The story of the loan if it is interesting, anything else that needs explaining such as income, credit usage, etc.

- Last paragraph: Recommendation

The standard template can be disregarded if the loan is uncomplicated and there is only one major point to be made. A short description of loan attributes and property is warranted when the major point is a complication; its significance should be put into perspective in the context of the full loan.

Do not oversell in the cover letter. Everything said should be true and credible. Not every loan is strong in every respect. Some fall into the "This loan has acceptable risk and should perform well" category.

Omit unnecessary detail. A lengthy letter may be taken as a cover-up for a flawed loan.

Personalizing the borrowers may require effort or research. For entertainment industry borrowers, I mentioned a few movie or television credits especially for borrowers with no name recognition. Current and sometimes future projects were included to demonstrate continuing demand for their talents. For self-employed borrowers in other industries, I included a few details about their businesses. For employed borrowers, I mentioned when the borrower had worked for the same employer for two decades or, equally pertinent, if she changed positions after a layoff or for a more responsible position.

If there is a good rapport with the cover letter's recipient, a personalized greeting can be included. Since the cover letter is a permanent part of the loan file, don't be too chatty or personal.

An abbreviated version of a cover letter is a good idea for denial recommendations. It should pinpoint deficiencies, give an accurate portrayal of the loan as a whole and conclude with a condensed statement explaining why approval is not justified.

Sample cover letter

Sara and Richard Thompson (B1 and B2) are purchasing their first home in Kearney, Nebraska with 30 year, fixed rate financing. Their credit scores are 763 and 688 and the combined debt ratio is 42%. Their 20% down payment is from personal savings, and they will have five months reserves.

The subject property is a detached residence with four bedrooms and two baths. The property was built in 1939 and has an updated kitchen and bathrooms. The appraisal is subject to repair of two broken windows and minor interior damages caused by the departing owners. Repairs will be verified as completed before closing.

Both borrowers have master's degrees. B1 has been teaching high school computer classes for six years and receives ten paychecks a year. Qualifying income was derived from annual base divided by twelve. B2 has been an independent agricultural engineer for six years. Self-employment started as a sole proprietorship but turned into a corporation almost two years ago. Qualifying income is averaged from the first corporate year and the final year's Schedule C. A twenty month average from first corporate year plus ten month P&L would reduce DTI to 36%. Qualifying ratios appear somewhat high, but the engineering business is increasing steadily in profitability. A letter of explanation states B1's score was impacted by a recent unpaid medical collection for which the employer-paid medical insurer is responsible. The credit report was drawn before the collection account was disputed.

Based on steadily increasing income, responsible credit use and proven ability to save, the borrowers should be responsible homeowners.

Eve Lynne Kay
Senior Underwriter

NOTE: This letter was originally written with "she" and "he" instead of B1 and B2. Then I learned that some current training advises elimination of female and male pronouns because they represent gender discrimination. The sample cover letter has been changed accordingly, but my opinion is that pronouns do not cause discrimination. If the promoters of neutralized verbiage sincerely believe narrow-minded people will ignore government monitoring data on the application and first names scattered throughout the file, they are naive. Energy is better spent removing people who make prejudiced decisions from loan origination.

See *Two sets of ratios*

Rebuttal letters

When a loan with merit is denied or an investor requests a repurchase, there is opportunity for a reconsideration with a rebuttal letter. Rebuttal letters require skill to compose and considerable tact. The letter must convincingly argue that whatever shortcomings were identified are either incorrect or inconsequential, without insulting the competency of the sender.

Tactics include:

• Providing additional information or a corroborating opinion from someone with expertise.

• Agreeing that the finding is valid but should be viewed in perspective.

- Placing blame on yourself, e.g., "I should have clarified that..."

- Discuss compensating factors, preferably new or restated so the letter is not an evident rehash of the original cover letter.

- Have another person compose the rebuttal presenting a different slant on the issue.

- The appeal should end with a tactful request for reconsideration.

Wholesale, retail and correspondent

All underwriting is not the same.

In Wholesale, brokers deal directly with the borrower and assemble the loan package. The package is sent on to the funding source, who re-underwrites the loan for completeness and quality. The underwriter in the broker shop has a difficult role—not torturing the borrower with unnecessary documentation requests but anticipating condition requests from the funding source's underwriter. A cover letter explaining any complications may increase the re-underwriter's comfort level, eliminate the need for additional documentation and facilitate quicker closing. Borrowers are attracted to wholesale operations, because with multiple funding sources, the broker can select the best fit based on borrower profile and pricing.

In Retail, the borrower likely is a customer of the financial institution. The loan officer and underwriter coordinate to assemble a complete loan package without tarnishing the customer experience. If the customer has a business banking relationship with the institution, the commercial group may already have financial documentation. The commercial relationship manager is a good contact point and can probably provide insight on the business. Borrowers are attracted to retail originators because of the established relationship.

In Correspondent, the underwriter reviews a closed loan. Obtaining additional documentation is problematic. The borrower may be uncooperative even after agreeing in writing to provide follow-up documentation at the beginning of the loan process. (A fruit basket or restaurant gift card may provide incentive.) The underwriter reviews for risk and essential documentation, recognizing that if the loan fails to perform or becomes a repurchase from the ultimate investor, the correspondent is contractually obligated and theoretically has the resources to repurchase. Since the borrower is detached from what occurs after closing, the customer is the originating lender, who values responsive service and competitive pricing.

These descriptions are admittedly over-simplified. Variations abound. The retail branch I managed received a majority of volume through real estate sales agents, although branch managers periodically advocated for depository customers. The commercial bank's mortgage division provided retail services for bank customers and wholesale services for brokers. The correspondent division assembled a prior approval team to process loans for select sellers. Diversification in services increases profitability.

Overly cautious underwriting

Some underwriters believe using the most conservative income approach is responsible underwriting. They think this practice minimizes the number of non-performing loans and protects their employer. Actually what is minimized is production volume and the resultant revenue; some declined loans are likely to perform. Overly cautious underwriting adversely affects the company, the borrower and the economy.

There is a spectrum of qualifying income—aggressive, realistic and justifiable, and overly-cautious—with gradations in between. The conservative approach to qualifying income is prudent on a higher-risk loan. More aggressive qualification is defendable when compensating factors are strong. In some situations, for example when deep equity, proven ability and impressive reserves are all in place, qualifying income plays a secondary role in driving performance.

Ultra-prudent underwriters adhere to rules too diligently. Consider a commissioned borrower employed for two years with a May 1 start date. An excessively cautious underwriter would ignore the four months' earnings in the most recent year and take a 24-month average from the two previous years less a 24-month average of expense write-offs. Justification would be that a two-year average from tax returns is required. I would use a 24-month average of commissioned earnings including year-to-date less a 20-month average of expenses. Commissioned earnings supported by pay-stubs are more credible than profit and loss statements. If the borrower were self-employed, I would not use year-to-date earnings but rather a 20-month average from tax returns after reviewing the P&L for credibility and profitability. Averaging 20 months of earnings over 24 months is especially unfair if the initial months of commission earnings show increasing momentum typical for new hires.

How to underwrite high risk loans

High risk covers government loan programs and any conventional product with shallow equity and non-stellar borrowers. Those searching for strong compensating factors may not find them.

These loans benefit the majority of borrowers, their families and the national economy. But much of the guidance in this book does not apply.

Two unbreakable rules apply to underwriting high risk loans:

1. Rigorous adherence to written guidelines and directives

2. Minimum if any benefit of the doubt

Why? For the borrower, indebtedness without the ability to repay is no favor at all. For the lender, deficient findings on non-performing high risk loans result in financial liability. Defaulted loans complying with guidelines have no repercussions.

When someone else reviews the appraisal

There is some justification for designating a specialist responsible for appraisal review. If the loan defaults, a weak appraisal may lead to financial loss. Appraisal analysis is complex, and some underwriters allocate most of their effort to borrower qualification. Post-meltdown reform limited lender involvement with the appraisal. But the intent of the reform was to stop coercion in regard to value, not to prevent underwriters from reading appraisals.

There are many reasons underwriters should read appraisals:

• Properties give insight to their owners or upcoming occupants. Whether the property is a good fit is a valid consideration. It is impossible to balance risk without considering occupancy.

• For refinances, commitment to the property is apparent in renovations and upkeep.

• Especially if the property is a move-down or a second home, review of the appraisal may cause conditioning for a motivation letter or eliminate the need for one.

• Whether a property is mainstream or not can affect how a loan is approved.

• Appraisals provide insight on unfamiliar areas and trends in new construction, They can distinguish meaningful from cosmetic remodels.

- Review of every appraisal expands the underwriter's knowledge base.

If an underwriter changes employment, proficiency may be expected. I finally resisted hiring alumni of one originator who were spared property review; despite retraining, they overlooked property-related complications more than their peers.

So start off by reading the *Appraisal* and *Property* chapters. They are intended to provide a comfort level. Consider touring open houses, watching HGTV and shadowing an appraiser. The ultimate steps are finding value and pleasure in reading appraisals, and demonstrating to management that appraisal review is good use of an underwriter's time.

Perspective and options

These two words were printed on a small pink Post-it attached to the edge of my computer screen for years. They illuminate two tests of risk too often ignored.

Perspective requires overview of the combined aspects of a loan. Evaluation of each individual element is necessary, but overall strength should be evaluated as well. Weaknesses may be acceptable if offset by compensating factors.

Options should be considered if a loan has a trace of marginality. If a life event like job loss occurs, default will be averted if the borrower has alternatives. Is replacement income likely, or are there ample reserves or sufficient equity to assure no loss to the lender? Stronger borrowers have several options; weaker borrowers have few.

Consideration of perspective and options is inappropriate for some lending programs, low and moderate earners, and high LTV loans. See *How to underwrite high risk loans*

Financial underwear

There are many reasons why underwriting is a fulfilling career. There is satisfaction in turning chaos into order as a loan package takes form and in judicious decisioning. Those who are curious by nature enjoy seeing people's financial underwear—the personal details unshared with one's closest relatives and friends.

When an underwriter reviews the loan package of a schoolmate, a coworker or a celebrity, insights are gained that few people are privy to. Even for anonymous strangers, seeing whether their finances are orderly or in disarray is interesting.

Admittedly, not all observations are pertinent to decisioning, Needless to say, discretion is essential.

I'm confused

An effective tactic in resolving inconsistent or unclear elements of a loan file is to admit you're confused. This places culpability on yourself while propelling the borrower or originator to amend the deficiency.

The flexibility spectrum

Underwriters vary in flexibility.

Most underwriters see merit in structure. Dedicated rule followers believe guidelines are sacred and even small deviations are unacceptable. Assuming some degree of flexibility is allowed (which depends on the investor and the regulatory climate), underwriters reluctant to loosen the reins may be more comfortable underwriting government loans and GSE affordable programs. On lower risk loans, they should consider the essentiality of each condition and make an effort to make complex but approvable loans work.

Some underwriters can rationalize anything. Rationalizers adapted very well during the years preceding the meltdown, viewing stable employment as a compensating factor for high ratios or substandard credit, and 85% as a below maximum LTV. There has been adequate time since the meltdown to readjust, recognizing that compensating factors should relate to the identified risk and understanding that not every loan merits approval.

Rule followers and **rationalizers** represent the two extremes of the flexibility spectrum. In the middle are the **risk evaluators**. They can identify the appropriate tipping point in the rules / risk balance for a specific loan. They understand that standardized guidelines for the largest investors were formulated to mitigate risk on higher loan-to-value loans.

The ability to balance risk usually comes with experience, although insight comes earlier to the gifted and may never be within the grasp of everyone.

Practices of effective underwriters

1. Reading the appraisal, except for generic text, to assess marketability.

2. Evaluating whether property renovations are cosmetic or meaningful.

3. Analyzing whether the subject property is appropriate for the borrower.

4. Calculating appreciation since purchase if rapid appreciation is at issue.

5. Evaluating credit beyond the credit score.

6. Considering accrued equity and other evidence of financial management.

7. Not assuming that assets on the application represent all the borrower's assets.

8. Evaluating whether use of cash-out is probable or improbable.

9. Determining whether occupancy is assured or in doubt.

10. Testing and/or trending income.

11. Assessing whether letters of explanation are credible.

12. Deciding whether the merits of the loan suggest conservative or more relaxed qualifying income, and more or less rigorous conditioning.

Final comment

This book can be useful when loan officers don't understand why you're requesting additional documentation or, even worse, denying a loan. It may clarify why your action is justified or at least spark a good discussion on loan specifics. If the loan officer is a reader, consider this book as a birthday or holiday present. Even if it is read just to humor you, it might benefit your working relationship.

CHAPTER 15

LOAN OFFICERS

The loan application

With a partially completed passport application, you don't expect a passport. For at least a decade, if a loan application was incomplete, it was pretty much business as usual. The processor reviewed documentation and researched online to fill in the gaps and, worst case, asked the borrower. Although passport and loan applications serve different purposes, both are critical documents. Even lower loan amounts involve a significant amount of money, and qualifying for a loan probably requires more thorough deliberation than qualifying for a passport.

The analogy has validity even though a mortgage is secured against real property. Lenders have loss exposure from increased servicing expense, insufficient equity, property damage, investor repurchase and REO costs. A diligently-completed application enables a better loan decision, resulting in profit to the lender and commissions to the loan officer—or a denial averting future loss.

Short-cut applications became acceptable as AUS decisioning caught on. The unofficial but enthusiastically adopted assumption was that any information not necessary for AUS input was superfluous. If this reasoning were valid, the 2016 application would be shorter instead of considerably longer. Every field in the application has a legitimate purpose, and decision-making should not be restricted to the AUS engine.

Incomplete applications are more attributable to laziness than improved customer experience. Most borrowers don't mind answering questions about themselves. It's requests for items like written statements explaining name variations with obvious spelling errors (e.g., George and Martha Washingtom) and probing questions about personal expenditures that annoy them.

Excessive conditioning is at least partially attributable to incomplete applications. If support obligations and real estate holdings are completed diligently, excessive scrutiny of depository statements and supplementary documentation on investment property may discontinue. Complete asset documentation may make the difference on a loan with high ratios or concerns about sustainable income. Ages of children justify whether cash-out for college tuition is credible or whether relocation is more likely. (One application I reviewed claimed cash-out for college expense when the oldest child was under ten.)

The loan application deserves to be filled out thoroughly, and those loan officers who facilitate it deserve commendation. A diligently completed application eases the process.

The benefit of a complete application

- **Rapport:** Borrowers don't want to be interrogated or have their time wasted but most understand their personal data is essential to obtaining a mortgage. Opportunity to bond can result in additional originations and referrals.

- **Repercussions:** There is likelihood that the short sale will show up on the credit report but candor earlier in the process can lead to opportunity. "I'm sorry, but you won't be able to qualify for our best pricing" delivered as the Declaration section is filled out can help educate the borrower ("I know we should have held on to that house") and turn into a discussion about financing alternatives. More probable than concealed major derogatory credit is support payments or property holdings surfacing during the underwriting process. If this occurs rarely, it is blamed on the borrower. If it occurs more frequently, the loan officer is viewed as less than diligent. Fewer catches during origination can also result in increased vigilance on bank statements for missing obligations. See *Intense Scrutiny of Depository Statements*

- **Accuracy:** For the benefit of all concerned parties—borrower, lender and loan officer—the application should reflect the truth, not an educated guess.

- **Responsibility:** The loan application is the core document in the loan package, and shepherding the borrower through the loan application is a core responsibility of the loan officer. The processor will be spared conditioning for data and the decisioning (AUS and human) will be based on comprehensive data. All parties will appreciate your diligence.

- **Speed and efficiency of processing:** A complete application means fewer follow-up questions and conditions.

Full asset disclosure

Loan officers concluded that full asset disclosure wasn't necessary after AUS approvals required only minimal reserves. The case was made that the application predated AUS decisioning, so did not specify what amount of disclosed assets was sufficient. The reluctance to fully disclose became somewhat defendable when post-meltdown paranoia resulted in intense scrutiny of undisclosed obligations and unsourced deposits. The industry should learn that scrutinizing bank statements is almost always a waste of time.

The redesigned application empowers borrowers to disclose which accounts they want considered to qualify for the loan. This allows borrowers to decide what is in their best interest.

Too many underwriters take applications literally, and the AUS decision always does. When savings are not evident, underwriters may conclude that no additional assets exist. With low depository rates, underwriters are unable to gauge asset depth from interest and dividend income. Disclosing more than minimal required reserves may make a positive difference in decisioning.

Especially with borrowers approaching the age when many people shift from income- to asset-based, ample savings can justify approval. Buyers with limited financial resources purchasing older properties or seasonal rentals can be worrisome to underwriters. Lack of diligence in documentation constitutes borrower neglect.

See *When reserves matter more or less*

The model loan officer

A local real estate agent referred me to his favorite loan officer. It didn't take long to understood why. Daniel returns phone calls within minutes, not hours or days. His knowledge of guidelines equals an underwriter's. He's able to predict whether a loan request will be approved or denied— and without a crystal ball. He's only missed twice, both on appraisal issues. Underwriters look forward to getting his files, since he obtains documentation they usually have to condition for.

Daniel is so knowledgable and responsive, no one minds he isn't present visually handing out business cards and donuts. He's too busy doing his job superbly.

Lesson: The best loan officers have competencies beyond sales.

Underwriters versus loan officers

Us versus them often seems inevitable. Underwriters and loan officers have different thought processes, motivations and personality types.

Underwriters tend to be rule followers. Loan officers tend to think bending rules is justified under appropriate circumstances.

Underwriters are governed by facts. Loan officers integrate gut feeling into decision-making.

Underwriters are detail-minded. Loan officers prefer the big picture.

Underwriters are afraid of auditors and non-performing loans. Loan officers fear jeopardizing relationships and being unable to pay their bills.

There is overlap. The best underwriters understand the big picture, and the best loan officers excel at follow-up which reflects detail-mindedness. I have worked with former underwriters who have successfully transitioned into sales, and at least one former loan officer who found greater fulfillment in underwriting. Each benefited from an expanded frame of reference.

In successful companies, underwriters and loan officers work together as partners rather than adversaries, at least most of the time. Both skill sets are valuable. Over-literal adherence to guidelines can result in denials of good loans; excessive flexibility can result in rampant foreclosures. Loan officers can help underwriters recognize a loan's merits, and underwriters can teach loan officers that diligence at the beginning can prevent frustrations later on.

A couple of jobs ago, a usually supportive sales manager pitched a loan for two recently married borrowers each with a previous (and unconnected) bankruptcy. "I have a feeling they're going to make it," he said. That day we disagreed.

To loan officers on behalf of underwriters

1. We admire your people skills. You're adept at dealing with borrowers, and much more fun in social situations than we are.

2. We sometimes wish loan officers had the same standard of consideration for underwriters as for borrowers.

3. You're not doing borrowers any favors by writing letters for them or even helping them with phrasing. We're usually able to tell the difference between letters written by the borrower and ones you've been overly involved with.

4. A complete application means our definition of complete.

5. Please don't blame requests for additional documentation on the underwriter. Many are investor- or government-driven. We're only trying to make your deals work.

6. Even though we may tease about your shorter workdays, we understand that you're on call seven days a week including evenings, vacations and holidays. (We trust you're aware that our workdays can extend for over eight hours and more than five days a week.)

7. We empathize with you on denials and cancellations, and understand that every lost loan has a direct effect on your paycheck.

8. Let's forge a trade-off. When we're slammed, please respect our time. In return we agree to prioritize whatever absolutely needs to be handled asap, as long as it doesn't include everything.

9. I'm glad we work together even though I don't always show it.

Beyond interest rate

To genuinely help the borrower, look beyond interest rate. For those in forever homes, the goal shouldn't be the lowest possible monthly payment but rather no payment at all. The ideal refinance reduces monthly payments with a loan term no longer than the existing loan's remaining term. For well qualified borrowers, an even shorter term can benefit. With extended ownership, most borrowers benefit more from a shorter term than extended deductibility. If affordability precludes a short term, borrowers should be coached that any amount over the minimum payment is applied to principal and repays the loan more quickly.

A 15-year loan term obtained a few years after purchase enabled my husband and me to have an unencumbered home less than 20 years after purchase. This explains my advocacy of fifteen year financing, although possibly less so after a thought-provoking discussion with the model loan officer. He favors a 30-year fixed term for flexibility with payments equivalent to fifteen year payments when the borrower is able.

Although borrowers understanding what best benefits them may generate fewer commissions from recurring refinances, you'll likely have referrals from their friends and relatives. That's what happens when borrowers are guided to smart financial decisions.

Final appeal

If you find this chapter helpful, consider reading the entire book. If there isn't time, dip into the *Borrower* chapter, also *Long-term obligations not on the credit report, When high ratios matter more or less, When reserves matter more or less*—or anything that catches your interest. Knowledge gained may provide ammunition to defend difficult loans or convince underwriters you are on the same team.

CHAPTER 16
LIFE LESSONS

The giant savings and loan

Norm ran the loan division for a savings and loan with over a hundred depository branches. His office was at the corporate headquarters in Beverly Hills. I'm not sure why he hired me. I had a degree in English from UCLA and a few years with investment companies, but not a clue about lending.

My official title was administrative assistant. Core responsibilities were researching and answering complaint letters and regulatory inquiries, and updating the underwriting manual. An executive secretary answered his phone and typed his letters.

As I investigated complaints, Norm taught me about mortgage risk. "I'd make that loan to a brown dog" meant deep equity making borrower qualification matter less. He began his career as an appraiser and considered the collateral as important as the borrower.

I also learned about low-key management. During the seven years we worked together, he only yelled at three people and two didn't know they were being yelled at.

Norm was happily married with two adopted children, was president of his church congregation ("which means when the plumbing doesn't work they call me") and was a middle-aged nerd before nerds had allure. He married late, admitting females weren't attracted to him until after they grew up.

After a few years as his assistant, I asked Norm if I could be a loan manager. I didn't like being thought of as a secretary, even though Norm's executive secretary sat across from me. My timing was fortuitous. The recently-hired loan manager down the hall didn't understand the difference between managing and bossing, which irritated the loan agents who lunched daily with Norm. I spent three weeks at a loan branch learning the mechanics of underwriting.

The first week was dedicated to shadowing three staff appraisers, two diligent and one slacker. The first house I walked through was bookless but had shelves filled with an extensive miniature liquor bottle collection. I was horrified. The appraiser instructed me to ignore furniture and interior decor, because if the homeowner moved, the furnishings left too. After inspecting and measuring the interior of the house, we viewed the comparable sales' exteriors. The second and third weeks, the branch manager and I dissected loan files.

I returned to corporate headquarters as manager of three loan agents and two clerks. My lending territory started at West Hollywood and went west to the beach. I was instructed to drive the properties when the office was quiet. I ended up knowing the area block by block.

I didn't try to be a boss. I made the best risk decisions I could, and when I wasn't sure Norm and I discussed the loan.

Most of our loans were jumbo, and many borrowers were self-employed. MI reps stopped dropping by after I told them I only had two insurable loans my first year. Salability was not a consideration. We were supposed to make prudent decisions and we did.

Everything changed when the frugal old man who was the chairman and major stockholder sold out his interest. There was no need for our corporate headquarters. Norm left to manage another loan division. He mentioned a possible position for me but I decided to go in my own direction. After seven years in the industry I was ready for a fresh start.

Lessons learned:

1. A knowledgeable and sharing mentor can ignite a career.

2. Employment in a company run by a miser worked to my advantage. I had greater responsibilities and more opportunities for advancement than in an organization with normal layers of management.

3. Managing differs from bossing.

4. Underwriting requires brains and insight. It was a job description I never wanted to graduate from.

5. A career, two close friendships still enduring, my first home purchase (from a feasibility study for condo conversion on Norm's desk) and my spouse were all found at one location.

The hard money shop

Despite seven years in the mortgage industry, I was blissfully unaware of hard money and subprime lending. The manager thought I wasn't right for the job but I asked for a chance and he gave it to me. During my brief tenure, I learned that loan approval was based on well-supported value because borrowers lacked strength. Payments were withheld from loan proceeds for the weakest borrowers, so the private investors were always paid on time. A well-known television actor whose long-running series had been cancelled told me about his credit problems. I hated the tales of woe and missed the decision-making. After crying on the way to a movie, I and my spouse-to-be decided I should find another job. I quit before my first month ended.

Lessons learned:

1. Hard money shops generate profit through points and fees. All interest goes to the investors.

2. Underwriter responsibilities were ensuring that equity position was supported and analyzing credit to determine whether payments would be made by the borrower or withheld from loan proceeds.

3. The manager was right. I was totally unsuited for hard money lending.

The neighborhood bank

My third mortgage industry employer was a small community bank whose lending decisions were made at a conference room table. There were residential loans and small business loans mostly on animal hospitals. I didn't understand why lending decisions needed a committee. I was let go during my first month.

Lessons learned:

1. If you don't buy into a company's culture, you shouldn't be working there.

2. Group decisioning can be an effective tool, although I didn't learn that lesson until much later.

3. Combined time in this and the previous position totaled about fifty days. Extended tenure elsewhere proved I wasn't a job-hopper. Bad fit can be identified by the employer or the employee and in the long run was a blessing.

The private conduit

The private conduit was a start-up aiming to be the Fannie Mae equivalent for second liens. Lenders throughout the country delivered closed loans, and my role was to ensure they were investor quality. I started out as the only underwriter, and ended up managing several regional underwriting teams. I transitioned from knowing my lending area street by street to evaluating loans in states I had only flown over.

The company grew. I traveled with Sales to unfamiliar states. My future husband, now self-employed, was hired to do marketing and advertising for the private conduit and several affiliated start-up companies. Everything went well until the new servicing system turned out to be poorly designed. Everyone from the receptionist to the president spent two hours daily manually setting up each adjustable rate loan.

After four years of rapid growth, the company had filed for bankruptcy. I told my future husband I was out of a job. He told me the company owed his company $75,000.

Lessons learned:

1. The same appraisal fundamentals apply everywhere.

2. Understanding how adjustable loans adjust paid off over a decade later.

3. The concept was good but execution wasn't. The company expanded too quickly and executive compensation was too generous.

4. Almost no one in the mortgage industry works for one company forever. Job security comes from proficiency and the respect of co-workers. At the beginning of a career, you search for your next position. After you become established, the positions search for you.

The show biz broker

A co-worker at the private conduit referred me to her father-in-law, who owned a brokerage two miles from my condo. He was in his sixties, 6'4" and charismatic. Shortly after I was hired, he sent us an expensive wedding present. Our Brentwood offices had fresh flower arrangements and entertainment industry publications in the waiting room. I reviewed tax returns for the names in the publications every day. Investors loved us because our loans were well packaged and soundly underwritten. Cover letters always included details about the borrower's past credits and current projects.

The downside was that the broker was a mean drunk. On good days his charisma and generosity made for a happy workplace, but we dreaded hearing the tinkle of ice cubes. On drinking days, employees who drank with him were treated better than those who continued working.

After a year and a half, I left for a longer commute and a $20,000 annual pay cut.

Lessons learned:

1. Entertainers with business managers almost always had sustainable careers and bought houses they could afford.

2. What looked like a dream job wasn't, with an alcoholic boss.

The country club savings and loan

I was hired by a small savings and loan about five miles from our home. My husband's former partner did their advertising. When I asked him about the company, he described corporate headquarters as a country club.

He was right. No one ever told me when the workday started or ended. I was hired to work alongside the long-ensconced chief underwriter because he lacked underwriting basics like tax-return analysis. He had a file card database including every culpable participant in every fraudulent loan transaction. His memorable talent was sneaking out of the office mid-afternoon without anyone seeing him. The consensus was that he climbed out through a window despite being middle-aged and bulky.

I reviewed larger loans and trained on current underwriting practices. Gradually I learned about office affairs. The two executives above the chief underwriter had been discovered consorting in the company gym. The gym was shut down, but they both held on to their jobs. The annual management retreat was known for social bonding and drunken escapades.

After seven months, I received a call from the sales manager who left shortly after my hire. He was starting up a mortgage division for a commercial bank. I accepted his job offer.

Shortly after I exited the country club, one of my office friends married the company president, and the company was taken over by the regulators. Not long after, I received the chief underwriter's resume with the entry "Languages Spoken: English and Danish."

Lessons learned:

1. When you have a strong work ethic, an unchallenging job can be a frustrating one.

2. A corporate culture with high tolerance for fraternization may have weak leadership in other respects.

The commercial bank

The commercial bank's customer base was local small- and mid-sized businesses, including some in the porn industry. Walk-ins approaching the new accounts desks usually exited when non-competitive account fees were disclosed, but service levels were first-rate.

The new mortgage division had a two-person management team. One handled administration, risk and retail volume while the other became a magnet for wholesale business. Both had enviable people skills. Bank customers were well qualified and wholesale brokers were drawn by our responsive service and competitive pricing. The new division was profitable from the beginning.

The investors loved us. One of the largest rated us their second highest-rated customer nationwide. The retail manager was disappointed with second place, but the rest of us were proud. We were appointed to advisory panels. In Minnesota, I marveled at snow falling sideways and scored a corporate letterman jacket still hanging in my husband's closet. I served on Fannie Mae's lender panel for two two-year terms.

During the bank years, credit scoring was adopted as a mortgage industry tool. I attacked the subject like a major term paper in college. This resulted in speaking engagements, first locally and then nationally including MBA National Underwriting Conferences.

The loan division's first failures occurred when we branched out. One manager had a following of brokers so loyal we were buried with loan files the day she started. Most were fraudulent. Another left her management position for a major investor to relocate to her home state, but couldn't attract a following. But for the most part our expansion efforts were so successful that the commercial bank sold off our division.

Our new parent company was a Midwestern bank whose board of directors looked like a mature male church choir. Business proceeded as usual except for quarterly stock distributions, until a disgruntled employee alleged a hostile working environment. Two executives were dispatched to babysit management. Corporate oversight changed our energy level from high to inert.

The retail manager left for a bigger company. The babysitters went home. After several of us defected, the bank shut down its mortgage acquisition.

Lessons learned:

1. Tag-team management can be very effective.

2. Growing pains affect businesses, not just teenagers.

3. You can tie a leader's hands behind his back but you can't make him stay.

The infamous mortgage banker

The retail manager from the commercial bank was hired to run the correspondent division. He led it to first place out of four divisions in quality and profitability. Growth was spurred by technology and a company-wide work ethic. The industry referred to it as a sweatshop and I called it the evil empire, but after accepting employment, my point of view shifted. Soon I found myself embracing the energy.

Our division was a cohesive and productive unit. Little did we know that two circumstances outside our division would lead to our company's demise. After the older of the two founders of the company retired from active management, his co-founder—the public face—propelled the company into more aggressive lending. And the forces of greed in the industry permeated even our divisional silo, with our company becoming the personification of abusive lending. It resulted in the company's demise.

Lessons learned:

1. A company unappealing from the outside can look better from the inside.

2. With good fit in senior management positions, there was mutual respect and a minimum of backbiting.

3. Even good apples become tainted if mixed with rotten apples.

The national bank

After the infamous mortgage banker shut down, I worked for a national bank, the antithesis to the infamous mortgage bank. Deliberate as opposed to bold, and controlled as opposed to entrepreneurial, the bank had multiple layers of oversight. After a few years, the national bank and I parted ways.

Lesson: If you don't trust the people doing the job, replace them with people you do trust.

Continuing education

To bridge the gap between college and a career, I decided to take evening classes. Luckily UCLA Extension offered relevant classes and my employer covered their cost.

My first course was Business English. Transitioning from literature to business writing seemed like a good idea. My classmates were mostly non-native English speakers trying to improve communication skills, but the class had useful content. I learned how to format memos and business letters, and most importantly to focus on what the reader needed to read rather than what I wanted to write.

Next I took every class pertinent to residential mortgage origination. Included were Real Estate Principles, Real Estate Law and Mortgages, Trust Deeds and Security Agreements (informative but a snoozer—I was running out of classes) but my two favorites were Appraisal and Residential Design and Structure.

Appraisal was compelling after a week driving around with appraisers. The high point was an on-site visit to a vacant rental property owned by a classmate. Our task was to appraise it. While the rest of the class listened to the instructor discussing landscaping, I sketched the floor plan and taped the rooms. A staff appraiser helped with the comparables and I easily completed the appraisal form.

Residential Design and Structure was taught by an architect who brought in floor plans every week. We analyzed what made each house more or less functional. I learned that bedroom closets muffled noise between rooms and that a sign of amateur design was a dining room not adjacent to the kitchen. The class focused on functional and non-functional floor plans. Every session also featured a different guest speaker—a landscape architect, an interior designer, developer, etc. The developer told us about a speech he delivered at an industry conference. Intending to drive the point of teamwork and leveraging talents, he began with the question "How many of you are geniuses?" Nearly everyone in the conference hall raised their hands.

The last class was available only at a community college. Escrow (the closing process in California and other states) was taught by the owner of a local escrow company. The class was enlightening since our closings were handled in another branch, but the lasting memory was from a conversation during break. The instructor knew where I worked and offered a cash incentive if our Human Resources department purchased training modules he had designed. I tactfully declined his offer.

These classes kickstarted my career in mortgage banking. The difference between a job and a career is understanding the why as well as the how. Although "mortgage professional" lost luster after the meltdown, a personal commitment to professionalism is worth the effort.

Diversity and inclusion

In my first industry position, I was hired to replace the first female vice president at the giant savings and loan. She was assertive before assertive women were appreciated. During our transition week before her exit, I discovered she was insulted with my hiring. She was a ground-breaker and her anger was legitimate, since I had no industry experience. She resented not being promoted to replace the deceased head of the mortgage division and my hiring as well.

A few years later, after promotion from administrative assistant to branch loan manager, I broke ground to a lesser extent. I became the second female loan manager in the company.

Origination management was integrated racially before women were promoted to leadership positions. My first district manager was black. The giant savings and loan was instrumental in opening the Home Loan Counseling Center, an industry-backed resource center in Los Angeles. It also opened an inner-city loan branch to increase minority homeownership. Additional black and Hispanic managers joined our ranks. My former district loan manager was promoted to a senior corporate position.

When I started in the industry, almost all underwriters were female. The appraisal staff and most of the mid-level managers were male. This pattern perpetuated until I was at the infamous mortgage bank. Loan volume increased and competent underwriters were in short supply so we decided to grow our own. College-graduate temporary employees identified with potential were drafted into an intense three-week underwriting training course. Those who passed the multi-hour final exam were teamed up with experienced underwriters. When they proved capable of making independent decisions, they were promoted to underwriters. Our successful candidates were male and female, multi-ethnic and diverse in age. We were fully integrated in every respect.

When the majority of underwriters were female, there was a noticeable presence of gay men to the extent that some straight male underwriters were assumed to be gay. Unfortunately, able gay men and lesbian women had limited success moving up to management. At the infamous mortgage bank, a gifted senior underwriter was promoted to loan manager but left the company after sensing a gay glass ceiling. He since has been promoted to senior vice president of a large bank. As for line underwriters and lower-level managers, some shared their orientation and others remained in the closet.

Post-meltdown when loan volume subsided, it was survival of the competent. Loan origination became a meritocracy. At least for the last decade or two, the industry has been tolerant and inclusive, based on my experience. As it should be.

Mentoring

Five people had major influence on my career. Although this book purposely excludes names of companies and most people, all deserve recognition. Norm MacLeod hired me into the industry and schooled me in risk. Doug Jones managed me (mostly indirectly) for 25 years at two companies, the first after his colleague told him the start-up mortgage division needed "an Anne Elliott type." Doug who hadn't yet met me responded "Why don't we just hire Anne Elliott." John Dixon was a business banker who morphed into a secondary guy and then led our division's operations and underwriting staffs. Jim Follette was a corporate transfer assigned to run the risk group. He tactfully moved me from people management to idea management, and a few years later, despite our company's industry reputation as a sweat shop, told me my work week ended at noon on Fridays. (I sometimes complied, rarely staying after 2:00.) The commonality is that none of the four had underwriting training, but all had perceptive risk acumen. Finally, Roy Downey was always open for discussing risk issues and "the why" behind guidelines, and appointed me to Fannie Mae's underwriting advisory panel.

In turn I have mentored. Transitory relationships have turned into friendships—three in particular. All live out of state but communicate by phone, letters or personal visits. Ashley Oberst Dingler has hiked with my husband. Beth McDow invited me to meet her family on the way home from Christmas with my husband's family. Matt Willard is an annual houseguest. Beth and Matt have flourished in the mortgage industry. Ashley worked in financial before marrying and starting a family. She opted for stay-at-home motherhood, and her letters, emails and phone calls radiate the joy of her choice.

Knowledge should be shared. There is benefit for both parties, and sometimes mentorship evolves from a good deed into a joy.

Technology

I've used the term Luddite to describe myself, but it's an overstatement. I don't hate technology; I struggle handling its implementation. And, on the whole, I believe technology has benefitted the mortgage industry.

Automated underwriting: LP and DU have expedited the approval process, protect originators on marginal loans that are AUS-approved and good loans that don't perform, and make valid decisions on the vast majority of loans.

Analytics: The mind-numbing process of manually compiling a spreadsheet has been replaced by a programmer populating a spreadsheet via data search. The result is useful information on pipeline management, reporting, pricing, fraud patterns, loan performance and numerous other areas of interest.

Electronic validation: Technology—specifically DU at this point—has facilitated validation of income, assets, employment and value. Fannie Mae has partnered with vendors to reduce originators' workloads and decrease exposure through reps and warranties protection. Eligibility is limited to specific transaction types, property types and borrower profiles.

Tax return pre-analysis: Within hours at an affordable price, LoanCraft performs the pre-analysis of tax returns necessary to calculate qualifying income. Years ago, this would have been accomplished with a warehouse filled with seasoned underwriters, each surrounded by towering piles of 1040s, 1120s and 1065s. Now, the culling of figures is accomplished through technology, followed by human review to assure accuracy. Scanners pick up select income and loss figures and insert them into a calculation template. The result is a compilation of relevant figures sorted into higher and lower approaches to qualifying income. Still recalling my first day in a long-past position pulling figures for a borrower with over fifty partnerships, I appreciate a service dispensing with the tedium and enabling the underwriter to concentrate on how qualifying income is most appropriately derived.

Credit scores: Before credit scoring, credit was largely assessed by tallying up derogatory credit and deciding whether the letter of explanation was the truth or a lie. Proficient underwriters did notice when there was sparse or new credit, or if the borrower was a heavy user.

Third party verifications: The debate whether VOES and VODS are preferable to pay-stubs, W2s and depository statements is less meaningful now that verifications can be obtained from some companies electronically.

Technology solves some problems and creates others. Everything is a double-edged sword.

My first home

My first home was in a condo conversion in a five-story building on a major traffic street. The unit had 575 square feet and was technically a studio because there was no walled-off bedroom. The original developer opted for several studio units to minimize the required subterranean parking spaces. I recognized the irony of purchasing a unit with impaired marketability in multiple respects.

Was it a bad decision on my part? Absolutely not. I wanted a unit after seeing the conversion feasibility study on Norm's desk. I was attracted to the desirable West Los Angeles neighborhood and the affordability of the smallest units. Norm connected me to the developer, who said there was a single unit available for rent. I told him I wanted to move in, then buy it. He insisted I look at the unit first.

The location was in Brentwood, and the traffic street was Sunset Boulevard. The building was U-shaped with the upper tips facing Sunset. Lush landscaping and fountains in the middle space in the U muted street noise. The building was soundly constructed with a brick exterior and brick walls between the units. My unit faced the street but was on the U's bottom bar. Between the fountains and brick construction, noise wasn't a problem. The developer repainted, re-carpeted and upgraded the kitchen in every unit, even for tenants who were purchasing.

The project has 93 units on five floors. Amenities include a front office, a common room, a roof-top sundeck, a swimming pool and a gym with a sauna. The gym's toilets and showers came in handy after a plumbing problem in my unit. The only other breakdown I recall is an inoperative elevator after a heavy rainstorm.

My unit included a kitchen with full-sized appliances, ample closet space and a bathroom with the sink separated by a closable door from the toilet/shower over tub. I purchased a two-sided bookcase to separate the sleeping area from the living room-dining area. I considered having a wall built to turn the unit into a one bedroom, but didn't. The unit comfortably accommodated Donald, me and most of our books when he moved in.

A property with multiple risk indicators can have good livability and marketability. I enjoyed being two short blocks from Brentwood Village, convenient when I was hungry or sick, and a ten-minute walk from San Vicente Boulevard where there was a parade every Memorial Day. My unit was large enough for small parties, and the meeting room could be reserved for the larger ones.

I knew I made a good choice at our first homeowners meeting when two attorneys, two accountants and a UCLA professor were elected to the board of directors. A consumer advocate didn't make the cut. I enjoyed the HOA meetings. They were Democracy in Action, and my neighbors were people I enjoyed knowing. There was a reasonable profit at sale, and I missed the location and closet space when we moved on to a detached residence.

The property was sold as a FSBO. I received advice from the appraisers at work and a broker friend across the hall, whose listings were on larger and more expensive properties. Advertising was a notice on the neighborhood grocery's bulletin board. I received a bid not long after the notice was posted and the buyer signed a simplified sales contract pirated from a loan file. The sales transaction closed smoothly.

Our first home

Donald and I bought our first home during a hot seller's market. That meant that even unappealing homes were snatched up quickly. We wanted to move closer to the beach but the only affordable option there was a mobile home park. So we spent weekends prowling every open house in the Palms and Mar Vista neighborhoods in West Los Angeles.

I recall only three. The first was a small house two lots away from a traffic street. It was affordable but its only appealing feature was vintage glass doorknobs. The second house was a two-bedroom one-bath home. Its selling point was the large lot. The third house lacked any interior visual appeal. Rooms featured different colors of shag carpeting, cottage cheese ceilings and dark wood paneling. The family room was awesome in the worst sense. It had a ceiling with dark cork panels, red shag carpet on the floor, and the dark wall panels alternated with strips of red shag carpeting. In the middle of the room was an affixed boat-shaped bar seating six and with in built-in blender.

This was the house we were able to purchase, probably because it took imagination to see past the ugliness. The house had three bedrooms, two bathrooms and a floor plan with good flow. It was on a quiet street, within our budget and almost 1,000 square feet larger than the Brentwood condo.

The first remodel removed most of the ugly. The ceilings were scraped, the walls painted white, the moldings unified, the 1939-vintage wooden floors restored and the house re-wired. The newer wing was re-carpeted, and the kitchen and bathroom floors and counters re-tiled in white. Every surface of the family room was stripped, and the boat-shaped bar was hauled away.

Our second remodel replaced every window and door in the the house, and a carpenter installed bookshelves in six rooms.

Our third remodel replaced the gravity heating system, added air conditioning, remodeled both bathrooms, replaced the white tile with darker tile in the kitchen and bathrooms, installed new wooden flooring everywhere else, and painted inside (still white) and out.

Living through three remodels, none adding any square footage, is the source of my annoyance with many homebuyers—first-timers, move-uppers and relocating retirees alike—desiring immediate gratification of unrealistic wish-lists. Older homes predate walk-in closets. Clothes can be stowed in closets of unassigned bedrooms (or in our case a guest room and library.) Walking to the bathroom not adjacent to the larger bedroom (un-master suite) does not constitute hardship. But every remodel improved livability.

The hot seller's market peaked soon after we closed. Five years after purchase our house was finally worth what we paid for it. Our equity position was deep, since my midwestern husband delayed moving up until our savings reached his goal. Even if our down payment had been smaller, default wouldn't have been considered. We love our house and our neighborhood—which explains why we remain there. The first remodel occurred while the house was valued at less than we paid for it. That didn't matter to us because we knew it would be our home for a long time.

Neighborhood update

Our neighborhood is transforming. For the first two decades of ownership, changes were subtle. Houses evolved through interior remodels, increased square footage or, to a lesser extent, tear-down and replacement by a new structure. Our neighborhood was aging gracefully. More recently, tear-downs and fully livable properties have been replaced by homes doubling original square footage. Our block started with only two two-story houses built custom built for relatives of the original landowner. Now nearly half the houses on our block have two stories.

Westside Village, a subsection of Palms, officially comprises about twelve hundred households, predominately single family detached. Three-quarters of the Village is on one side of an arterial street and one-quarter (including our house) is on the other. Our block-wide swath traditionally sold for slightly lower prices. The two-block-wide mix of apartment buildings and SFRs south of our block sold for even less. Their south border is a major traffic street lined with low-rise retail, discount clinics and used auto sales.

In 2015 our zip code appeared in a front page Los Angeles Times article as one of ten zip codes with the highest appreciation in the county. More recently, Palms/Mar Vista placed fourth out of fifty-one local communities in annual appreciation.

Values have appreciated for several reasons. The national economic recovery and proximity to Silicon Beach—an unofficial designation for tech companies sited in nearby coastal communities gradually spreading eastward—have increased demand. Light rail now extends to West Los Angeles. This positively impacted local neighborhoods even prior to its completion, as did installation of bike lanes throughout Los Angeles. A vacant supermarket is being replaced by a high-density condo project, and a discount store on a short-term lease is expected to as well.

Which brings us to walkability. Two years ago I was unaware of the term. After a housing risk conference in Washington, D.C. and a Bloomberg Business Week article, the term became familiar. Walkable neighborhoods allow people to live, eat out, shop and socialize locally. Even in auto-dependent Los Angeles, walkability has become closer to reality.

First-time home buyers in our extended neighborhood are mostly young professionals, many working for tech companies, preferring to buy smaller and older homes closer to work and with the means to afford them. Seasoned residents are changing their habits as well. Donald rides his bike to business meetings in Venice, and I'm considering taking light rail to visit friends who work downtown and my cousin in an adjacent county.

Redfin has rolled out a Walk Score which rates neighborhoods on a walkability scale of 1 to 100. Los Angeles has an overall Walk Score of 66.3, and its most walkable neighborhoods—Koreatown, Silverlake and downtown (with only Silverlake being trendy a decade ago)—have Walk Scores over 90, representing the top 2% of the city's active home listings.

A decade or two from now, the Walk Score may be replaced by a more pertinent indicator. The remaining economic life of houses lasts considerably longer than buyers' priorities.

See *Tracts decades later*

Personal adventures in financing

Applying for a loan was part of my industry education. Filling out the application was challenging, even though I had looked at hundreds before my first loan and thousands by the last. But what I remember most in retrospect are the interest rates.

The rate on my first mortgage loan was 14%. It wasn't subprime. It was the most competitive rate available in the early 1980s. Six months later after interest rates settled down I refinanced at 10%. With updated comparables, LTV decreased from 90% to 80%, and the loan remained on the books until the condo was sold seven years later. Interest rates had decreased further, but the mortgage was small and I was content with a 4% rate reduction and no private mortgage insurance.

When Donald and I bought our house in 1988, interest rates were around 7%, lower than the condo loan but exorbitant currently. We refinanced a few years later for a reduced rate and a 15-year term. We held on to that mortgage for ten years or so, paying as much as we could afford in the later years. We finally refinanced into a 3/1 ARM, a program I never anticipated buying into. With checks equal to our previous payment level, our house was free and clear over a year before the fixed period expired.

Donald and I made good decisions. We were never tempted to cash out, move up or speculate. As stated previously, we are content.

My first book

Mortage Risk Blueprint is not my first book on mortgage risk. I wrote *The Loan Underwriting Handbook* around 1980 as a gift for Norm MacLeod, who hired me into the lending industry and help formulate my risk philosophy. The book had 63 pages but only slightly more than two hundred words. It was bound inexpensively.

Most of the opinions expressed were from the chairman of the giant savings and loan. His risk philosophy consisted of damning every borrower or property type that resulted in default or unpleasantness during the origination process.

The chairman had many acquaintances who became loan applicants. Since my office was located in our corporate headquarters, their loans were handed off to me. They thought leveraging their relationship would improve the outcome. Little did they know the experience would be better without his intervention.

Footnotes are included for clarity.

LOAN UNDERWRITING HANDBOOK

I. BORROWER CONSIDERATIONS

Do not make loans to:

> Lawyers,
> doctors,
> dentists,
> real estate agents,
> builders,
> developers

or anyone in the construction industry
even hod-carriers,
borrowers who have second trust deeds
or will be getting second trust deeds,
movie producers,
directors,
musicians,
actors or
anyone with needle marks,
wheelers and dealers,
speculators,
pyramiders, (1)
old people,
young people,
poor people,
people who haven't owned property,
people who already own property,
people without proof of citizenship,
people in unstable industries,
people who will lose their jobs,
people who will go bankrupt,
people who will get divorced,
employees,
relatives,
personal friends
(ex-friends, that is),
chronic delinquents,
or people willing to pay what you're offering.

II. PROPERTY CONSIDERATIONS

Do not make loans on:

Older properties,
properties on a mountainside,
properties on a hillside,
properties below a hillside,
properties in a canyon,
properties near an ocean,
properties near a river,
properties near a stream,
properties adjacent to creeks or ravines,

properties in areas that will be flooded, (2)
or mudded,
or properties that will slide
or be slid upon,
or burned in a fire,
or properties on a flag lot,
or in rural areas,
or without adequate sewers,
or without adequate cash flow,
and especially when our quota is filled. (3)

III. THE MOST IMPORTANT CONSIDERATION OF ALL

How big is the lot? (4)

IV. HOW TO ESTABLISH LOAN RATES (5)

Find out what Reliable Mortgage is charging...
Or higher.

Footnotes:

1. Pyramiders was the chairman's term for borrowers converting equity into cash to buy other properties.

2. Designated flood zones were not yet devised.

3. "Our quota" referred to brush and slide areas in my lending territory. The quota was applied by the chairman exclusively on loans he was involved with.

4. "How big is the lot?" came up during a prolonged interrogation with the chairman about a loan for his tailor. His assistant had warned me there would be questions about property insurance, so I entered his office well-prepared. I didn't anticipate questioning would continue until he found one I was unprepared to answer, which was "How big is the lot?" I didn't check on that because if the residence burned down, the lot size would remain the same.

5. Our standard rate sheet covered conforming and jumbo pricing, but the chairman's acquaintances often required super jumbo pricing. Reliable Mortgage was a local loan company catering to borrowers ineligible with mainstream lending institutions, principally because of substandard credit.

CHAPTER 17
UNDERWRITING MANAGEMENT

For new managers

1. Since underwriters typically behave like adults, managers shouldn't have to be drill sergeants or referees. Personnel management should dominate only during review season which, if your team is capable, is more painful for you than them. Reviews should emphasize positives as well as constructive criticism and include tangible steps for improvement for those with deficiencies or seeking advancement. No one should be surprised when review results are discussed face to face.

2. Managing underwriters involves more than guidance in decision-making. When workflow is managed effectively, turn-times meet goals, underwriters don't return from days off to ignored files and frustrated borrowers, and the most accommodating underwriter doesn't go home hours after everyone else. When workflow can't be managed effectively because of sustained high volume, discuss solutions with your manager.

3. Idea management covers everything from group training to trending to individual loan decisions. Every day is an opportunity for a learning experience.

4. Team meetings should consist of more than applause for birthdays and service anniversaries. When you find a good teaching file, have everyone review it independently and then discuss it as a group. If there isn't enough time to dissect a loan, condense it into bullet points or pick an interesting appraisal. The more hands-on your meetings are, the more content will be remembered.

5. There is a difference between bossing and managing. The best leaders teach and motivate without being bossy.

6. Don't counsel employees on their personal lives. The more you encourage them to bring their problems to the office, the more they will.

7. Do ask for help from co-managers. Their management styles may help formulate yours, and having manager-friends is a positive.

8. Be aware that every change in personnel changes equilibrium.

9. Listen!

Underwriters by classification

Underwriters tend to be analytical, detail-minded, comfortable with following rules and skeptical by nature. Beyond the standard underwriter profile, there are various subspecies:

Tree-counters: Metaphorically, they can't see the forest because they are too busy counting trees. This group underwrites mechanically and appreciates the guidance of checklists. They see benefit in calculating income to the penny and DTI with decimal points. They believe every detail matters, and their devotion to precision confirms their excellence.

Big picture underwriters: They have the ability to put the pieces together but may miss out on the details. They never over-condition. Auditors love reviewing their files because there are inevitably findings, often more inconsequential than meaningful. These underwriters often can be effective in lead or manager positions, as long as they are not supervising other big picture underwriters.

The more conservative the better: These overly-cautious underwriters believe responsible underwriting requires taking the most conservative approach to every facet of the file. They see themselves as guardians of risk, but don't understand that excessive vigilance negatively affects the company's profitability and reputation.

Insightful: These underwriters can identify fraud without a list of red flags, can discern between the atypical and the unlikely, and problem-solve until concerns are resolved. They counter-offer more often than others, prefer non-standardized conditions and seldom over-condition unless attempting to give a poorly-packaged loan the opportunity to close. They don't always agree with the AUS decision; if consistently overruled, they may move on to another company. They were born to underwrite and joyous to discover their calling.

Fraud hounds: These underwriters are preoccupied with fraud. Often their suspicions are not well-founded. What they enjoy more than crafting a closable loan is identifying a loan that shouldn't be closed.

Journeymen: Butchers and other tradespeople progress professionally from apprentice to journeyman to master. Tradespeople may achieve master designation after an established number of years, but senior underwriter should be a title evidencing competency, not longevity.

Built for speed: These underwriters are a production manager's dream and, for some, the auditor's as well. The best balance speed with quality. Others may be capable of balancing quantity with quality, but only if their priorities change. Adding a quality component to compensation may do the trick.

Good at potlucks: Members of this group are apt to be appreciated more for their social skills than their risk acumen. They should be at least competent. Unless they are insightful, they should not be promoted despite extended tenure, unless to a position where people skills matter more than analytical skills.

Risk-blind: I didn't understand that risk acumen couldn't be taught until the year after my in-laws moved. I wanted to go to a store we visited the previous year. Donald grabbed the car keys and headed to the front door. "Don't you need directions?" I asked. "Not unless it moved." This incident taught me that my limited sense of direction is similar to some underwriters' inability to identify risk. It's a talent not everyone is born with.

Some underwriters overlap between two classifications. Some of the classifications are better suited to certain product types. Tree-Counters and Journeymen are a good fit for government, affordable and manufactured housing loans, also for compliance. They are less desirable for non-conforming production where over-conditioning or lack of vision can turn a low-risk loan into a cancellation.

Once underwriters have been classified, the next step is figuring out how to implement improvement. If you believe people's fundamental natures can be changed, try pairing up underwriters with different strengths and ask them to co-underwrite. Tree-Counters, The More Conservative and Risk-Blind underwriters can be matched with Big Picture underwriters. Working together may benefit both. Built for Speed and Tree-Counters can improve each other, unless the Built for Speed underwriters are already built for quality. Insightful underwriters can be paired with anyone.

Not everyone is capable of improving. Less-seasoned Risk-Blind have greater potential than well seasoned Journeymen. The More Conservative underwriters may lack capacity to reason out the best income approach. Pairing is better attempted in lower volume periods, since it adversely affects productivity.

Underwriters not in need of improvement deserve recognition and opportunity. A file with several inches of tax returns can be overwhelming or drudgery to most underwriters, but a welcome challenge to the best. Assuming they are willing to share expertise, competent underwriters should be utilized as team leads or managers. Even less outgoing underwriters may enjoy and be effective in one-to-one mentoring situations.

Only a fraction of insightful underwriters can judiciously decision exceptions. This requires risk acumen without being bound by written guidelines.

Another distinctive talent is the ability to identify patterns within a population of loans prior to default or inability to sell. Most companies can withstand losses on isolated loans but even sizable companies struggle with large-scale losses resulting from organized fraud or deficient underwriting. These specially skilled underwriters should find satisfaction in (and benefit their employers from) analyzing populations of rather than individual loans.

See *Mentor underwriters, Feast or famine* and *Not terminating employees*

The underwriter litmus test

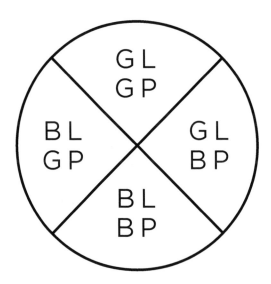

The litmus test is the underwriter's ability to distinguish among four categories of loans. Starting at the top counter-clockwise, the categories are

- Good loan, good packaging

- Bad loan, good packaging

- Bad loan, bad packaging

- Good loan, bad packaging

Even unseasoned underwriters should be able to tell the difference between a good loan with good packaging and a bad loan with bad packaging. The harder test is distinguishing a good loan with bad packaging from a bad loan with good packaging. Some seasoned underwriters are flummoxed by the east and west quadrants, which results in good loans being denied and bad loans being approved.

This suggests a training exercise, probably best reserved for lulls in submissions. Select two cancelled or denied loans, one each from the east and west quadrants. It is preferable but not required that the complicating factors for both loans are similar, e.g., appraisal or self-employment issues. Ideally participants should review key documents first, or the loans can be summarized. Discuss each loan consecutively, then if necessary explain what the critical difference is. The aim of the exercise is making underwriters aware that good loans with bad packaging are worth fixing, and bad loans with good packaging are irredeemable.

Managing underwriters

Underwriters shouldn't need much managing. Employees paid for judgment skills should act like mature and responsible adults. That means work hours need not be uniform as long as there is adequate coverage for phone calls, accessibility to borrowers and loan officers, and attendance at meetings and training sessions. Leaving early for parent-teacher conferences, appointments or special occasions should be accommodated unless there is a pattern of taking advantage. Likewise, underwriters at companies where month-end requires concerted all-hands-on effort should try to avoid parent-teacher conferences and days off during those times. As a manager addicted to travel, I tried to distinguish between trips that can be re-scheduled and events like family reunions which cannot. Pre-booked flights are a judgment call. The employee optimally should check before booking.

The manager's day-to-day responsibilities should include making sure the workload is fairly distributed, expertise is shared, the team is motivated, and escalations and emergencies are decisioned quickly (whenever possible) and well (always).

A good underwriting manager praises as well as admonishes, although only when justified. Underwriters who don't meet standards in terms of quality, productivity or attitude should be given a finite period of time to improve and if not they should be managed out. If there is minimum possibility of improvement, a history of unsatisfactory performance or lack of integrity, manage out immediately.

Pre-hire testing for underwriters

I advocate pre-hire testing but find true/false or fill in the blank tests a waste of time. Objective tests don't assess judgment skills. Even mediocre underwriters can calculate LTV. Questions like "If Jacob's Schedule C had net earnings of $47,832 and depreciation of $4,335 two years ago and net earnings of $42,475 and depreciation of $4,598 last year, what is qualifying income?" are slightly better. However, the salient issue is Jacob's declining income.

The more worthwhile approach is analysis of a loan file sanitized to protect the privacy of the borrowers. (Leave in first names and street names. Obscure social security numbers, the last four digits of phone numbers, etc.) Selected loans should include judgment issues and be neither easy approvals nor easy denials. The first section of written responses should be more objective: qualifying income and method of calculation for each borrower, loan score, debt ratios, verified assets and reserves. The subjective section should be open-ended: "Comment on the borrower's credit," "How would you decision this loan and why?" The candidate's test responses should be integrated into the interview: "What made you feel comfortable with the 16-month job gap?" Written responses and verbal discussion test essential job skills without opportunity for editing, polishing or coaching, unless a single loan is used for an extended period of time. File analysis requires more time and effort for the interviewee and interviewer but provides greater insight on candidates.

There is another pre-hire test for underwriters. Reviewing candidates' credit reports was someone else's idea, but I endorsed it. Underwriters with lax credit usage are apt to consider marginal borrowers normal.

The commercial bank that prohibited hiring underwriters with bankruptcies allowed an exception to policy. The underwriter had a strong resume and came highly recommended. She, her ex-husband and two children had a normal family life until the husband started acting erratically. He was diagnosed with a brain tumor. His behavior deteriorated, and the underwriter feared for her young children. She filed for divorce, and her husband moved in with his parents. Debt had accumulated, both medical bills and consumer debt, as the husband's earnings plummeted. She sold the house and filed for bankruptcy. Her decision to declare bankruptcy and the company's decision to hire her demonstrated that decisions justified by special circumstances aren't confined to loans.

Worst case underwriting

My favorite loan for testing underwriting candidates was a purchase transaction for a couple who had relocated 20 months earlier. The attorney was employed by a law firm, earning salary and bonus. He also taught at a local law school and received buyout payments on his former practice. The dental hygienist increased her work schedule from two to three days weekly and sold paintings at art fairs. All sources of income were documented. Their credit was good, and the 20% down payment came from savings and seasoned sale proceeds from their midwest residence.

Qualifying income identified overly conservative and overly aggressive candidates. The borrowers didn't need every source of their current income to qualify, but needed more than his base and her earnings for two days weekly. With decent equity, good income potential and overall creditworthiness, the only obstacle was unseasoned income. That obstacle could be surmounted with a prudent amount of flexibility.

Pre-hire testing for underwriters should involve judgment skills as well as general industry knowledge and technical precision. A well selected sample loan measures all three.

Younger and older

This subject is politically incorrect but bears mentioning. The attributes vary by person. Some or all may be totally inapplicable to people you deal with. Because of these caveats, my usual qualifiers (e.g., usually, often, sometimes) are largely omitted.

Younger underwriters:

- are energetic and have potential to grow

- may be college graduates with analytic skills

- are comfortable with technology

- may think well-established approaches are outdated

- have fewer bad habits to unlearn

Older underwriters:

- have looked at thousands of files, know how to handle the unusual and discern the scary

- may have graduated from processing

- are less adept at technology

- may be unwilling to take direction

- may have memory issues. This may be manageable with post-it reminders or to-do lists.

In-house underwriter training

For maximum benefit to employees and employer, promoting from within should target employees with the greatest upward potential. Work with HR to identify underutilized employees from positions not restricted to processing who are ready for more challenging responsibilities. Or consider hiring college graduates with analytic skills. For those new to the industry or the origination process, offer an introductory training or a short-term support position to provide familiarity with basic lingo and origination documents. This also allows opportunity to consider whether the mortgage industry is a good fit before training begins. Some will decide they'd prefer doing something else.

Although the traditional approach to underwriter training is one-on-one mentoring, a more formalized structure works when several people are being trained simultaneously. Trainers should be knowledgable and good communicators, and specialists should present on their areas of expertise. In addition to key points from presentations interspersed with space for notes, training materials can be gathered from real loan files. Start with applications, then credit reports and gradually work up to full loan packages. Lessons should begin with a presentation on fundamentals leading to hands-on learning. Although borrowers' personal data should not be shared with job candidates, those on the payroll should be trusted with actual files. Explain that only notes may be taken out of the training room.

Do not do tax return training all in one day. I learned from experience that a better method is to handle the less complicated basics (Schedule Cs, rental cash flow, unreimbursed expenses, and forgiven debt) during the initial training and the complicated parts later.

Consider bringing in outside experts like appraisers and title officers. Do not let any outside expert be the sole source of training. Trainee underwriters will benefit from hearing about how an appraisal is conducted as well as about memorable, unusual or challenging properties. They should learn appraisal analysis from an underwriter.

If the training group is small or there are available and willing appraisers, at least half a day in the field with an appraiser is invaluable.

A critical element of training is testing. I recommend quizzes at least weekly and a multi-hour, timed final exam requiring analysis of loan files and appraisals. Being tested on several appraisals and files works to the trainee's advantage; one wrong call matters less and a pattern of errors counts more. A time limit is important because productivity is a critical part of the business. I usually allowed three or four hours, and found that the best learners usually finished earlier. Communicating final exam results, both good and bad, may be best handled by the participant's immediate supervisor. As heartless as it sounds, unless there is a life event causing temporary loss of concentration second chances are a bad idea. No company needs mediocre underwriters.

After formal coursework ends, the hands-on phase begins. As an experienced manager told me when I was starting out "You're not really an underwriter until you've looked at a thousand loans." He was correct. A co-underwriting or mentoring phase is necessary. Select mentors who understand risk as well as technicalities and have good communication skills. Some underwriters are better at dissecting a loan file than sharing insights, but some unimpressive communicators share knowledge effectively one-to-one .

Fledgling underwriters should be encouraged to ask questions—many questions. Winging it is inappropriate for the first year or two, at least. Underwriting remains a collaborative effort, and newbies should be aware that there is no stigma at any stage of proficiency in asking for a second opinion. Every loan file presents different issues, and some issues arise infrequently.

Testing during the mentoring phase is accomplished through file review. If an area of deficiency is identified, partner the newbie with a mentor who has proficiency in that area. (This strategy can apply to experienced underwriters as well. I fondly recall an underwriter competent in every aspect of the loan package except for appraisal.) Switching mentors from time to time isn't a bad idea whatever the circumstances. Different perspectives and life experiences can provide tangible benefit.

As loan volume increased in the years before the meltdown, the correspondent division of infamous mortgage banker resorted to turning temporary employees who demonstrated potential into underwriters. Most of the temps who passed the tough final exam and survived the hands-on training phase turned into capable underwriters of closed loans, despite limited industry experience. Many have transitioned into front-line origination, and the best have turned into leaders.

Managing underwriting support

Effective underwriting assistants, junior underwriters or processors (whatever their title is) should have similar attributes to underwriters. They should be detail-minded, have good interpersonal skills and not be intimidated by math. Rudimentary knowledge of loan origination should increase. Teaming up assistants with underwriters is the standard way of increasing efficiency and proficiency. Periodic switch-ups can help, although change is distressing to some.

An essential teaching point is recognizing when issues should be escalated. It usually starts with a displeased loan officer or a resistant borrower. Assistants should understand that difficulties they are unable to resolve should be referred upward. Underwriters should have greater discretionary authority than assistants. When the resolution will not please the applicant, the communicator should be someone who is firm but conciliatory.

The most capable assistants should be candidates for underwriter training. They may not be the most seasoned. Promoting from within is admirable but should be merit-based and take into account that underwriting requires judgment skills. If processors with potential resist promotion, wait patiently and ask again, reiterating their strengths. But do not force the unwilling into underwriting positions. Some juniors want to be juniors forever, and the industry does not need underwriters who prefer doing something else.

The processor quandary

There are two common alternatives in filling open processor positions. Both have limitations.

1. Hire promotable processors. They should have attributes suitable for underwriting, notably math aptitude, an organized mind and the potential for good decision-making. At least some should turn into underwriting candidates. The downside is that those who are promoted must be replaced, and those who aren't may be discontent.

2. Hire career processors. Some will be dependable, and others will have potential but be responsibility-adverse. The downside is that less seasoned employees with more authority may be resented.

There are career processors who perform superbly. Cherish them. With open positions, consider both alternatives.

The botched origination

The jumbo loan was a rush, and the processor did her best to expedite it. Most of her efforts went toward completing the Schedule of Real Estate Owned for two properties acquired in the last year. When the file was finally passed on to the underwriter, timing was even more critical. She noticed that corporate returns for the restaurant opened two decades ago showed an $8,000 profit two years ago but a $45,000 loss last year, yielding debt ratios of 69%/72%.

The branch manager asked me to review the loan with the processor. To prepare, I was handed the 1008, the loan application and a three page cash flow analysis completed by the underwriter. While profitability decreased, salaried income from the restaurant increased from $50,000 to $71,000. The borrowers were moving up from a $600,000 house to a $855,000 house with housing expense increasing from $2,750 to $4,725.

Since debt ratios at 80% LTV were unworkable, the loan was counter-offered to the conforming maximum, reducing LTV to 49%.

Lessons:

1. *Too much concentration on individual trees may cause the forest to be missed.*

2. *The story of the loan indicates that the borrowers not only had a suffering business, but simultaneously were making questionable financial decisions. The acquisition of two rental properties and the conversion of their current residence (acquired only two years ago) into a third rental suggested they were transitioning from income-based to asset-based—a normal transition for those approaching retirement age. At 80% LTV, the new house was unaffordable. At 49% LTV, with acceptable ratios and a deep equity position risk was acceptable.*

3. *A process that doesn't involve the underwriter until the file is ready for approval reduces overhead, but can result in unhappy borrowers or expensive mistakes.*

Pre-hire testing for processors

Hiring processors has almost as many pitfalls as hiring underwriters. The counterintuitive part is the more experienced the processor, the more questions there are to be asked.

Since the most proficient processors get promoted to underwriting positions, a critical issue in interviewing a current processor is a tactful version of "Why are you still a processor?" Usually either the processor wants a job with limited responsibility because of other priorities or is unqualified for promotion. Those falling into the second category may not be aware of their limitations. If they are, they won't tell you.

Checking references can be handled two ways. Talking to the processing supervisor may yield an edited response. Chatting with loan officers may be more useful. Ask about accuracy, frequency of screw-ups, communication with borrowers and willingness to pitch in during high volume periods. The more candid answer will probably come from the L.O.

An objective test could be constructed for processors. Depending on the client base, the ability to dissect complex tax returns is either unnecessary or essential. With business banking customers or wealthy clientele, sanitized tax returns with some complexity are an effective test of a candidate's competency.

Processor to underwriter

A promotion from processor to underwriter encompasses more than a change in job title. A change in orientation is necessary as well. Processors take care of the details; they are task-oriented. Underwriters—at least the most competent ones—are able to mentally integrate the various elements of the file, view the loan as a whole and thus evaluate risk.

A change of focus from micro to macro is necessary.

A worthwhile exercise for promoted processors is composing cover letters. The task enables the transition coach to assess strengths and weaknesses. Underwriters-in-training not traumatized by the experience may also learn that composing a cover letter benefits the writer as well as the reader.

Pre-underwriting orientation

An underwriter's point of view is influenced by previous industry experience. Former loan servicers envision loans turning into foreclosures, former appraisers focus on the property and ex-processors tend to dwell on the mechanical aspects of the origination.

Managers should be aware that reorientation may be necessary. The challenge is figuring out how to retrain mindset. Underwriting is seldom an entry level position; those with industry experience cannot help but apply prior knowledge to their new role.

Training can help. A change of perspective is necessary for a former processor who notices the credit reports is outdated but not recurring cash-out refinances, or the former servicer who correlates new employment with default. Teaming newer underwriters with underwriters who have different work experience can expand the risk perceptions of both.

Feast or famine

No one likes to discuss layoffs. They are inevitable in the mortgage industry where average volume seems unusual. Workload is either overwhelming or so sparse employees fear staff reductions.

Reducing staff is horrific. As soon as the list was finalized, the near-departed transformed into ghosts and I became haunted by their imminent disappearance. My sleep quality deteriorated. But I also believe layoffs benefit a company. The lowest performers hopefully find another position for which they are better suited. Probably if the bottom 20% percent left simultaneously, the quality and volume of work wouldn't suffer much. Trimming staff improves everyone's work ethic and productivity.

The fairest way of reducing staff is not by seniority. The standard approach for government and union workers isn't best for the private sector. In fact, the converse is true. The seniority system protects complacent and mediocre performers. The goal should be retention of the most valued employees and managers, both seasoned and with strong potential.

Promotability

My seat-mate during a flight to South America was Hispanic with a fluent command of English. He was returning home to Lima, Peru. As we chatted, I learned he previously lived in the U.S. and held a management position in the restaurant industry. He didn't know English when he started his career and had no formal culinary education. But he arrived at work before his shift started, came up with money-saving suggestions, and discouraged a co-worker from stretching out his job in order to save work for the following day. He also spoke of turning down a higher-paying job out of loyalty to the employer who promoted him, and mentioned that his restaurant in central California would be turned over to his nephew in two years.

One of management's core responsibilities is identifying whom to promote. I learned early on that employees with intelligence, work ethic and people skills are the keepers. Employees with two of the three probably can hang on, and employees with only one are dispensable. The lessons are:

1. Employees with intelligence, work ethic and people skills are the best candidates for promotion.

2. A meaningful loan lesson can have nothing to do with lending.

Terminating employees

Firing someone is never easy. The act is painful even when termination is justified. The most helpful observation to assuage guilt came from a colleague who advised "I don't fire people. They fire themselves."

Volume-related staffing reductions differ somewhat. Job loss is distressing whether it is the employee's fault or the economy, but layoffs are easier on the conscience.

There are two approaches to group layoffs. The prolonged ordeal involves meeting with each affected employee individually. The efficient ordeal is shepherding the affected employees as a group into a conference room and communicating en masse. For the employees, the benefit of individual delivery is privacy during an emotional moment. The benefit of group delivery is visual proof that others were impacted too. The group approach is less painful for the unaffected who are spared from wondering who will be called in next. Supervisors should be advised before the event, possibly sitting in and accompanying people to their desks. With either approach, the survivors deserve communication immediately after.

Management sometimes waits until Friday afternoon so everyone will have the weekend to recover, or until the end of a pay period or on a recurring mid-week date. The worst time is before a holiday, public or personal. The celebration date will be tainted for the affected long-term and for those not directly affected for at least the following year. My preference, particularly for group events, is mid-day so belongings can be packed up with a limited audience.

Criteria for layoff should be contributory value, not tenure. Exceptions are justified if someone volunteers, is relocating or has announced other career plans.

For the employee, termination can have long-term benefit. The horticultural metaphor is replanting a plant that fails to flower into a different garden where it may flourish. A good example is my own. An entry-level clerical position was the best this recently graduated English major could do in a depressed job market. My transgression was complaining about a malfunctioning cooler where the all-female support staff stowed their lunches. My firing propelled me into the mortgage industry.

Not terminating employees

Retaining an unsatisfactory employee can create more damage than firing that person. Some organizations are hesitant to fire employees who haven't demonstrated gross inadequacy. They fear legal repercussions and creating a climate of insecurity for other employees. They distinguish mediocre performers from failures, and rationalize retention to avoid the admittedly arduous process of finding a replacement.

The overwhelmingly substandard employee is easier to terminate. The undistinguished performers with no chance of promotion, those with attitude problems and troublemakers tend to stay until they decide to leave. They should be asked to leave.

Bad employees are resented by good employees because they contribute less, or are annoying or toxic. They decrease other people's productivity because frustrations are inevitably vented. They create a hostile working environment for their supervisors.

When bad people stay, good people leave.

Incentive compensation

Incentive compensation elevates morale during high-volume periods and downplays the disparity between high-earning loan officers and most everyone else. Before class action lawsuits made underwriters non-exempt despite their decision-making authority, production bonuses replaced overtime for many. Now some line underwriters earn overtime and production incentives.

In my first industry position as a loan manager, I was urged to leave the office at least two afternoons a week to drive properties and comparable sales. The stated purpose was to improve decision-making, but the unstated purpose was to augment paychecks through mileage reimbursement. Since my lending area was small, it took considerable effort to generate a low dollar benefit.

The company also introduced an incentive program in partnership with an insurance company. Branch managers who passed state-mandated testing could sell hazard insurance on loan originations. Again my lending territory worked against me. Expensive properties required coverage over company limits, and canyon areas were off-limits because of brush fire risk. The insurance company didn't insure non-married couples. For those combined reasons my sales were negligible, while the tract loan manager booked policy after policy. This didn't bother me much. Early on, I consciously chose a job I enjoyed over higher earnings.

In the course of my career, I've seen various forms of incentive compensation—monthly bonuses for line underwriters, annual bonuses for managers, auto allowances and production incentives based on number of closed loans—all in addition to fairly equitable base salaries. Some incentives yield better results than others. The key is rewarding extra effort but not compromising quality.

Mentor underwriters

This is an underwriting position I was unable to implement because of bureaucratic inertia. The why of underwriting traditionally has been handed down verbally. Certain seasoned underwriters generously share accumulated wisdom without formal management acknowledgment. They deserve recognition and compensation for benefits provided.

Underwriter, risk and underwriting managers

Underwriter managers are general managers at large companies that believe managers are interchangeable. Some have impressive management skills. But having no insight into what underwriters do, they are of little help when it comes to decisioning. People managers are best utilized for groups that perform rote tasks, assemblers and other step-followers. Mentor underwriters can bridge the gap, but preferably underwriters should be led by someone who understands what they do.

Risk managers understand guidelines and can assess risk. They may enjoy working with people but are better utilized concentrating on loan issues rather than on workflow, time cards and personnel problems.

Underwriting managers can handle both people and loans.

How managers are utilized depends on the size of the department and company needs. But optimally for the manager and the team, managers should find fulfillment in their responsibilities.

At one point my reports were reduced from many to few with the provision that I spend most of my time "thinking about risk." Those three words comprised the core of my new job description. The decision was inspired and I was blissful. I finally had time to concentrate on individual and categories of loans, ones that weren't performing or had the potential for fraud or poor performance, attempting to find commonalities. Single loans sometimes led to related loans and identification of larger patterns. I worked closely with the team responsible for reporting analytics, who worked adjacent to my team. We looked at escalations and problem loans, and identified trends and patterned fraud. Many of our discoveries were fodder for training. Sometimes we discovered less, which was positive and reassuring.

Few in the mortgage industry think about risk as their core responsibility. Creating risk positions should improve loan quality. Recommended improvements could simplify rather than complicate origination, benefitting originators, borrowers and accountants alike.

File review by expertise

An inarguably brilliant co-worker believed complex files were best reviewed by specialists—tax return experts handling income, credit experts evaluating credit and so on. A division of responsibilities more commonly implemented is having the underwriter qualify the borrower and a property expert evaluate the appraisal.

Having a specialist review appraisals for quality, identifying critical findings and highlighting key points, is justified to some extent. Appraisals are lengthy, and review by two knowledgable people may be better than one. The underwriter looks for property eligibility, acceptable marketability, likelihood of occupancy and other risk-related details. Knowledge of the property is essential to understanding the transaction. Cash-out for home improvement should be assessed to determine whether improvements are necessary or seem contrived.

Efficiencies can leverage specific expertise and reduce underwriter tedium. Complex tax returns are best handled by internal experts or external resources like LoanCraft's Income Portal which produces results in hours with affordable pricing. LoanCraft also expedites review when volume is overwhelming. In either instance, the underwriter with the best command of a loan's risk should determine which components of qualifying income are used.

Cooperative review does not alleviate the underwriter's responsibility for making a sound decision on a full file. Support can be provided by those familiar with compensation structures for various lines of work, obscure title issues or specific geographic areas. Critical issues like misrepresentation and compensating factors can be missed when underwriters separately review components of a file.

From an underwriter's point of view, being a designated expert could be less interesting and fulfilling than underwriting a file end to end. The most proficient underwriters crave understanding the full picture despite being the expert on a single aspect.

File review – correspondent version

Correspondent lenders ensure quality by sampling files submitted for purchase. Selection ranges from 100% to much less. In the interest of efficiency or to cope with increased volume, there are inevitably periodic attempts to expedite the process. Risk and quality control managers see this as a compromise, but it may not necessarily be so. One solution is to make the review process smarter.

There are multiple approaches to gauge loan quality. The default approach is selecting loans with the highest risk attributes, possibly combined with originator strength and track record. Time of closing should be factored in; seasoned loans may have been declined by another investor. File thickness gauges complexity but industry controls have turned uncomplicated loans into documentary nightmares, and fraudulent loans may be simplified into brevity.

A fraction of submissions should be selected randomly for review of core documentation by a skilled screener. A loan with acceptable risk or an identified risk that has been resolved should be signed off. If there are concerns, a thorough review should be conducted.

Needless to say, thorough review of all non-performing loans is critical. A pattern of deficient origination should intensify the review of incoming product, if the relationship continues.

Conditioning

Conditioning is a craft. Underwriters strive to be comprehensive, seldom considering resultant complications for the borrower. Originators should have a conditioning philosophy, established after due consideration of the following:

Standardization can assure conditions that are clear, with no misspelled words or lapses in punctuation. The best standardized conditions allow for free-form insert of specifics and modifications.

Non-standard conditions evidence an underwriter's proficiency. Companies that discourage non-standard conditions don't take into account that every loan is unique. An insightful underwriter can structure creative conditions that save good loans from denial.

Clarify is my favorite conditioning word. Asking for clarification can provide insight on such issues as a request for cash proceeds shortly after purchase, irregular rental income and unstable employment.

Some issues are better handled in a phone conversation than a written condition. The underwriter has the option of adding "Our conversation has really helped me understand that situation. Could you please put that in writing?" or convert the conversation into a processor's or underwriter's certification. A verbal equivalent of the needing clarification is "I'm confused."

Some lenders format conditions to expedite sign-off. Asking for seven K-1s becomes seven conditions, in case the borrower doesn't submit all simultaneously. Efficiency in sign-off should not outweigh customer experience. The visual impact of a lengthy list of conditions is disheartening. With applications at more than one lender, the length of the condition list is a prime consideration.

Intrusive conditions should be avoided whenever possible. The borrower is entitled to privacy on matters that are not the underwriter's concern, unless the lending program requires the information. See *Intense scrutiny of depository statements*

Killing with conditions can be effective when an underwriter believes a loan has minimal chance of approval but wants to give the benefit of the doubt. The "If I can get everything I'm asking for, this loan could be doable" approach may rescue a complex or poorly packaged loan. But when every loan includes an exhaustive list of conditions, the real problem may be the underwriter.

The over-conditioned loan

All Cousin Gail wanted was enough loan proceeds to pay for a bathroom remodel. She was a national director for a company selling kitchen products through in-home parties and direct sales for over 20 years. After providing the lender with two years' tax returns, a profit and loss statement, a balance sheet and a letter from the company confirming continued employment, the lender asked for a written statement from one of her customers. "When will this ever end?" she asked me.

I wrote the letter not mentioning the family relationship. I was one of her customers and wanted to alleviate her frustration. I repressed the urge to call the underwriter and ask him about the purpose of the condition. It was reminiscent of an outdated practice of requiring customer letters to validate self-prepared tax returns or on stated programs when self-employment couldn't be confirmed online. But with full documentation it wasn't necessary. Stability was adequately demonstrated, tax transcripts were a better option, and risk was mitigated by an LTV under 25% and a score level close to 800.

The underwriter's motivation most likely was strengthening the file. That additional strength wasn't needed didn't cross his mind.

Lessons:

1. *The underwriter failed to consider the purpose of the condition. If he had, it would have been retracted.*

2. *Over-conditioning is as bad as under-conditioning. It sends the message to borrowers that the loan process is painful, they're not trusted, and maybe they should apply with another lender.*

Micro-conditioning.

Micro-conditioning is a subset of over-conditioning. It is the triumph of triviality over substance. Examples are:

Complete depository statements: Meaningful data—the breakdown of account statuses and a summary page—is usually found at the front of the statement. The back pages are sales pitches and other fluff. Unless depositories start placing meaningful data in the midst of the fluff, the first page of fluff should be sufficient. The possibility of bank loans on supplemental pages is remote. They are relatively infrequent and, unless in the name of the borrower's business, should be reported to credit bureaus. Requiring superfluous pages of a bank statement is post-meltdown overkill and results in petty audit errors, needless investor conditions and considerable wasted energy for borrowers, many of whom dispose of or fail to submit pages with unnecessary content.

Fully readable depository statements: One or two letters on the left margin cut off during printing with no dollar amounts obscured should be acceptable. An underwriter, auditor or investor should have the expertise to mentally reconstruct what's missing. If this ability is lacking, consider replacing the underwriter, auditor or investor.

Sourced funds for revolving account overpayment: This is not the same as account payoff to reduce ratios. A borrower had an 801 score, earned five figures monthly, and had below maximum ratios and ample verified reserves. Her offense was paying more than the outstanding balance on a revolving account. Possibly she applied her expense reimbursement to the next month's bill or paid extra so part of her return-from-vacation expenses would be paid in advance. Whatever the case, it shouldn't matter.

Micro-conditioning has elements of zealotry. Fixation on

inconsequential details may be motivated by fear of audit errors or management criticism. It also can be construed as abuse of power. Triple dotting every "i" is wasted effort, does not improve loan performance, should not make loans unsalable and makes for bad customer service.

On the topic of irritating customers, a mortgage division should not require the borrower to provide documentation obtainable internally from their depository division. Customers easily conclude that their inconvenience isn't important. Some institutions have more accessible internal systems than others. If internal systems are blocked for privacy, there should be interdepartmental cooperation (after presentation of the applicant's authorization to release documentation, of course) so the borrower is not bothered needlessly.

Underwriters who expend energy on trivial details are apt to overlook larger issues.

See *Superfluous documentation*

The condition experiment

During a lull in volume,I selected a loan that was relatively straightforward and easily approvable, asked a dozen underwriters on-site to review it independently and bring their notes into a conference room. Approve or deny? I asked. Everyone agreed on approval. What about conditions? I asked moving towards the whiteboard. As the underwriters called out conditions, I listed them. Any more? Any more? After a lengthy list had been compiled, the underwriters were asked to place themselves in the borrower's position after receiving all the conditions listed. Cancel the loan was the consensus. So what can we eliminate? I asked and started erasing one by one. After the list had been culled from thirty or so to less than ten, the conditioning exercise was over.

Some underwriters can come up with a seemingly endless number of conditions. Conditions can't turn a bad loan good or ensure loan performance. Managers should consider auditing conditions of over-zealous underwriters prior to communication with the borrower.

I'd be tempted to get $100 of crisp dollar bills and let managers distribute them to underwriters who identify their own unnecessary conditions, or to team leads after identifying conditions that serve no purpose.

The qualifying experiment

On the loan featured in *The condition experiment*, I asked the same dozen underwriters for their figure used as qualifying income. There were two borrowers on the loan, neither self-employed or with a base salary. Each response was listed from high to low on the whiteboard. Only a few figures were duplicated, but most were within a relatively narrow range with a few outliers above or below.

There can be more than a single correct answer to qualifying income. When plausible answers fall within a relatively narrow range, the variations make minimal difference unless DTI is high.

When income is complex, qualification should be dependent on the overall risk of the loan. Conservative income is appropriate on marginal loans. A less moderate approach is justifiable when there is ample equity, ample liquid reserves and overall borrower strength.

Signing off conditions

In many companies underwriters sign off the complicated conditions and processors or assistants sign off the rest. This approach makes sense most of the time. Underwriters can usually distinguish those conditions they want to sign off; reviewing pedestrian conditions wastes their time and expertise. Quality may be compromised, however. Less knowledgable staff may fail to recognize hedged or suspicious responses. The least trained or able sign off on anything remotely resembling an outstanding condition, despite its content.

The solution is to have periodic pre-closing audits of condition sign-offs. The less experienced or consistent the employee, the more frequent and intensive the audit. Whether the audit is conducted by the employee's supervisor, the underwriter or a dedicated team within or outside the underwriting group is up to management. This is another good use of time during lower volume periods.

Superfluous documentation

There are three classifications of underwriting documentation:

Core: Anything required in the AUS decision. These same items were core before automated underwriting was conceived.

Supporting: Anything that expands on or clarifies core documentation or addresses other essential aspects of the loan.

Superfluous: Anything that provides no or negligible value to the file. Some are investor-specific requirements; others are obtained because "we've always asked for that" or they theoretically protect the company from liability. Admittedly, some items are considered mandatory by investors. However, in the interest of not wasting effort for borrowers, origination staff and those who review loans after closing, thoughtful reexamination of what documentation provides value and what does not would be worthwhile.

Examples of superfluous documentation are:

1. Access to funds letters: A co-vested checking or savings account by definition gives full access to each vestee. Custodian or power of attorney status should be indicated on the account statement. For retirement assets, the account holder has full access to IRA and 401(k) accounts. Access may be restricted on pension accounts, especially for public employees without social security contributions.

2. Gift letter from spouse on a co-vested account.

3. Sourced funds on a gift.

4. CPA letters regarding use of business funds: CPAs unless on the borrower's company payroll probably have no personal involvement with business accounts. These letters in essence provide CPA confirmation that the borrower is not an idiot.

5. Board of director resolution on a corporation verified to be solely owned by the borrower or where the borrower has an ownership interest of 50% or higher.

6. Final pages on depository statements - Depository statements pack pertinent account information in the initial pages. The product pitches and bureaucratic small print occupy the final pages. A complete version of the most recent account statement and the pertinent pages of the more dated ones is an acceptable compromise.

7. Written customer confirmations that a business relationship remains operative or the housekeeper continues to provide services. This is a holdover from the stated income era.

8. Current taxes and insurance on investment properties. Using last year's rental income, taxes and insurance proportionally represents current net income. Prorate if appropriate. Plugging in current taxes and insurance with last year's gross rent is unduly conservative.

9. Accounts or loans held by the originator.

10. Interim profit and loss statements on established businesses with confirmed stable or appreciating income. Year-end profit and loss statements have more justification.

11. Balance sheets, particularly for sole proprietorships or pass-through corporations.

12. Explanations for underwriter-identified potential recurring obligations on depository statements. Most long-term obligations register on credit reports or through search engines like MERS. (Originators should quantify actual long-term obligations discovered and time spent on dissecting depository statements. If results are nonexistent or negligible, the practice should be discontinued.)

13. Swimming pool letters, safety latch letters and the like unless non-isolated and reasonably recent monetary losses or costs of litigation can be verified.

14. Verified date of retirement for a retiree already receiving benefits.

15. Proof of a pattern of savings withdrawals for borrower not yet needing to withdraw.

16. Letters of explanation for dated addresses, easily-identifiable addresses or when a property search verifies the borrower has no ownership position.

An industry that requires superfluous documentation but accepts a two word explanation ("home improvement") from a borrower yielding major cash proceeds should rethink which is more critical. Risk is controlled by good decision-making, not excessive documentation.

See *Micro-conditioning*

The superfluous documentation contest

The list provided above is partial. It could be longer, much longer. Organize a contest to lengthen the list. Give prizes for insightful additions. Distribute the list and email it to this author at MRB@digitology.com. The contest will serve several purposes—eliminating needless documentation, improving the customer experience and, if the nominated documentation serves a valid purpose, explaining the necessity.

Excessive diligence

A major force in residential lending replaced the industry standard two-year average with a one-year average of the weaker year for non-conforming loans. This stringency is applied to each individual source of qualifying income, ignoring that borrowers may strategically decrease one source of income when another source of income increases, or vice versa. If the weaker year is the most recent year, income may not be used at all. Worst case underwriting becomes inequitable when creditworthy borrowers are denied financing. See *The entertainer with declining income*

There are occasions when traditional documentation is less essential. A profit and loss statement from a handyman with demonstrated stable income is onerous for the borrower and contributes little to the risk decision. A letter of explanation for a minor name variation or a dated address provides little clarity. Approving a loan omitting knee-jerk documentation shouldn't be confused with approving substandard loans.

In my experience, excessive prudence and preoccupation with precision are accompanied by inability to assess overall risk.

Credit committee

Post-meltdown, after the contraction of guidelines and the resultant complaints by customers who thought acceptable loans were being denied, Credit Committee was created to discuss and decision recommended denials for the infamous mortgage banker's correspondent division.

Credit Committee met twice daily in the two national underwriting centers. Participants were the manager who chaired the meetings, a record-keeper who kept track of decisions, available senior managers, the underwriters presenting recommended denials and any newly hired or promoted underwriters. When volume was high, underwriters could leave after their own presentation. When visitors attended, identifiers were omitted to preserve privacy. The original format included an advocate to make sure individual loan strengths were taken into account and to devise ways of making good loans work. After a while, several of us handled that role.

Credit Committee had a standardized format: a recitation of loan attributes, contributory factors and why the loan was recommended for denial. Presentation was followed by discussion, sometimes prolonged and sometimes a quick "Kill it!" Occasionally the loan was so ugly the decision to deny interrupted the presentation. Early on we decided eligibility violations could be denied outside the meeting with manager approval.

Decision quality was best when at least one person beside the presenting underwriter previewed the loan before the meeting. Previewing involved a cursory review of the loan application, credit and documentation pertinent to the denial recommendation. Potential previewers were the underwriter's supervisor, the meeting chair and preferably the advocate. All received a list of loan numbers and presenters an hour or two before the meeting.

Credit Committee improved the quality of decisions. Escalations from customers to management decreased. Reconsiderations were allowed when additional documentation or clarification was provided, or when very senior management requested it. The latter was typically handled outside the standard meeting format and required a non-cursory review.

Benefits exceeded customer satisfaction. Underwriters put more thought into their recommendations and learned through discussions of other underwriters' loans. Newly hired or newly promoted underwriters were exposed to management thought process. Their participation was encouraged, and some impressed us with their contributions. Overall competency level increased. Some decisions surprised the room.

Loan officers can serve as effective advocates, possibly with a limited allotment of appearances. They see the most positive aspects of a loan; underwriters sometimes do not. Hopefully even when Credit Committee decided against approval, the loan officer left the meeting with increased insight or, at minimum, learned that denial was not a casual decision.

Credit Committee is not viable for all companies but before any loan is declined, due consideration should be given.

The fraud team

Most underwriters find fraud riveting, but some have the ability to identify it more readily than others. Consider enlisting those with the keenest ability to smell fraud to review suspect files with the underwriter before escalating upward. This can increase the skill level of line underwriters and give recognition to members of the team. To avoid instances where the fraud team member is less convinced or isn't aware of an emerging pattern, I would urge at least a short incident report so potential fraud can be tracked. This team can be scattered at the site level, but preferably should meet in person at least annually.

Fraud reporting and afterward

Reporting fraud is not optional. Underwriters with a reasonable suspicion should escalate; verified proof should not be required at time of initial suspicion.

Specialists confirm the presence of fraud and explore whether the incident is isolated or part of a pattern. If fraud is confirmed, findings should be escalated to law enforcement and industry fraud control alliances. Criminal action against the perpetrators and media coverage of punitive measures may deter similar attempts.

Feedback should be given to the underwriter—unless there is the possibility of internal complicity—and shared on a larger scale as well. Most underwriters are fascinated by fraud. Fraud training keeps the attention level high at underwriting meetings.

Internal complicity plays a part in some fraud efforts. Those involved may be unaware of their role. If internal fraud is identified and those involved remain employed, consider escalating to a higher level of management or to the police, IRS or FBI. Privacy should be protected. Companies are not allowed to retaliate, and law enforcement agencies protect their sources.

The major league blunder

The borrower worked in the payroll department of a major league team. The source of down payment was pay-out for the team's very successful season. The underwriter was not a sports fan but thought a bonus several times base pay seemed improbably high.

The underwriter was right. The majority of the down payment had been diverted to the borrower from other bonuses. The employer caught on when a letter signed by the team's H.R. manager was sent to the team for confirmation, and responded that the letter was forged.

Lesson: The improbable sometimes can be perceived beyond a thoughtful underwriter's usual frame of reference.

Quality control audits

Auditors have a meaningful role in origination. Sloppiness and poor decisions should be identified. Unfortunately, in my experience many underwriters eager to transition into auditing are checklist underwriters best able to identify technical mistakes. A protocol that evaluates both technical and decision-making aspects of loan origination should be feasible to design.

Auditing the auditors is a good idea. Checklist underwriters may lack the ability to catch over-conditioning, questionable sign-offs and other errors in judgment. As a manager whose duties included reviewing audit reports, I invented a single-player game called "Who's the Idiot" with me deciding whether the idiot was the underwriter or the auditor.

If logistically possible, auditors should be seated at some distance from the people they audit.

Too low reserves?

An oversight group responsible for auditing exceptions took issue with an approval because of low reserves. I felt that $9,000 was acceptable proportionate to the $100,000 loan amount, but exception criteria required strong compensating factors. Evidently $9,000 was inadequate, at least to one member of the oversight group.

The exception was relatively inconsequential, a minor repair pended until the Minnesota winter was over. Otherwise the loan was very low risk. There was a high credit score, stable employment, good debt ratios and a $130,000 down payment on a $230,000 sales price.

The most difficult part of constructing the audit rebuttal was avoiding sarcasm. "Which would you prefer, a lower equity position or higher reserves?" would be rude. My final draft stated that $9,000 reserves represented 15 months' PITI, 13 months over minimum, and should be viewed in relation to the ample down payment and the 43.5% loan-to-value.

The finding was successfully rebutted.

Lesson: For this loan, the idiot was the auditor. See Quality control audits

Outside audits

Originators are subject to audit by regulators and investors. Although no one enjoys being audited, the positive is that they can reveal areas of deficiency and opportunities for improvement.

In preparing for an outside audit, the standard advice is to answer questions succinctly, saying as little as possible. Attempt to establish rapport and demonstrate sincere commitment for quality. "How can we improve?" may sound like a kiss-up question, but if suggestions are implemented in good faith it could make future audits less painful.

Evidence of sloppy origination results in intensified scrutiny. Auditors should be given well-organized files. Complicated aspects should preferably be addressed during origination while the rationale is fresh or, if not, identified and addressed during a quick pre-closing review of the loan file.

Repurchase and default audits

Every company should have an established review process for loans that are repurchased or don't perform. Loans should be dissected on an individual and spreadsheet basis, determining whether each default was predictable and whether any patterns were identified such as fraud, underwriter oversights and inability to recognize layered risk, and source (loan officer, broker or other originator.) The cause of default is important. Default may result from unanticipated causes, for reasons undisclosed to loan servicing, from errors during origination, or from programs that tolerate marginal qualification. Feedback should begin with the underwriting manager and be selectively shared with the underwriter if default is related to deficient underwriting or if other underwriter deficiencies come to light.

Spreadsheet or snowflake?

There are two opposite views of how to evaluate mortgage loans. The first group believes that loans can be effectively encapsulated on a spreadsheet, while the second group believes every loan is a snowflake. Although I align with the snowflake faction, I admit that most loans (notably those in the John and Mary Buy a House category) can be captured sufficiently on a spreadsheet. But loans scrutinized on an individual basis give insight on origination quality, which explains why at least some sampling is critical.

Spreadsheets and portfolio quality

Back when stated programs were being retracted, a seasoned underwriter was assigned to review one originator's post-deadline submissions on a discontinued program. I was surprised she recommended almost all the loans for purchase, so I requested a spreadsheet on the submissions.

Several columns caught my attention. The properties were located in a variety of neighborhoods with an average range of sales prices. A disproportionate number of borrowers had management-level job titles; their numbers reflected an organization chart turned upside down. On those loans, our underwriter comments consistently started with "Stated income appears high but...." My conclusion was that job titles were enhanced to justify inflated income.

Before reviewing the spreadsheet, I believed that the best test of loan quality was a close review of the loan. Afterwards, I realized that looking at loans as a group could give insight on a larger scale.

Pattern analysis is an effective tool, especially on suspected fraudulent loans based on either property location or originator.

Lack of capacity

Guidelines typically preclude lending to borrowers under eighteen or lacking the mental capacity to understand the loan documents. These controls protect both the borrower and the lender. On the rare occasions that someone lacking capacity applies for a loan, the situation has to be handled correctly.

On a mishandled loan, a borrower's spouse signed documents under a power of attorney. The spouse provided a letter explaining that the borrower had dementia. The loan had high risk because cash-out was at maximum, and declared use of proceeds was for borrower care, which could entail a change of occupancy. More importantly, the loan was ineligible because disclosure of dementia confirmed the borrower lacked capacity. Unfortunately, a coworker with authority but unaware of the capacity guideline signed off the general power of attorney, so the loan purchase went through.

Not long after that debacle there was a non-compliant loan that deserved to be made. The applicant had been driving on a military base when her car was crashed into, leaving her braindead. The settlement provided lifetime healthcare plus personal and living expenses. The award covered a sizable down payment on a home for the applicant and her nursing support. If risk and compassion were the only considerations, approval would be easy. However, since the loan breached eligibility guidelines and was unsalable, it was regretfully denied with lack of capacity referenced in the denial. The borrower's congressional representative contacted Fannie Mae, who agreed that the loan should be purchased. The story had an happy ending, thanks to reasonability triumphing over rules.

There are deserving loans that do not fit into the box.

The aged mother

The borrower was in her mid-70s and lived on social security and pension benefits. She and her decreased husband had purchased their home 20 years ago for $54,000, and $132,000 was currently owed on it. The loan request was for $199,000 cash-out at 60% LTV. The borrower had a 762 score and $7,750 in an account vested in the name of her son as guardian.

The loan was submitted for exception because the application was signed by the borrower's guardian, not a power of attorney. We declined the request. It was a low risk loan, but the guardianship indicated lack of capacity and there was no assurance that proceeds would be used for the borrower's benefit. If proceeds were for out-of-home care, owner occupancy was at issue.

Lesson: There are some situations that a letter of explanation cannot cure.

Infrequent encounters

The more unusual an aspect of underwriting, the more likely it will be mishandled. New York City underwriters should understand the intricacies of co-ops but not manufactured housing and Hawaiian lava zones. Those familiar with the entertainment industry should know that lower-level workers are paid only while a project is in production, while top performers receive a lump sum.

Intermittent exposure may never turn into expertise. My sole recollection regarding Texas (a)(6) refinances is that a loan deemed cash-out according to Texas law could be closed as a rate and term if it met GSE guidelines.

The best way to minimize errors is creating an environment where employees—even senior underwriters—aren't embarrassed to ask questions. Limited knowledge on obscure issues doesn't demonstrate lack of competency. Those with backgrounds in other geographic areas or in other professions can serve as experts, and checklists can be designed to identify key points. However, over-dependence on checklists results in employees ticking off boxes by their pattern, not their content.

The brokered loan

Todd and Kerry expected that purchase of their third home would run smoothly. Their credit scores were above 800. Todd was still self-employed as a screenwriter and Kerry was still salaried in a management position. They had a 20% down payment (10% more than on their first home) and reserves three or four times the down payment amount. But their mortgage broker repetitively requested details about irregular checking account deposits, which were from Todd's royalties. The broker explained that they had to prove deposits weren't gifts or loans.

Borrowers with ample reserves don't need gifts or loans. There was a logical relationship between royalty income and Todd's employment, and scant chance year-to-date income was used in qualification. The most significant risk issue was one borrower's self-employment, but it was seasoned. There was a history of appreciating income supported by tax returns and consecutive move-ups from their first to their new residence.

Three years after purchase, Todd and Kerry haven't forgotten the bad experience.

Lessons:

1. **Underwriters handling higher loan amounts should understand or research how non-salaried earners are compensated.**

2. **Thicker files aren't necessarily better files.**

3. **Whether over-documentation was the broker's or the lender's fault, it reflects poorly on our industry.**

Loan-specific questions

My favorite response to loan-specific questions is "It depends," followed by "Tell me about the loan" or better yet "Let's look at the loan together." The best decisions require loan-specific details, not just loan attributes. Working out a loan together is a teaching opportunity. Less experienced or less insightful underwriters deserve help in structuring conditions, evaluating risk or enabling a worthy loan to become approvable.

Not everyone wants a discussion. Some loan officers and production-driven underwriters prefer a one-word answer, preferably "Yes." They don't understand that good underwriting requires analysis.

Overlays – management view

It is tempting to use investor guidelines as a starting point and narrow down at will. Aside from criteria where the investor is willing to have higher exposure (like lower credit scores), more obscure property types (like co-ops) or unfamiliar geographic areas, try to resist. You may be protecting your company too well.

Consider overlays from the point of view of those sending you business. This includes real estate agents, mortgage brokers and financial advisors. The longer the list and the tighter the restrictions, the more likely volume will be diverted to another source with more generic guidelines.

So consider the number of items on your overlay list and the relative obscurity of each issue. If you can't remember why an overlay is on the list (possibly because of a single ugly loan), remove it. If the list expanded when borrowers acted less responsibly, it may be time to shorten it. Retain the essentials and reconsider the rest. It will give your sales team a welcome message to deliver.

Lack of expertise is a legitimate reason for overlays. If there are no or few co-ops or manufactured houses in your lending area, classify them as ineligible. Your customer base shouldn't care much, and the inevitable errors occurring with low proficiency will be avoided.

For recommended denials because of overlays, consider first having the exception team review the loans for overall risk. This requires underwriters to be aware of what is or isn't an overlay. If risk is acceptable and a loan is salable, the loan should be approved. When exceptions for a particular overlay are consistently approved, consider removing it from the list.

See *Overlays*

The inexplicable denial

With twenty years' experience in loan origination, Adam thought the refinance would be an easy approval. Two years earlier, an investment property had been deeded to him from a family member unable to finance repairs. Adam took over mortgage payments and paid for the repairs out of pocket. The quit claim deed conveying title had been recorded only two months ago, but was notarized.

The unrecorded deed admittedly complicated matters, but Adam never anticipated loan denial. LTV on the rate and term transaction was about 50%, the score over 700 and tax returns verified positive cash flow.

The loan was denied because of continuity of obligation, despite documentation including a copy of the notarized deed and depository statements proving timely payments for the last 24 months.

After venting his frustration to an industry friend, Adam learned that Fannie Mae had eliminated their continuity of obligation restrictions about six months earlier.

Lesson: Inability to recognize the difference between rules meriting enforcement, rules waivable under the right circumstances and investor rules no longer in force can result in the denial of easily approvable loans.

The non-conforming profile

Non-conforming loans differ from conforming loans by more than loan amount. There is overlap, often with complex loans in lower cost areas and relatively simple loans in higher cost areas.

Aspects more apt to be found in non-conforming loans are:

- Higher probability of self-employment

- Thicker tax returns

- Multiple or inconsistent sources of income

- Higher probability of business funds

- Diversified investments

- Higher probability of alimony

- More qualified first-time home buyers

- Assets exceeding those verified

- Higher outstanding consumer debt, which should be viewed proportionate to annual income

- Higher net worth

- Business expense write-offs, which may be paid off on a monthly basis

- Non-mainstream properties, more custom and less tract

- Urban housing, unimpressive in square footage but with high land value

Since the average non-conforming loan is more complex than the average conforming loan, non-conforming underwriters should be more knowledgeable and have greater insight, not just years of experience. Ideally, they should prefer, not resent, challenging loans. Complex conforming loans should be assigned to underwriters capable of handling them. Keeping less complex non-conforming loans with non-conforming underwriting specialists is justified because of higher loss exposure and to allow periodic respite from thicker files.

Loan assignment

It is preferable to assign loans so that the more able underwriters aren't bored and the less able ones aren't overwhelmed. It's also considerate to give underwriters who've been burdened with ugly or complex loans an uncomplicated loan or two. Ideally, the assignment process should start with a manager able to assess a file's complexity early in the process. Another method is teaming up loan officers with underwriters, even though relationships can turn adversarial or overly-accommodating.

It is tempting to assign loans by loan amount correlating to signing authority. Product type is another convenient method. But lower loan amounts may have minimum equity and very high risk. The exception to not assigning by product type is government loans, where precise adherence to guidelines outweighs other considerations.

Assessment for manual assignment should start with the core transaction. The departure point is how far removed a loan is from the most basic transaction, which I call "John and Mary Buy a House." A basic transaction could be Mary by herself, or John and Jim who have been together for many years. If the down payment comes from borrower savings, the transaction is less complex than if there is a gift. If John and Mary are both salaried employees, the transaction remains relatively simple. If Mary is a partner in a law firm and John owns part of a family business, the transaction is no longer simple. If John is a 20-year-old and Mary is his grandmother planning to rent out her long-term residence and move in with her grandson, with the down payment coming from a recent cash-out refinance on her residence, the transaction is complex.

Assessment criteria should include:

- Income which ranges from straight salaried to corporate and partnership returns several inches thick

- Assets, which range from straight personal savings to gifted funds, inheritances, gifts of equity, trust distributions, sale of personal property and deferred exchange accounts

- Credit complications such as foreclosure equivalents and other major derogatory credit, shallow credit, non-representative scores, borrowers with authorized user or disputed accounts

- Multiple borrowers excluding married couples or partners with a history of living together

- Occupancy other than owner-occupied

- Property type other than single family detached

- Properties with complicating factors such as rapid appreciation, over-improvements, non-residential zoning, impaired marketability or unconventional outbuildings

- Non-arm's length transactions, purchases of short sales

- Locations with increased potential for default or fraud

This all sounds daunting, but a quick review of the application, credit report and appraisal can usually reveal a loan's complexity. The page-count of documentation and loan amount are also tip-offs. Underwriters should be encouraged to advise when a loan is beyond their depth, and either co-underwrite or receive guidance afterwards on how complications were resolved.

When volume is low, assigning loans to be co-underwritten can improve the skills of the inexperienced, the overly picky and those who miss critical points. Mentor relationships can increase overall quality.

Alternative methods are random assignment or self-assignment from the queue. Random assignment works well if underwriters are equally skilled, and self-assignment from the queue works well if underwriters are equally skilled and no one cherry-picks.

Horses versus zebras

A senior manager was fond of the expression "Solve for horses, not zebras." What she was saying is that management should concentrate on the major issues. Unfortunately, resolution for some issues never occurred.

The origin of the phrase is a medical adage, "If you hear hoof beats, think of horses not zebras." This translates to considering the most common diagnoses before remote possibilities. It doesn't advise sending patients home if they don't have common diseases. As for its application to mortgage lending, it's management responsibility to find solutions for loans not fitting the mold.

Exception philosophy

The post-meltdown distrust of exceptions has some justification. Rampant flexibility in the mortgage industry escalated into financial devastation worldwide. But the remedy for excessive flexibility should not be complete lack of flexibility.

Disregarding rules can backfire legally, morally and in everyday living. Tampering with proportions in baking can produce inedible results. Ignoring traffic laws endangers lives. Disregarding game rules is cheating.

With mortgage origination, rules are implemented to control risk on some loans intrinsically risky to begin with. GSE guidelines are designed for loans with minimal equity positions and for borrowers with limited strength. FHA and VA guidelines are based on an even higher risk equation.

Conventional guidance for exception approval is strong compensating factors and a high probability of performance. Strong compensating factors may not be necessary if an exception is minor or the rule being violated lacks pertinence. An enlightened view is that approval should rest on willingness to purchase a hundred similar loans.

Attempts to control risk by quantifying the number of exceptions proportionate to volume are probably wasted effort. Although metrics and quantification serve a good purpose, the assumption behind exception metrics is flawed. A more valid test would be comparing performance of approved exceptions to performance of the general population of loans originated under the same program. If exception performance is not inferior, there is no increased risk from exception approvals. If profitability on exception decisions rendered unsalable is not inferior, there is both improved risk and improved profitability.

Those with limited hands-on exposure to mortgages may view all exceptions as having enhanced risk. Like felonies and misdemeanors or venial and mortal sins, mortgage exceptions range in severity. A low-risk loan with an exception probably remains a low-risk loan. Part of the stigma may be terminology. An approved exception sounds like a pardon after being found guilty of a crime. Merit-based decision would be a fitting and less judgmental term.

The co-signing mother

Major derogatory credit should not be disregarded casually. No matter how credible and persuasive the letter of explanation, if the event was not dated, loan approval is rarely justified. But in one case, I ended up with a different perspective.

The loan request was from a 70-year-old woman. LTV was below 60% and cash-out was minimal. But there was a short sale a few years ago on a loan co-signed for her adult son. The woman had about $150,000 in verified savings and otherwise flawless credit. Although excusing bad behavior too often encourages recurring bad behavior, this borrower's loan request was approved. Should she deplete her life savings to pay off the mortgage obligation? Morally, maybe. Was there any possibility of default on the current loan? Not really—there was acceptable equity, stable retirement income and a consistent history of responsible repayment, except for the co-signed mortgage. This loan merited exception approval.

Lesson: Major derogatory credit is seldom ignorable, but in this case was highly unlikely to recur.

The football rookie with almost no credit

This borrower was an early round draft choice after a successful football career with my university's cross-town rival. He was an authorized user on two of his parents' accounts and had an unseasoned revolving account with a major bank. Non-traditional credit was a rental rating for his final year in college paid by his "full ride" athletic scholarship. He had limited credit history, the football season hadn't started yet, and he was requesting an 80% purchase money loan.

After prolonged deliberation, I ended up seeing merit in this request. The borrower had a multiyear, no-cut contract, but this was not nearly enough to justify approval. Less obvious factors were a virtually intact signing bonus several months after receipt and a new upper-end tract home as his choice of property. These choices evidenced good judgment, as did his limited credit history. No doubt this borrower could have obtained credit cards during his college years, bought a car or two with his signing bonus and purchased a mansion. The act of not spending large proved his creditworthiness. It turned out that his father and grandfather had gone through college on football scholarships. Their coaching led him in the right direction.

Lesson: In rare instances the absence of credit can be offset by evidence of financial management skills and prudent choices.

Exception Types

Matrix exceptions encompass spreadsheet attributes like LTVs, debt ratios and credit scores. Only a fraction of exceptions fall into this category. (The size of the fraction depends on the lender.) Matrix exceptions were freely disbursed in the years prior to the meltdown. Increased risk was quantified into pricing adds, an approach proven ill-conceived. Higher adds were required on larger exceptions or double exceptions, such as above-maximum LTV combined with a below-minimum credit score. Unfortunately pricing couldn't mitigate risk on a loan with minimal equity and substandard credit. Post-meltdown, matrix exceptions decreased in availability.

Policy exceptions appear as risky as matrix exceptions. Examples are properties outside of normal lending boundaries, and waiving private mortgage insurance coverage. However, the property could be in a familiar area and appraised by a credentialed appraiser. The absence of private mortgage insurance could result from high CLTV caused by a subordinated SBA loan. Exception approval on policy exceptions typically requires senior management approval.

Guideline exceptions enable tolerance on timing, seasoning, required documentation and other non-matrix issues. Allowing a 22-month history of overtime earnings or waiving K-1s on partnerships yielding a few dollars of taxable earnings should not compromise risk on an otherwise acceptable loan.

Deviations from internal processes are borderline exceptions, since increased risk is not at issue. As long as there is no compromise to regulatory requirements or inadequate staffing to handle the rush or delay, the exception should be granted.

Property exceptions deal with various issues such as eligibility, warrantability or seasonality. Some are cut and dried; some are judgment calls. On GSE product, single loan variances could be available on non-warrantable projects.

Judgment exceptions are non black-and-white issues such as marketability or stability. Although these decisions often can be made outside of the exception process, exception teams often pitch in on decisioning when others are unavailable or unwilling.

Unclassifiable exceptions. A handful of exception requests defy classification. Since every loan is a snowflake, it follows that a few exceptions will be one-of-a-kind. Different is not necessarily bad.

Accommodations are sometimes classified as exceptions, but approval is less based on risk than senior management decision because of missteps in origination or customer relationship. Internal mistakes can be handled with pricing penalties to the originating unit (or on correspondent loans, pricing adjustments and / or indemnification.) Accommodations should be differentiated from true exceptions in performance metrics.

These exception classifications are admittedly contrived and arbitrary. An exception can fall into one category, more than one or none. What constitutes an exception varies from institution to institution. Some underwriters, team leads and managers have authority to approve exceptions documented in the write-up, but not always tracked and consolidated for reporting purposes. Classifications are set forth only to demonstrate that exception exposure ranges from none to considerable. Since unworthy requests can be turned down and the true test of decisioning is performance, exceptions should not be uniformly feared.

Portfolio, escalation and exception underwriting

Portfolio, escalation and exception underwriters have much in common. All deal to some extent with out-of-the-box loans. Portfolio underwriters follow portfolio guidelines, which typically allow more discretion and flexibility than investor guidelines. Escalation underwriters deal with loans that line underwriters cannot or do not want to decision. Exception underwriters decision loans that don't meet guidelines.

All require underwriters in the Insightful group, who usually have years—if not decades—of experience. The more seasoned the underwriter, the greater the exposure to the atypical and complex. Excluded are seasoned underwriters with limited product experience, limited appraisal analysis and those who are rules-bound.

Portfolio underwriting may require less risk acumen since guidelines have wider tolerance. Escalation underwriters may have authority to bend the rules. Both may need management concurrence when there is higher exposure. Only a fraction of underwriters are capable of decisioning exception loans. Underwriters by nature tend to respect rules and have a natural predilection against non-compliant loans. Only a small percentage have the judgment skills to identify a good loan that is outside the box.

The ability to write convincingly and with proficiency is important, since some second readers can't distinguish between good judgment skills and unimpressive writing skills.

All three underwriting roles may be pressured to allow a higher degree of flexibility for relationship borrowers. This can prove disastrous if the only compensating factor is relationship.

The term "risk appetite" sometimes comes up in discussions of exception and escalation tolerances. For some institutions, over a decade after the meltdown risk appetite is virtually nonexistent. But the assumption that exceptions by nature have high risk is fallacious. Exception requests on high-risk loans should not be approved. Approved exceptions and escalated approvals should perform at least as well as non-exception originations and very possibly better because of compensating factors.

See *Underwriters by classification.*

Portfolio lending

Portfolio loans are retained rather than sold on the secondary market. They may meet investor guidelines, internal guidelines or both.

It is tempting to retain salable loans with the lowest risk, but this tactic is not appreciated by investors.

Portfolio loans are originated for many reasons. Some borrowers find a less rigid approach to documentary requirements with portfolio lenders. There often is a well established and valued customer relationship with the originator and a complication causing more reasonably priced financing to be unavailable. Examples are non-conforming loan amounts, short-term construction financing, ineligible borrowers, ineligible properties or property ownership over the maximum allowed per investor guidelines. After closing, the lender can hold loans as long-term bank-held investments or for sale at a later date.

When loans do not comply with industry norms, origination should be justified by a detailed written analysis. This statement may be useful during audit or if at a future date there is a desire to sell seasoned portfolio loans, although loan performance should outweigh dated observations. The intangible factor in performance is mutual loyalty, ideally present between a financial institution and its customers.

Some loans may be placed in portfolio for reasons unanticipated at time of origination—repurchases and those rendered unsalable because of incurable errors. These loans can be refinanced immediately or after the flaw can be overcome.

But it's my best broker (or seller)

The considerations are similar when a real estate agent or seller on the correspondent side submits a substandard closed or a have-to-close loan. What matters besides the flaw is the quality of other submissions received from that source. If the last 99 loans were high quality, very possibly the hundredth should be purchased, sold if it is salable (with the deficiency addressed and extra attention to packaging) and retained for portfolio if it is not. Indemnification should be considered in either case.

There must be a track record of quality before favors are justifiable. Mistakes are inevitable but some originators commit to deficient loans as a matter of course. Purchase a marginal loan from a marginal originator, and additional low-quality loan submissions will follow. There are brokers or originators who wear out their welcome with one lender, make convincing promises of volume to the next, and the pattern continues until they're back sweet-talking the first lender hoping their memory is short. If solemn assurances of reform are made, thoroughly review at least several dozen submissions prior to purchase to ensure that quality promised is quality delivered.

Buying one flawed loan from a quality originator is supporting a business partner. Buying quantities of loans from a mediocre originator is poor judgment.

How not to run an underwriting department

1. Have uniform guidelines for conforming and non-conforming to simplify the underwriting process. If simplification is necessary, consider separate underwriting teams or hiring brighter underwriters.

2. Assume that any loan not in full compliance with guidelines has high risk.

3. Believe that an AUS approval outweighs an insightful underwriter's recommendation. Technology is a tool, not a replacement for risk analysis.

4. Believe that fear of audit errors improves origination quality, and that technical audit errors matter as much as those that impair salability or are risk-related.

5. Believe that underwriting means following process steps, not assessing risk.

6. Believe restrictive overlays are necessary to control quality.

7. Believe that post-meltdown guidelines established to control and punish the industry have continuing benefit. (This includes oppressive documentation and excludes stated programs combined with minimal equity and/or marginal credit.)

How to build a strong team

1. Recruit for diverse life experiences. This includes older underwriters who learned the craft before AUS decisioning and credit scoring.

2. Recruit for intelligence, also people skills and strong work ethic.

3. Understand that ability to identify risk is not universally bestowed or in all cases trainable.

4. Understand that hands-on training is more effective than lecturing, no matter how knowledgable the lecturer is.

5. When gifted employees are identified, allow reasonable accommodations to retain them. Part-time employment or job sharing may be the solution for those with school-aged children or retirees wanting a limited work schedule.

6. Understand that management's role is not only to meet production goals and cure systemic deficiencies, but also to nurture, encourage and praise when warranted.

7. Help H.R. partners to understand that employees with negative attitudes are as bad for the work environment as those with poor productivity, unsalable loans or excessive audit errors.

8. Understand that a manager's bad mood or discontent directly effects the team.

9. Help educate your sales team, both on a group and loan-level basis. While writing this book, I asked a seasoned loan rep for examples of excessive conditioning and the response was "roof inspections." Based on her industry tenure and financial success, I surmise she is not stupid, but either doesn't understand why roof inspections benefit the lender and the borrower—or doesn't care. (If loan officers understood risk as well as products, the atrocities committed on stated income programs may never have occurred.)

10. Understand that underwriting sometimes is a collaborative activity, and that discussing loans with management or coworkers should be encouraged.

11. Establish a forum to rescue loans too good to be denied. Even when the advocate has a weak case, discussion may increase competency. See *Credit committee*

How to find the bathroom

Using process steps:
1. From the door of the office, turn right and walk 15 steps.
2. Turn left and walk 76 steps.
3. Turn right and walk 17 steps.
4. Turn left and walk 13 steps. The restroom will be on your left.

Control advocates believe these process steps require only the ability to count and to distinguish left from right. Since these skills are commonly acquired during a child's first six years, the approach should be foolproof.

Thought advocates believe these process steps are better in theory than in practice. They are ineffective for people who are interrupted or get distracted. If steps are miscounted, bruises may result from bumping into work stations or walls. Errors can be particularly harmful for people unable to reach their destination.

Using thought:
"See that large opening across the room? (Point to it.) Walk through it and down the hall. The restroom will be on your left."

Control advocates believe that without very specific instructions, people might never reach their destination.

Thought advocates believe that with a competent staff, empowerment fosters quality and a more satisfied workforce.

CHAPTER 18

FORTY YEARS, THREE LOAN LESSONS

The 1976 purchase

Bob and Diane, a CPA and accountant respectively, purchased their first house in 1976. They had a 20% down payment and an accepted bid on a $50,000 house an hour out of Cincinnati. Their real estate agent recommended a local community bank, so they walked in and were introduced to the head of the bank, who guided them through the loan application and compiled a list of required documentation. He said he'd get back to them in a few days, but called the following day saying credit committee approved their loan subject to the requested documentation. Documentation must have been satisfactory, since loan closed on schedule.

Lessons:

1. *This loan was originated before the efficiencies of credit scoring and AUS decisioning. Loan approval was speedy and origination was painless.*

2. *Bob compared his experience to a more recent transaction where, after promotion, he was asked for complete partnership returns for an international accounting firm where the K-1 verified his ownership interest as less than 1%. The requirement was waived only after his conversation with management.*

The 2015 equity loan

Two sisters, both retired teachers, wanted to update their kitchen so applied for a $20,000 equity loan. The balance on their first lien was about $30,000 and their house was worth about $500,000. After four months of documentation requests, the loan was finally ready to fund. At 4:30 PM on the closing date, they were asked to send over just a bit more documentation. "Forget it!" one sister replied.

The next day, they were informed the loan had closed, proceeds had been disbursed and no additional documentation was required.

Lesson: A system this broken needs fixing.

In 2016, Happy was happy

Her nickname was Happy. When she mentioned she had purchased her first house six months earlier, I asked how the loan process went. Mostly okay, she said. She had started out with a loan rep whose assistant was the intermediary. Questions were answered after a call-back from the assistant and follow-up questions required waiting for another return call. After Happy changed to a more responsive rep, the process became less painful. She was pre-approved (as opposed to pre-qualified) before she found the right property. There were only two requests for follow-up documentation, a copy of the reverse side of her green card, and a third depository statement, both annoying but easy to provide.

Lessons:

1. *A responsive broker can make the difference.*

2. *With only two follow-up items, maybe there's hope.*

Acronym Cheat Sheet

ARM	adjustable rate mortgage. The interest rate on a 5/1 ARM is fixed for the first five years and adjusts annually thereafter.
AUS	automated underwriting system
AVM	automated valuation model
BPO	broker's price opinion
CC&Rs	covenants, conditions and restrictions
CD	certificate of deposit
CLTV	combined loan-to-value
CPA	certified public accountant
CU	Collateral Underwriter, Fannie Mae's appraisal review system
DE	Direct Endorsement for FHA underwriting
DTI	debt-to-income ratio
DU	Fannie Mae's automated underwriting system
FHA	Federal Housing Administration
FICO	originally Fair Isaacs Company, renamed FICO. Sometimes used as a synonym for credit score.
FSBO	for sale by owner
FTHB	first-time home buyer
GSE	government sponsored entity, i.e., Fannie Mae or Freddie Mac
HCLTV	combined loan-to-value when the subordinate lien is a HELOC
HELOC	home equity line of credit
HOA	home owners' association
HP-12C	Hewlett Packard financial calculator
IRA	individual retirement account
LLC	limited liability corporation
LO	loan officer
LP	Freddie Mac's automated underwriting system
LPA	Loan Product Advisor, previously LP
LTV	loan-to-value

MERS	Mortgage Electronic Registration System, a company and its system that tracks property ownership
MLS	Multiple Listing Service, as distinguished from a private or pocket listing
PAL	passive activity loss
PITIA or PITI	principal, interest, taxes, insurance and association fees or principal, interest taxes and insurance (old school), i.e., the total of housing expenses
PUD	planned unit development
P&L	profit and loss statement
SFR	single family residence
TILA-RESPA	Truth in Lending Act – Real Estate Settlement Procedures Act
TRID	TILA-RESPA Integrated Disclosure
VA	Veteran's Administration
VOD	verification of deposit, a GSE form
VOE	verification of employment, a GSE form
4506	borrower consent form used to validate tax returns

To quote John Dixon: "I don't speak acronym."

List of Loan Lessons

Index

Photo by Andy Comins

Anne Elliott studied mortgage risk from inside the industry for nearly four decades. Hours during lengthy commutes and periods of insomnia were spent mulling over compelling loans. Anne lives in Los Angeles with her husband Donald. Since leaving full-time employment, she writes and consults. For relaxation, she reads, travels and plays Scrabble on her iPad. Contact her at MRB@digitology.com.

Made in the USA
Columbia, SC
23 October 2018